Agreements, Forms and Checklists for Risk Managers

A Companion to
Legal Risk Management for
In-House Counsel and Managers

Bryan E. Hopkins

PARTRIDGE
A Penguin Random House Company

Library of Congress Control Number: 2014937446

ISBN: Hardcover 978-1-4828-9642-8
Softcover 978-1-4828-9641-1
eBook 978-1-4828-9643-5

To order additional copies of this book, contact
Toll Free 800 101 2657 (Singapore)
Toll Free 1 800 81 7340 (Malaysia)
orders.singapore@partridgepublishing.com

www.partridgepublishing.com/singapore

To my wonderful wife Yeong Hee, my son Geoffrey, and daughter Christine who are always in my thoughts-thank you for your love

To Rod Manning, Esq., a fabulous lawyer and good friend

To Won Young, Won Kyung, Justin, Andrew, and others I have mentored or helped along the way— keep up the good work and pass it on

To Jaechan Park, whose tireless efforts made this book possible

Contents

Preface

Risk management has become popular in recent years due to various corporate scandals, government investigations, disasters, and fines. Though some in the risk management industry often refer to enterprise risk management (ERM) when discussing risk management, it is in my opinion that risk management is in reality a process to reduce and minimize the legal risk that is found in many areas. Such legal issues include class actions, product liability claims and lawsuits, government investigations and fines, shareholder actions, and often other legal-related matters. Hence, this book is really about the study of legal and corporate risk or legal risk management (LRM) and what issues, concerns, processes, and procedures should be discussed and implemented when instituting a legal risk management program.

The main role of in-house counsel in corporations or legal entities is, of course, to mitigate legal risk in connection with the sale of products or services provided by the company. In essence how the company protects its success will be based in part on its ability to manage, control, and minimize legal risk, especially in a litigious society such as the US marketplace. Legal counsel must take an active effort in developing strategies, systems, and processes that will minimize the legal risks faced by the company on a daily basis.

In order for the LRM program to be successful in any organization, management must be involved. It is hoped that corporate managers will also take an interest in this vital area, as a successful risk management program or LRM program greatly depends on executive ownership of risk management. Only with the buy-in of executive management will legal risk management be embedded in the strategic decision-making processes of the organization.

This book describes many of the processes that have been developed through my experience to manage and control legal risks faced by most companies today. It also contains many sample forms, agreements, checklists and contracts needed to implement a comprehensive LRM program. Though the forms and agreements contained in this book are not meant to be exhaustive or all-encompassing, they do encompass most of the processes and steps needed to implement a well-rounded legal risk management program. Of particular note is the loss control forms, contract management forms and compliance documents that I deem necessary for a robust LRM program. These would help any risk manager, corporate manager, or in-house counsel should they consider trying to minimize legal risk and exposure.

It should be noted that I will often refer to legal risk management as the acronym LRM throughout this book. I cannot emphasize enough the fact that risk management itself is interconnected with legal risk. All risk management issues at the end are connected to and quantifiable by the legal exposure faced by a company. Therefore, for a company to protect its bottom line, an aggressive LRM program should be implemented on a daily basis.

This book is intended to supplement the concepts and ideas reflected in my first book—"Legal Risk Management for In-House Counsel and Managers." It can be considered a companion to the book. This book offers a practical step by step process with forms and agreements to implement all the processes I discussed in my first book on legal risk management. It is not intended to be an exhaustive form book but a form book that can be used by in-house or corporate managers alike when they have issues on how to implement a basic LRM program. Because this is form book containing checklists, agreements and sample contracts, it is not an exhaustive textbook or treatise. The forms and agreements contained within this book are a culmination of the forms and documents I've had to use during my career to implement the risk management processes I have discussed earlier. As I've said before, it is my experience that I offer to you, the reader. At the beginning of many chapters in this book I first describe the basic process or legal issues that in house counsel or risk managers must consider and then offer sample forms, checklists, and other tools that should be utilized.

I hope this helps all concerned to address the risk management issues they face and help them implement processes that can or will protect their respective companies and organizations.

1. Conducting a Legal Risk Assessment

1.1 LRM Investigation

Conducting a Legal Risk Management investigation is of major importance to a company. Many companies have not conducted a proper LRM investigation of its departments to determine what legal risks need to be identified and minimized. It is recommended that initial LRM investigations be conducted in departments that have major dealings with the public or are heavily regulated, as these departments or divisions will have more legal exposure than most.

Human Resources (HR) is a prime example of a department within a company that not only comes into contact with the public, but that in many countries has to deal with many employment laws and regulations. A sample HR audit follows.

1.2 Sample Employment Policies and Processes Audit

I. Audit Objectives

The primary objectives of the audit can be stated as follows:

1. To review current Employment Policies and identify policies that require modification;

2. To gather data that will enable XXX to identify and evaluate the problems and/or issues that appear to be of present concern to the employees;
3. To identify those facts that will aid XXX in determining its relative strengths and weaknesses in maintaining an environment that inhibits litigious activity;
4. To collect sufficient information so that XXX can clearly define any problems that may exist and be in a better position to develop the relevant, feasible, pro-active countermeasures that will help XXX achieve and maintain the level of employee commitment, loyalty, enthusiasm, and general morale that is needed to maintain a productive and efficient work environment;

II. Audit Objectives

During __________, Risk Management shall employment policies in place at XXX, the current processes in place shall review and conduct numerous private, confidential interviews of employees in supervisory positions (managers, senior managers and vice presidents). The purpose of these confidential interviews is to learn facts and obtain impressions and perceptions of the issues that currently exist at the various locations. The interviewees will be asked a series of open-ended questions intended to allow discussion of any issue or concern which the individual chose to address. The open-ended technique is designed to ensure that the interviewees will feel comfortable and be more willing to discuss the issues of greatest concern to them.

During the interviews, many topics with the interviewees, including their views on the extent of wages, fringe benefits, communication, and working conditions shall be discussed.

The audit will identify issues of concern to supervisors and/or employees as relayed to the supervisors, discuss the ramifications of each issue and consider as to how XXX might best address the issues.

III. Employment Policies and Procedures

A. Policy Review

There are a number of policies that need to be updated and revised to provide direction to the Human Resources department, supervisors and employees.

- Section 1 Employment

  Recommendation:

  Revise the policies to clarify the Job Posting Policy, the Employee Referral Program Policy and the Employment Termination Policy definitions and explanation.

- Section 2 Performance Management

  Recommendation:

  Revise the Performance Evaluation Policy to clarify the role of the managers and expand upon the need for regular feedback to employees to avoid issues that can arise with an employee who does not receive regular feedback who needs to be managed through the Corrective Action Plan

  With regard to the Attendance and Punctuality Policy, we need to review this in conjunction with other policies in place to ensure consistency.

  Several issues regarding policy inconsistencies are discussed in subsequent sections of this report.

- Reward and Recognition

  Recommendation:

  The Promotions Policy needs to be revised to allow more flexibility within the area of promotions.

- Employee Relations

  Recommendation: Several policies in this section require revision.

  With regard to the Sexual Harassment and Anti-Harassment Policies, these need to be revised to provide details as required by the law. A clarification of the complaint procedures and examples of sexual harassment are integral components of these policies. Moreover, references to the training requirements should also be incorporated.

  With regard to the Affirmative Action Policy, this entire process needs to be reviewed and revised to ensure compliance and accurate data maintenance.

  With regard to the Drug and Alcohol Policy, this policy should be revised to ensure compliance with the law. Additionally, consideration should be given to random drug testing within the company.

- Personnel Records

  Recommendation:

  The policies in this section are in compliance with the current state of the law in the relevant jurisdictions.

- Personnel Records

  Recommendation:

  With regard to the Security Inspection Policies, although these policies are compliant with the current state of the law, we need to exerclse extreme caution if the need arises to implement this policy.

- Health and Safety

  Recommendation:

  The policies in this section are in compliance with the current state of the law.

- General Employee Information

  Recommendation:

  With regard to the Business Travel and Expenses Policy, this policy should be revised conform to the current Compliance Policy.

B. Employment Document Review

- Section 3 Compensation and Benefits

  Recommendation: A number of policies require revision in this section.

  Specifically, the Time Keeping Policy require clarification regarding who can input time changes and the issue of adjustments to non-exempt employee time reports. There must be increased awareness regarding employees who come in early and/or work through lunch without properly swiping

With regard to the Employee Benefits Policy, this policy should be revised once the relevant plan documents have been reviewed and finalized.

With regard to the Family and Medical Leave Policy, this policy needs to be revised to give further detail and explanation to employees.

With regard to the Personal Leave Policy, this policy should be revised to clarify the terms of the personal leave and its interactions with other types of applicable leaves (e.g. FMLA, disability leave).

- Employment Application Form

  This form needs to be modified to rectify some issues regarding the information that is elicited as well as proper waivers for XXX to obtain necessary information.

- Employee Evaluation Form

  The Employee Evaluation Form has been recently revised. The main area of concern in this area is the lack of effort and thoroughness from the evaluating employees. Currently, we have a program in place to provide guidance to evaluating employees.

- FMLA Policies and Procedures

  This is an area that requires a significant amount of attention. The current policy must be reviewed and the process must be modified to ensure timeliness, efficiency and compliance with the law.

C. Process Review

Numerous employment processes that are currently in place should be reviewed including:

- Payroll and Recordkeeping Practices

  The general payroll practices should be audited to ensure compliance. For example, the requirements for final paychecks made to employees in California, if any, are quite strict and issues like overpaid commissions must be dealt with in advance of the final paychecks.

  There must be increased recordkeeping in all of the locations to ensure that the records are properly retained (e.g. I-9 forms in separate files; medical leave documentation in separate files) and retained for an adequate period of time.

- Job Descriptions

  The area of job descriptions is one that requires significant attention. This is an issue at all of the locations, with some locations having minimal problems and others having significant deficiencies.

- Selection/Interview Process

  The Selection and Interview Process need to be improved upon to minimize exposure to failure to hire and discrimination claims. It is recommended that XXX require mandatory interview training for any individual who participates in the interview process. There needs to be increased consistency in the interview process and this will be facilitated by the online training program.

- Orientation

  The New Hire Orientation is managed by Human Resource Professionals in their respective locations. This should be checked to ensure there is not significant inconsistency in the programs presented, the duration of the orientation and the materials distributed.

- Promotions

  The Promotions Policy needs to be revised to offer some flexibility for promotions. Historically, there have been deviations from this process and this can lead to disparate treatment claims, regardless of merit.

IV. Supervisor Interviews

Interviews of various managers at the various XXX locations should be conducted regarding:

A. Communication

The underlying reason for many of the employee relation issues may revolve around communication. This includes both the perceived lack of communication and miscommunication between headquarters and the various locations. The failure to communicate or ineffective communication often exacerbates other problems faced by a company.

For the most part, the managers at the different locations believe they do not receive effective communications from the next level.

B. Supervisor Morale

Generally, supervisor morale is low. While most supervisors seem to enjoy working for XXX, at times, they feel frustrated and without support from upper management. A number of things are driving supervisor's morale down. The lack of communication and inclusion for those locations outside of HQ is a source of concern for many supervisors.

C. Favoritism in the Workplace

There is a general sense at the various location that some employees are favored over others.

D. Physical Environment

The majority of the locations had limited complaints regarding the physical environment.

E. Training and Advancement

There was generally good feedback on the issue of training. Supervisors felt there was adequate training for their position.

As for advancement, some issues were raised regarding the inconsistency in the promotion process (addressed above). This will continue to be an issue until we revise the current Promotions Policy and move in the direction of more consistency in this process.

F. Discipline/Corrective Action

This is an area that requires significant attention. There are issues with lack of communication and lack of consistency with this process. Oftentimes, these decisions are not based on metrics, but rather, other objective and subjective criteria that must be documented to support a termination. This has led to frustration on the part of Human Resources in other locations as well as the business managers because they may need to retain a mediocre employee simply because the corrective action process was not properly managed.

Summary of Audit Process

1. Employment Manual Revisions

    - Job Posting Policy
    - Performance Management Policy
    - Timekeeping/Overtime Policy
    - Pay Deductions Policy
    - Employee Benefits Policy
        - Family and Medical Leave Policies

- Vacation Policy
- Personal Leave Policy
- Promotions Policy
- Sexual Harassment Policy
- Anti-Harassment Policy
- EEO Policy
- Affirmative Action Policy
    - Corrective Action Policy (to conform to new Corrective Action Plan for managers)
- E-mail/Computer Policy
- Business and Travel Policy

2. Application/Recruitment Process/Job Descriptions

   Review and streamline the application and recruitment process to ensure that it is uniform and compliant with the law.

3. Leaves of Absence

   This process needs to be streamlined, including revisions of the current Leave of Absence Forms (including but not limited to FMLA leaves).

4. Temporary Workforce

   Legal and Human Resources must continue our review of the temporary workforce and action plan regarding the significant temporary worker population within XXX.

5. Independent Contractors

   Revise the current Consultants Agreement and reinforce to managers that all independent contractor candidates be discussed with the Legal Department to ensure that they are truly independent contractors.

6. Corrective Action/Discipline

   Revise Corrective Action Policy to conform to new Correction Actions developed by Legal and Human Resources.

7. Training

   Implement new training programs as provided by the Law Department and a new Investigation Training program for all Human Resources Professionals.

8. Restrictive Covenants

   Implement a uniform restrictive covenant policy for all applicable employees.

9. Payroll/Recordkeeping Practices

   Review and streamline the recordkeeping process to ensure that all records are kept in an organized fashion and for the time required by law.

10. New Hire Orientation

    This process needs to be revised to ensure uniformity and avoid different basic programs being utilized at different locations.

11. Improved Communication

    Improved communication between management and subordinates to minimize the general perception that employees, including high level supervisors, are not included in vital decision-making.

2. General Product Liability Considerations

2.1 Product Liability Concerns and Costs

Product liability claims, product recall cases, and related litigation, besides hurting the company's brand, image, and reputation, will entail many costs, expenses, and legal fees such as:

- Costs related to product incidents, including recall, retrofit, management and employee time, and lost profits
- Legal costs, including litigation costs
- Increased insurance costs
- Costs including those associated with a loss control program and other risk management—related processes

In order to implement a risk management program that covers all legal issues related to product liability in a specific jurisdiction or country, companies must consider the various legal theories related to product liability in that jurisdiction or country before implementing a risk mitigation program. In the United States, such legal theories include:

2.1.1 Typical Legal Theories on which a Plaintiff May Base a Product Liability Claim and/or Class Action

- Breach of express warranty
    - Express warranty can be created by:
        - "Affirmation of fact or promise" made by the seller to the buyer, which relates to the product and becomes part of the basis of the bargain
        - Advertisements, labels, literature, samples or models, catalogues, and brochures
- Breach of implied warranty
    - Implied warranty of merchantability is implied by law in every contract with a merchant for the sale of goods—a guarantee that product will be merchantable (of commercially acceptable quality).
    - Implied warranty of fitness for particular purpose arises when the seller has reason to know that buyer wants goods for a particular purpose and buyer is relying on seller's skill to select suitable goods.
- Negligence

A manufacturer of goods has a duty to use reasonable care in the design of goods so as to protect those who will use them from an unreasonable risk of harm while the goods are being used for their intended purpose, or for any purpose, which could reasonably be expected. This duty extends to unintended yet reasonably foreseeable uses, as well as intended uses.

- Strict liability

In the United States, the Restatement of Torts Section 402 sets forth the special liability of the seller of a product in a defective condition resulting in physical harm to the consumer.

- 402A. Special Liability of Seller of Product in a defective condition unreasonably dangerous to the user or consumer or to his property is subject to liability for physical harm thereby caused to the ultimate user or consumer, or to his property, if the seller is engaged in the business of selling such a product, and it is expected to and does reach the user or consumer without substantial change in the condition in which it is sold.[1]

- Deceptive and unfair trade practices (DUTP)
    - In the United States, every state has a statue prohibiting deceptive trade practices.
    - DUTP claims are not based on contract; contractual limitations on liability, therefore, do not apply.
    - Claims are not based on warranty, so disclaimers of warranty do not apply.
    - DUTP can include:
        - Failure to disclose information
        - Oral and written misrepresentations
        - Ambiguous representations
        - Breach of warranty obligations
        - US consumer class actions against manufacturers

2.2 Sources of Product Liability Risk

There are a number of areas that a company's Risk Management Department (RMD) or related divisions must consider when implementing a comprehensive legal risk management program to address product liability concerns. The main concerns are sources of risk, whether departmental or process oriented. Each step of the design, manufacturing, sales, and distribution chain contains numerous risks, including:

2.2.1 Potential Sources of Product Liability

- Product design
    - Performance specifications
    - Safety analysis and features
    - Labeling
    - Instructions for use
    - Warnings and cautions
    - Detectability of malfunctions

---

1 Restatement of Torts (Second), Section 402, 1964.

    - Serviceability
    - Product warranty
- Manufacturing and distribution
    - Manufactured to specifications
    - Components meet design specification
    - Product testing
    - Product packaging
    - Record-keeping procedures
    - Suppliers
    - Contractors
    - "OEM" or "VAR" customers
    - Distributors
- Product promotion and service
    - Advertising copy
    - Product literature
    - Marketing and promotional material
    - Service and repair procedures

2.3 Possible Defenses to Product Liability Exposure

Though consumer warranties in the United States are governed for the most part under the Magnuson-Moss Act, the Uniform Commercial Code (UCC) addresses warranties when used in the sale of goods. The proactive use of warranties can be seen as another tool to limit product liability exposure when dealing with the sale of goods in the United States. Such defenses include:

- Breach of express warranty
    - Possible defenses to a breach of express warranty claim include:
        - Lack of causation
        - Lack of damages
        - Disclaimers: UCC §2-316 provides that a disclaimer will be effective only to the extent that it can be read consistently with any express warranties made.
- Assumption of risk: UCC §2-715 indicates that when the plaintiff assumes the risk by using a product while aware of the breach of

warranty, any resulting injuries are not proximately caused by the breach.

- Contributory negligence: Courts in contributory negligence jurisdictions have adopted an approach similar to that used in strict liability in tort—that unreasonable failure to discover the defect does not bar recovery, but that unreasonable conduct after discovery does bar recovery.
- Breach of implied warranty
    - Possible defenses to a breach of implied warranties claim:
        - Assumption of risk: UCC §2-715 indicates that when the plaintiff assumes the risk by using a product while aware of the breach of warranty, any resulting injuries are not proximately caused by the breach.
        - Contributory negligence: Courts in contributory negligence jurisdictions have adopted an approach similar to that used in strict liability in tort—that unreasonable failure to discover the defect does not bar recovery, but that unreasonable conduct after discovery does bar recovery.
        - Comparative negligence: Courts in comparative negligence jurisdictions use comparative fault notions in warranty cases to reduce damage awards in the same way as in strict liability cases.
        - Disclaimer: Disclaimers of liability for breach of implied warranty must be specific and are narrowly construed. See UCC §2-316.
        - Notice of breach: UCC §2-607 requires the buyer to give the seller notice within a reasonable time after the buyer discovers or should have discovered the breach.
        - Lack of privity: The implied warranties most likely will extend only to the buyer and his or her family and not the third parties.
        - Statute of limitations.

The following forms and policies should be implemented when creating a product liability risk mitigation program. The policies cover everything from a basic product liability policy to the creation of a product loss control committee and implementation of a claims management process. It is through these processes that a company can mitigate product liability.

2.4 Forms

The following forms and policies a company should consider are helpful when creating product liability defense processes.

2.4.1 Product Liability Policy

PURPOSE:

To increase customer satisfaction, protect the XXX brand and limit the potential for liability by (a) providing safe and reliable products that comply with all regulatory requirements and (b) appropriately identifying product features and benefits, describing proper use and operation and advising of potential risks in associated product materials and advertising.

POLICY

To ensure customer satisfaction, XXX brand protection and limitation of potential liability, the Company shall implement a Product Liability Program ("Program") that shall include at least the following:

- Product Design/Manufacturing: Verify product compliance with rules of applicable regulatory agencies, standards bodies and industry best practices. Design product specifications that define acceptable ranges of variation for each product characteristic. Assess likelihood of customer misuse and reduce misuse possibility through design features, safety features and/or labeling. Validate test procedures, test to ensure that products meet specifications and document and maintain test results. Document and maintain records regarding quality assurance and control practices. Monitor industry practices and design changes to keep current on appropriate solutions. Apply best practices solutions across all products in a product category to the extent design platforms will allow.

- Product Marketing: Create and provide to customers product user manuals and/or data sheets, as applicable, that detail product technical or functional specifications as appropriate, correct product use, warranties, disclaimers and warnings or contraindications taking into consideration the user's level of expected expertise (such as technical versus non-technical). Use product labels where indicated to warn against risks and educate users on consequences of improper use. Design product packaging to clearly and accurately identify package contents and characteristics. Publish advertising that clearly and accurately reflects product characteristics. All information provided, regardless of form or medium, should be complete, visible and easily understood. Consistency of information should be confirmed to avoid misleading users or creating misunderstandings. Train all in-house sales and marketing teams and customer sales teams on proper product characterization.

- Product Complaints: Create and maintain an easily accessible service log that identifies complaints and what solution is provided. Require all third party service providers to document, maintain and provide on request all product repair records. Evaluate all reported failures and malfunctions to determine cause and take corrective action. Document and retain test results and engineering change notices that are issued to correct any problem found.

RESPONSIBILITY:

The Company shall define what group or groups within the organization shall be responsible for each part of the Program. For Companies that do not manufacture products but import them from Korea, it is recognized that the Product Design/Manufacturing responsibilities portion of the Program shall be a cooperative effort with the factory.

PROCEDURE:

Product complaints involving potential safety issues must be reviewed by the group(s) designated by the Company. If a product complaint is made that involves personal injury or property damage, the complaint must also be reported immediately to the Company's General Counsel for action, (if a company or business unit does not have its own General Counsel, then complaints must be reported to the Risk Manager.) If a lawsuit develops as a result of a product claim, all documentation relative to the product and circumstances must be retained as directed by the General Counsel, even if the Company's records retention guidelines would normally allow record destruction.

Reporting to regulatory agencies governing the product/s at issue shall be made consistent with applicable law.

POLICY VIOLATIONS:

Failure to follow the Policy can result in customer dissatisfaction, injury to the XXX brand, regulatory investigations with potentially serious penalties and individual and class action litigation with potentially large damage claims against the Company. Violation of the Policy will result in corrective action and may result in disciplinary action up to and including termination for individual Company employees.

2.4.2 Claims Management Program

I. INTRODUCTION AND OVERVIEW OF THE PROGRAM

II. PRODUCT LOSS CONTROL COMMITTEE ("PLCC")

a. Purpose
   b. Members of the PLCC
   c. Actions of the PLCC

III. COMMUNICATIONS RESPECTING PRODUCT PERFORMANCE

   a. Customer contact with the customer service center

b. Reports from field personnel
c. Reports from OEM Customers
d. Reports from Authorized Service Centers

IV. DETERMINATIONS RESPECTING CORRECTIVE ACTIONS

I. XXX CLAIMS MANAGEMENT PROGRAM

a. The company encourages users of its products to provide feedback respecting its products performance.
b. One method for obtaining feedback is through the Customer Service communications system that permits customers to contact the company directly.
c. A key element in any product loss control management program includes a well-documented system, which sets forth guidelines and procedures for the collection, recording and evaluation of information respecting incidents and accidents and the performance of the company's products in the marketplace. Such a system enables the company to identify issues respecting its products at the earliest possible time and to select an appropriate form of corrective action before increasing numbers of the product are introduced into the marketplace.

II. PRODUCT LOSS CONTROL COMMITTEE ("PLCC")

a. The PLCC functions as XXX's focal point for gathering information respecting product performance in the marketplace. The PLCC is responsible for identifying and providing the analysis of performance issues respecting the company's products in the marketplace and to make and monitor decisions respecting product safety issues.
b. The PLCC is chaired by the Vice President of Customer Service. Other members of the PLCC include: Manager of Customer Service, Product Engineering, Marketing, Legal and Insurance.
c. **The PLCC's responsibilities include:**

   - Establish guidelines and criteria for the evaluation of product hazards.

- Assessing the impact of and the resolution of product safety issues.
- Developing a system for reporting and recording product accidents, incidents, and customer or user complaints.
- Arranging for and issuing notifications to governmental agencies respecting product defects or non-compliance with safety standards.
- Determining whether a product recall or other corrective action is required and implementing and managing the process.

d. **Action of PLCC:**

- The PLCC shall meet on a weekly basis to review Incident Reports
    - Matters to be considered include:
        - Notice to the insurance carrier
        - Was the incident or accident allegedly caused by a failure of the product or human error or both;
        - If the product is alleged to have failed, how exactly did it fail;
        - What kinds of alleged defects caused the alleged failure;
        - If the incident/accident was due primarily to human error, was it foreseeable and preventable;
        - What instructions did the consumer receive in the use of the product;
        - If the incident was allegedly caused by fire, whether the fire was one which the product was designed to withstand or one against which the product was not designed to provide protection;
        - Whether there is any evidence that the product ceased to function'
        - What possible explanations for the incident exist other than a design or production defect;
        - Any other relevant facts concerning the product or incident.

- The PLCC shall, following an analysis of a products' deviation from its standards and a determination of the probability and magnitude of a potential product safety hazard, recommend to a course of action, (i.e., Recall retrofit, safety bulletin, change in instruction manual), respecting the affected product.

III. **<u>COMMUNICATIONS RESPECTING PRODUCT PERFORMANCE</u>**

a. **<u>Customer contact with the XXX Customer Service Center</u>**

- Information that should be collected respecting an incident or accident involving one of the company's products includes:
    - Consumer names and addresses.
    - All possible witnesses and their addresses.
    - The precise location and date of the incident.
    - A description of the exact nature of the problem including: (i) whether the product was correctly assembled, installed, maintained, repaired; (ii) whether the product had been modified or altered in any way; (iii) whether instructions or warnings were furnished and followed; (iv) how long the product had been in use; (v) whether any physical, deterioration in the product was noticeable; (vi) if the problem was gradual; (vii) when it first developed; (viii) when the problem became apparent.
    - A description of what the injured person was doing at the time of the incident.
    - The circumstances surrounding the incident
    - It the incident involved injury, determine the source of the injury and the nature of the injury. The present condition of the injured person.
    - The current location of the involved product.
    - The serial number and model number of the product.
    - Whether any photographs were taken of the incident and whether any diagrams or reports were prepared.

- Was the accident caused by alleged failure of the product or human error or both?
- If the product allegedly failed, how exactly did it fail?

b. **Report from XXX Field Personnel**

- XXX Sales and Technical Support personnel shall promptly report to the PLCC:
    - All incidents and accidents allegedly caused by the company's product that they become aware of. Such reports shall be made.
    - Information respecting consumer misuse, abuse and alteration of products.
    - Incidents in which the company's products were involved, but not allegedly the cause.
    - User complaints of product deficiencies.

c. **Reports from OEM Customers**

- All OEM agreements shall include an obligation that the OEM customer shall provide the company with regular reports, in a form set forth in the OEM agreement, respecting incidents, accidents and reports respecting the performance of the company's products in the marketplace.

d. **Reports from Authorized Service Centers**

- All ASC Agreements shall include an obligation that the ASC shall provide the company with regular reports, in a form set forth in the ASC agreement, respecting incidents, accidents and reports respecting the performance of the company's products in the marketplace.

IV. **Determination respecting corrective actions**

a. **PLCC analysis respecting the alleged failure of the product to meet performance standards or that product may contain a safety related defect.**

- Obligations under Tort Law
- Obligations under Statute
- Consumer Product Safety Commission
- National Highway Traffic Safety Administration
- Other federal and state regulations

b. **PLCC analysis of options respecting corrective actions:**

- **Warn**

    - Warning or instruction labels, manuals
    - Product safety notice or hazard communications
    - Press Release

- **Retrofit**

    - Redesign of product and provision of free retrofit kit

- **Recall**

2.4.3 Product Loss Control Policy

LOSS CONTROL
POLICY AND PROCEDURE MANUAL

• Policy statement

It is, and shall continue to be, a primary objective of and each of its divisions and subsidiaries to provide customers with safe and reliable products and services. Our employees must be committed to fulfilling these needs. Each operating division is responsible for maintaining effective control of the conditions necessary to meet the safety needs of our customers and control product claim losses.

• Program objective

To increase the awareness and effectiveness of Product Loss Control and Claims Defense Programming through the development and application of effective procedures and controls.

• Organization—responsibility

Company Vice Presidents and Officers are responsible for the development, application, and maintenance of Products Loss Control—Claim Defense Programs, consistent with the guidelines of this policy, at each of their respective operating locations.

In turn, the administration application, and maintenance of such programs on a current and continuous basis rests with the individual company/division chief operating officers.

Depending upon circumstances, a company/division chief operating officer may appoint a representative to coordinate activities on their behalf.

All policy statements, Products Loss Control Programs, and related formal announcements and directives concerning individual programs should be approved and signed by the respective company/division chief operating officer. (See sample Policy Statement—exhibit A attached.)

Will issue general policies and procedures, monitor activity, and provide coordinating assistance with the broker and insurance company.

• Products loss control—claim defense committee

Each division/subsidiary should, either independently or in conjunction with related group members, establish a Products Loss Control—Claim Defense Committee. The company/division officer, or where applicable their appointed representative, should chair the Committee.

Committee membership will vary depending on the type of operation (manufacturing, service, etc.) and the size of the operation. Each Committee should include the company/division representative (chairperson), the loss control representative, and sufficient membership to provide representation from all strategic departments (i.e., R&D, engineering, design, QA, QC, manufacturing, marketing, service, purchasing, shipping & receiving).

It is anticipated that most Committees will have a membership of from three to seven. The minimum is two active members.

Joint Committees formed within a related group shall consist of a minimum of one member representative from each involved operating location. Under these conditions each of the company/division representatives must serve to coordinate the program directly with all affected departments and personnel within their operation. Joint Committees should also include representatives of all strategic departments.

The purpose of the Products Loss Control—Claim Defense Committee is to:

- Develop a formal written program
- Implement the program through education and training
- Provide administrative surveillance and technical product safety assistance and guidance throughout the operation
- Monitor claims activity
- Identify real or potential problem areas and institute corrective activity

[Note: ADD MORE ITEMS HERE]

Committee meetings should be scheduled and conducted on a regular basis. It is anticipated that, depending upon need, meetings will be scheduled either monthly, semi-monthly, quarterly, or semi-annually. Each operation should, at a minimum, conduct semi-annual meetings to review their program. All operations should prepare complete minutes of all meetings and forward copies to the Director of Litigation and Risk Management.

- RESEARCH—DESIGN—DEVELOPMENT

Research, design, and development of products and services should include both safety and reliability considerations.

Personnel assigned to these activities should possess necessary academic and experience qualifications and meet applicable registration or certification requirements.

Formal hazard/failure evaluations should be conducted on all new products and services. Every possible hazard/failure that could result from use, misuse, or modification should be identified and eliminated whenever possible. Identified danger that cannot be designed out should be identified and given individual attention in the form of special warnings and instructions.

Design efforts should be directed towards meeting or exceeding all applicable safety standards and regulations. These may include federal, state and local codes and regulation, industry and trade standard, technical society standards, and others that may be applicable to a given product or service.

Laboratory and field tests should be conducted to verify product and service safety and reliability. Where required (or desirable) independent laboratory testing and/or certification should be utilized. Product and service certification by industry or trade association should also be considered.

All tests, evaluations, findings, and decisions relating to the above should be documented and retained.

Modification of design of existing products and revision of service procedures should include the same considerations.

Procedures should be developed for regular review of established product and service lines to insure that they continue to meet subsequent safety and reliability standards and regulations.

- QUALITY CONTROL—STANDARDS AND PROCEDURES

Written quality control standards, including specifications, should be developed for all components, materials, and processes critical to product and service safety and reliability. Material specifications should comply with national and/or company standards and meet the requirements of all applicable safety standards.

All purchases should include specifications, regulatory standards, and all other company acceptance criteria that must be adhered to by the supplier. Incoming materials and components should be checked to insure that they meet minimum standards. Purchase orders should contain provisions for warranties as to the fitness of the products and/or services, compliance with applicable standards, and indemnity agreements to either eliminate or transfer the risk from.

Formal procedures for process controls and quality checks should be established. The standards and procedures should be made available for control use in the form of a quality control manual. Educational and training programs should be established as necessary to insure effective performance.

Quality checks and final tests should be conducted as often as necessary to insure that applicable standards and specifications are met. Employees conducting checks and tests must possess the necessary skills to certify acceptance. All equipment and tools used for quality control should meet current requirements for product safety and reliability and be maintained in proper operating condition.

Quality checks and final test date relating to the safety and reliability characteristics of products and services should be recorded and maintained so that, within the bounds of good practice, the condition of the products of service can be verified.

As necessary and feasible parts, materials, units, packages, tools and equipment crucial to safety should be permanently identified.

- CERTIFICATE OF INSURANCE—VENDORS ENDORSEMENT—HOLD HARMLESS (IDEMNIFICATION) AGREEMENTS

Selection of subcontractors and suppliers should include consideration of their financial responsibility for liability losses.

A certificate of insurance should be obtained from every subcontractor. Certificates should include specific coverages (i.e., products, completed operations, automobile, contractual coverages, etc.) and certify amounts of liability of not less than limits currently carried by.

An individual analysis of the extent of potential liability should be conducted whenever a subcontractor's coverage is less than that of.

When the loss liability potential is greater than the amount of coverage, the subcontractor should be requested to increase coverage, or other subcontractors with satisfactory insurance coverages should be solicited.

A determination of a vendor's insurance coverage should be made prior to the purchase of products for eventual resale. If it is determined that sufficient coverage exists to provide acceptable insurance protection for the risk involved a vendor endorsement should be requested and obtained before actual resale of any items. If sufficient insurance is not available the vendor should be requested to supply adequate coverage, or other vendors with satisfactory insurance coverages should be solicited.

In many instances and its subsidiaries are required to enter into contracts containing some form of hold harmless (indemnification) agreement. Although there are many types of Hold Harmless Agreements, they generally fall into three broad categories.

- Limited forms hold the other contracting party harmless for claims arising out of your negligence.
- Intermediate forms hold the other party to the contract harmless against claims where both of you may be jointly negligent
- Broad forms indemnify the other party to the contract even where he is solely responsible (negligent) for the loss

[NOTE: ADD MORE INSURANCE PROCESSES HERE]

- MANUALS, INSTURCTIONS, AND LABELS

Operator's instruction manuals should be developed for all equipment. They should provide instruction for safe use, storage, operation, and maintenance.

The manual should identify the standards of performance in respect to safety which the product should achieve after proper preparation.

Operating instructions should be complete and easily understandable. They should contain special instruction in the use of safety devices and protective equipment. All associated hazards should be clearly identified. The operating instructions should detail the procedures which will protect against these hazards, in direct and understandable language and, as necessary, illustrations.

Operating instructions should include maintenance instructions and parts lists servicing instructions should clearly specify the steps necessary to assemble, install, use, and maintain the product in a safe and reliable conditions. Special attention should be given to the care of safety devices. All service work performed by the company should be fully documented and retained.

Warnings and caution statements should be included in the manual and on the products and/or the product container in the form of labels or tags. They should, for example, contain statements that:

- Highlight correct methods for assembly, installation, use, and maintenance. Indicate level of skill or training needed
- Stress the dangers of not following the printed procedures and instructions
- Describe the products limitations
- Warn against modification of the product and parts substitution
- Warn of misuse and hazard to the user
- Specify maintenance procedures and frequency
- Project the useful life of the product
- Instruct the user in the care and use of safety devices and protective equipment and warn of potential consequences
- Recommend antidotes or emergency procedures when applicable

Labels and warnings must comply with federal, state, local, and industry regulations and standards. The copy should be clear, conspicuous, and complete. Special attention should be given to the physical durability of the materials used for labeling and warning.

Manuals and labels should be reviewed regularly to insure compliance with regulations and standards. They should be maintained current to warn users of ne dangers discovered. Previous purchasers should be warned by the best means available when future developments make a change necessary for safety purpose.

All manuals and labels should be reviewed and approved by the Product Loss Control Committee and legal counsel before actual use.

• MARKETING—SALES AND ADVERTISING

Sales and advertising materials should accurately describe products and services. Literature and exhibit used in sales promotion, advertising, or public relations should judiciously reflect necessary accident prevention features, such as safe operating practices, proper projective devices, and approved guarding.

Sales, distributor, dealer, installation, and service personnel should accurately picture products and services. They should be included in educational activities concerned with product safety responsibilities. Sales and other technical representatives should not be misrepresented as being more expert than they, in fact, are.

All proposed advertising literature should be reviewed for technical accuracy and exaggerated statements. Terms such as "maintenance free," "absolutely safe," "fool-proof," and "nontoxic" should be avoided. All sales and advertising materials should be reviewed on a regular basis.

Disclaimers and limitations of warranties should be incorporated into sales literature and sales agreements whenever possible.

All advertising should be reviewed and approved by the Products Loss Control Committee and legal counsel before distribution.

• PACKAGING AND SHIPPING

Written standards should be developed for the packaging and shipping of products. Applicable federal and state standards and regulations governing the identification, packaging, and shipment of regulated products must be included. Company safe packaging and shipping standards should be developed for all products.

Formal procedures should be developed to insure completeness of shipments, including compliance with shipping and safety standards. Special attention should be directed towards insuring that all information and instruction manuals, labels, warnings, and safety devices are included in the shipment. It is recommended that final inspection checklists be developed and utilized.

Education and training programs should be established as necessary to insure effective performance of shipping personnel.

• COMMUNICATIONS

Product safety should periodically be an agenda item for operations and staff meetings at all organization levels.

A program for timely investigation and dissemination of information regarding product incidents, safety suggestions, complaints, accidents, and claims should be developed and communicated throughout all departments and field activities.

• COMPLAINTS AND CLAIM HANDLING

The definition of a complaint or claim is, for the purposes of this program, any verbal or written report of personal injury, property damage, or other claimed loss allegedly resulting from a direct or related failure of any company provided material, product, work, or service. Also include for control purposes all apparent or alleged malfunctions or failures regardless of the presence of an actual claim for loss.

Conversely, complaints of claims which do not relate to the functional use or safety of a product should be excluded.

A written procedure for handling product or service complaints and claims should be developed. Included should be effective controls to insure that:

- All complaints and claims are immediately referred to an individual expressly designated to receive claims
- Each incident is properly described and accurately recorded
- All complaints and claims are immediately recorded on an incident log
- Each complaint or claim is promptly and thoroughly investigated and processed
- Whenever possible the product is obtained for examination
- Each incident is reviewed by the Product Loss Control Committee
- A determination of action necessary is made and corrective action taken

- All employees, sales representatives, dealers, and installation and service personnel are informed of the procedure for handling complaints and claims
- All information relating to complaints and claims and subsequent investigations, discussions, decisions, and corrective or follow-up activity is properly recorded and preserved

[NOTE: ADD MORE CONTROLS HERE]

• CLAIM PROCESSING

All claims are to be processed in accordance with. Immediate notification by telephone is required on all bodily injury and serious property damage liability claims.

Internal reporting procedures should be developed to insure that all claims are properly processed.

The names of individuals assigned reporting responsibilities should be properly communicated.

• RECORD KEEPING

Formal guidelines should be established for record retention. Specific instructions should be communicated to employees for their guidance in dealing with the preparation, storage, and retention of records, samples, and test results that related to product/service loss control.

The basic "rule of thumb" for record retention is at least the life of the product.

Product/service loss control records should not be destroyed without the express permission of the Products Loss Control—Claim Defense Committee. If in doubt the Committee should seek counsel's advice.

• LEGAL

Legal counsel should be utilized to alert the Products Loss Control—Claim Defense Committee and local management of existing laws and changes affecting Product Loss Control.

Counsel should review all contract and sales agreements for elements of potential liability.

All printed material such as labeling, advertising, operating or maintenance manuals should be approved by counsel. All warranties should also be reviewed.

Counsel's approval should be secured before printed material or product information is actually disseminated.

Review assistance is also available from the Company's insurance broker.

POLICY STATEMENT

XXX, an operating division of recognizes its responsibility to provide customers and consumers with safe and reliable products and services.

2.4.4 Claims Investigation and Procedure

CLAIMS MANAGEMENT PROGRAM

A key element in any product liability management program includes a carefully delineated system of handling customer complaints and potential or actual claims. A program with specific guidelines and procedures for handling complaints and/or claims with respect to the product is being developed and implemented.

A. <u>XXX Claims Management Program Overview</u>

CLAIMS MANAGEMENT PROGRAM

This program is designed as a guideline to enable XXX or its subsidiaries, to react promptly and prudently to any complaint involving a product. The scope of this plan is confined to the immediate steps, which XXX should undertake once a complaint is received; the plan does not discuss the strategy or tactics of preparing for trial or a product liability action.

The earlier XXX is aware of a complaint involving appliances, tv's, etc or any type of injury, the better it will be able to react to such a complaint. Therefore, XXX should encourage its customers to report to XXX any incident involving its products. This should, of course be done without suggesting that it is likely that any such incident will occur. Sales representatives will be instructed to tell purchasers that XXX stands behind its products and wants to learn promptly of any incident in which one of its products is involved. When such an incident occurs, the following procedures are to be followed:

1. When a salesman receives a complaint concerning potential fire or any injury, the customer making the complaint should be referred to the XXX Customer Service Manager or the Claims Manager. If the customer does not want to discuss his complaint with the Customer Service Manager or Claims Manager, the salesman must complete an Initial Incident Report, (see attached), and forward same to the Claims or Customer Service Manager. The Claims or Customer Service Manager will then contact the customer for further discussion.
2. After discussing complaint with the customer, the Customer Service Manager or Claims Manager will complete or add to the initial Incident Report and distribute accordingly.
3. The Loss Control Claim Defense Committee (LCCD), or Director of Risk Management, will review all Incident Reports and decide whether further action is warranted. All further inquiries will be made under the direction of XXX Legal in order to preserve the privileged status of any documents generated in the investigation.
4. If no further action is necessary, the Report is filed.
5. If further action is needed, the action to be taken is noted on the bottom of the Incident Report.
6. It may be necessary to notify the insurance company.
7. After completion of further action/investigation, the LCCD will meet again to (1) determine the cause of the incident; and (2) develop a recommendation for prevention of further incidences by initiating a memo to and receiving a response from Engineering. During the meeting, the following questions should be addressed:
   a. What is the likelihood that the injured party will file a suit against XXX and what is the amount of damages likely to be sought;
   b. What instructions the injured worker received in the use of the product;

c. Whether XXX would wish to conduct any test or analysis on the product;
d. If the injury was allegedly caused by fire, whether the alleged fire appears to be one which the product was designed to withstand or one against which the product is not designed to provide protection;
e. Whether there is any evidence that any part of the product ceased to function;
f. What possible explanations for the injury exist other than a design or production defect;
g. Any other relevant fact concerning the product or incident which is the subject of this investigation.

B. Proposed Claims Investigation Questions Checklist

INVESTIGATION QUESTIONS CHECKLIST

During an investigation of an incident/injury, obtain the following information:

1. The precise location and date of the incident;
2. The identity of all person(s) injured, their addresses and all possible witnesses and their addresses;
3. A description of what the injured party was doing at the time of the incident;
4. The circumstances surrounding the incident;
   A. If the incident involved injury, determine the following:
      i. the source of the injury
      ii. the nature of the injury

5. The present condition of the injured worker, what medical attention he has received and where treated;
6. Location of the involved product;
7. The condition of the product prior to the incident
8. The present condition of the product and whether it has been subjected to any test or analysis;

9. Whether any photographs were taken of the incident or after the incident; and whether any diagrams or reports have been prepared;
10. An attempt should be made to examine the product, take photographs and record the serial number and model number.
11. The injured party should also be interviewed, if possible. Prior to setting up the interview, an attempt must be made to determine whether the party is represented by counsel. If so, his counsel must be consulted prior to contacting the party. If not, the investigator should contact the party and inform him the investigation is being conducted on behalf of the manufacturer. The above questions should be asked of the employee;
12. An attempt should be made to interview each and every witness. The above questions should be asked of each and every witness;
13. Photographs of the site and all relevant objects should be made, if possible.

C. **Proposed Claims Report Checklist**

INVESTIGATION QUESTIONS CHECKLIST

1. State only the facts using "it is alleged".
2. Identify all contributors or other independent investigators. Include names, addresses, purpose of investigation by independent investigators and attach copies of their reports.
3. Attach copies of operating and maintenance manuals. Code or explain pertinent sections.
4. Identify any written or unwritten procedures or work instructions. Any labels, identification symbols or codes should be included.
5. Identify and clearly explain all photographs.
6. Include statements from witnesses and their names and addresses. Distinguish between those who actually "witnessed" and those who are passing on hearsay.
7. Include a glossary of terms when attaching technical documents or literature.
8. Keep master list of all evidence, including:
    A. names and addresses of witnesses;

B. location of all non-attached evidence;

C. content and availability of photographs;

As well as retrieval procedures for above.

9. Obtain duplicates of products involved for examination, analysis, testing and comparison.
10. List and attach copies of any relevant laws, standards and regulations. Include title, jurisdiction, section and paragraph.
11. Mark each page of the Report as "Attorney-Client Privileged Information"

3. Product Design Risks, Labels and Warnings

When designing products, manufacturing companies need to be very detailed to avoid product liability litigation in the United States. Product planning is a very detailed process involving many departments, as we have seen. As part of an overall plan to reduce risks of product liability litigation as well as class actions and government investigations raised by CPSC or FTC concerns, it is recommended manufacturing companies develop a detailed design risk program or "DRP." Such processes can minimize, reduce, or prevent liability when claims are brought. A checklist should be developed to cover such issues. Checklists are another handy tool to use when looking at processes and procedures to minimize legal liability. Product planning and design process considerations should normally include the following:

3.1 Product Design Issues and Considerations

- Written procedures for the design program, including:
  - Design choices—consideration of alternative designs
  - Specifications—definition of specifications used in designing the product
  - Establishment of a design review committee

- Establishment of written procedures for the development of specifications, which verify that specifications are accurately reflected in the designs.
- Establishment of procedures for construction and testing and prototypes.
- During the design: Evaluation and consideration of:
    - Determine types of people likely to be exposed to the product, consider unique risks to these groups
    - Tailor labeling and develop safety features to address the unique risks to the intended users
    - Risks of intended use—test and evaluate to determine what risks are presented if the product is used as intended; reduce these risks through design changes, safety features, and/or labeling.
- Assess the likelihood that products will be misused; identify and reduce through design features, safety features, and/or labeling.
- Malfunction: Incorporate features that prevent critical failure or malfunction. Is it safe to use? If not, what features can render it safe?
- Design manufacturing considerations: Can the product be manufactured in accordance with the specifications?
- Serviceability: Are the products so difficult to service or maintain correctly?
- Consider the materials, components, equipment, and software that should be used in manufacturing the device.
- Assure that designs comply with applicable code certifications and standards. Are they appropriate? Do they comply with governmental and industry standards?
- If using an outside company to develop or provide product designs, review and evaluate the designs.
- Monitoring of designs, including continued research and testing and review of new information respecting the products.
- Record-keeping of all product designs and processes to show all the above processes were considered.
- Is everyone in the design department familiar with all design procedures and processes?

3.2 Forms and Checklists

3.2.1 Checklists for Product Design

Designers Guidelines for New Product Introduction

1. **Concern for safety**

   Your design should clearly show that you were concerned about user safety. Juries have little sympathy for manufacturers who do not exhibit a primary concern for safety.

2. **Safety margins**

   Failing to meet standards is invariably fatal to the defense of a product case. Conversely, merely meeting a standard does little affirmatively for the case's defense. The wise route is to exceed standards.

3. **Safety margins and material specifications**

   You must establish clearly defined criteria that support the decision leading to fulfilling this responsibility.

4. **Documentation of analyses and tests**

   This is a particularly crucial step since analysis and sufficient testing are often key issues for the jury.

5. **Life or accelerated testing**

   The designer must be able to demonstrate a comprehensive understanding of both the limits and maximum capabilities of the product.

6. **Failure and hazard analysis**

   These engineering fundamentals are equally important in the courtroom. It's no longer sufficient to argue that the injury or accident was "unanticipated."

7. **Worst case analysis**

   This effort is particularly useful in the defense of products litigation.

8. **Fail safe design**

   Reasonably foreseeable uses (and misuses) must be anticipated and potential resulting injuries should be designed out of the product.

9. **Hazards (use and misuse)**

   Since the designer has anticipated foreseeable uses and misuses of the product and also the potential resulting injuries from these uses, the designer must lend particular heed to the magnitude of the potential injury or damage.

10. **Warnings and instructions**

    The plaintiff's bar has focused on this aspect recently in developing a case against the manufacturer. Clear, comprehensive adequate warnings are a must.

11. **Inspection and quality control**

    It is important to be able to demonstrate to the jury that the product and its components left the manufacturer in good functional condition.

12. **Evaluation by independent laboratory**

    This tends to remove some of the natural bias that a jury may develop against the manufacturer's in-house testing.

13. **Product performance feedback**

    Empirical testing and assessment of the results reported both in the laboratory and in the courtroom.

14. **Documentation of risk-utility considerations**

    This responsibility must be undertaken both at the outset of product development and intermittently hereafter as incident reports of claims are received. These 14 points generally outline the designer's responsibilities from an engineering standpoint and to satisfy a jury.

3.2.2 Checklists for Warnings and Labels

I. <u>Warnings</u>

1. Are warnings adequate?
2. Do warnings address misuse of product?
3. Do warnings cover inherent hazards?
4. Are hazards properly covered?
5. Do warnings warn users against obvious risks?
6. Do warnings clearly state the consequences of improper use?
7. Do warnings warn users against all risks?
8. Do warnings reasonably communicate the seriousness of harm that may result from improper use?
9. Do warnings adequately indicate the scope of danger?
10. Do warnings indicate the level of hazard seriousness?
11. Do warnings indicate the likelihood of the hazard resulting in harm?
12. Do warnings adequately alert a reasonably prudent person to the danger?

II. Labels

1. Is the label accurate complete, visible and understood?
2. Is the label easy to understand?
3. If the label is incomplete, does it state that other materials will provide full information?
4. Are labels and warnings consistent?
5. Does the label mislead consumers in any way?
6. Do labels include how and where to obtain service?
7. Do labels contain information:
    i. Maintenance
    ii. Service
    iii. Alterations
8. Do labels comply with governmental requirements?
9. Are labels monitored for accuracy and adequacy?
10. What are labeling practices in the industry?
11. Are labels monitored for legal requirements?
12. Are label-history files being maintained?
13. Are changes in labels reported to the label design committee if there is one?
14. Do labels comply with food manufacturing standards?

3.2.3 Checklists for New Product Planning

OUTLINE RESPECTING NEW PRODUCT INTRODUCTION

I. Potential claims can arise from Breach of Warranty or State Deceptive and Unfair Trade Practices Statutes.

II. Creation of Warranties: Express and Implied.

III. Limiting Liability through disclaimer of warranty, limitation of remedy and product information, warning and cautionary statements.

NEW PRODUCT INTRODUCTION

I. Potential Claims Can Arise From
  A. Breach of Warranty
  B. State Deceptive and Unfair Trade Practices Statute ("DUTPA")
II. Warranties
  A. Express Warranty
  1. Magnuson Moss Warranty Act
    a) Written Warranty—must be designated as "full" or "limited" (requirement applies to all written warranties on consumer products costing more than $10).
    b) Written Warranty—must meet one of following conditions:
      (i) Statement or Promise that material or workmanship is defect free or will meet specified level of performance over a specific period of time or
      (ii) an undertaking in writing to refund, repair or replace or take other remedial action in the event that the product fails to meet specifications promised.
    c) Disclosure and pre-sale availability rules apply to all written warranties on consumer products costing more than $15.
    d) Required disclosures must be clearly and conspicuously disclosed in a single document in a simple and readily understood language.
  2. Uniform Commercial Code ("UCC")
    a) Under UCC the following can create an express warranty:
      (i) Express affirmation or promise (2-313(a))
      (ii) Description of the goods (2-313(b))
      (iii) Sample or model (2-313(c))
    b) Some UCC Express Warranties will be Magnuson Moss "Written Warranties."
    c) Express Warranties can be oral and can arise from advertisements, catalogues, brochures, pamphlets, and labels.
  B. Implied Warranties
  1. Under Magnuson Moss Warranty Act an "Implied Warranty" means an implied warranty arising under State Law.

2. Uniform Commercial Code
    a) Implied Warranty of merchantability is implied by law in every contract with a merchant for the sale of goods; a guarantee that product will be merchantable (of commercially acceptable quality).
    b) Implied Warranty of fitness for a particular purpose—arises when the seller has reason to know that buyer wants goods for a particular purpose and buyer is relying on seller's skill to select suitable goods.

III. Deceptive and Unfair Trade Practices ("DUTPA")

A. Every state has a statute prohibiting deceptive trade practices

1. DUTPA claims not based on contract; contractual limitations on liability do not apply.
2. Claims are not based on warranty so disclaimers of warranty do not apply.
3. Deceptive and Unfair Trade Practices can include:
    a) failure to disclose information
    b) oral and written misrepresentations
    c) ambiguous representations
    d) breach of warranty obligations
    e) failure to comply with certain federal or state laws or regulatory requirements.

IV. Limiting Liability

A. Disclaimer of Warranty

1. Magnuson Moss
    a) Full Warranty may not exclude or limit consequential damages for breach of express or implied warranty unless exclusion or limitation appears conspicuously on the face of the warranty.
    b) Cannot disclaim implied warranty to a consumer when (i) a Written Warranty is given on a product or (ii) when consumer enters into a Service contract with supplier at the time of sale or within ninety (90) days after sale.
    c) Implied Warranties may be limited to the duration of a written warranty of reasonable duration.
        (i) any limitation on duration must include the statement "some states do not allow limitations on how long an

implied warranty lasts, so the above limitations may not apply to you."

d) Can limit remedies available for breach of express or implied warranty. The limitation must be clearly and conspicuously disclosed in the document.

e) Any limitation on remedies must include the statements

(i) "some states do not allow the exclusion or limitation of incidental or consequential damages, so the above limitation or exclusion may not apply to you."

(ii) "this warranty gives you specific legal rights, and you may also have other rights which vary from state to state."

2. Uniform Commercial Code ("UCC")

a) UCC generally permits disclaimers and modification of warranty liability (2-316)

b) Cannot disclaim express warranties (2-316(1))

c) Specific language is required ". . . to exclude or modify the implied warranty of merchantability or any part of it the language must mention merchantability . . ."

B. Limitation of Remedies

1. Magnuson Moss Warranty Act ("Act")

a) Under the Act, the term "remedy" means whichever of the following the warrantor elects:

(i) refund;

(ii) repair,

(iii) replacement.

b) "Warrantor cannot elect refund unless (i) the warrantor is unable to provide replacement and repair is not commercially practicable or cannot be timely made or (ii) the consumer is willing to accept such refund."

c) Must clearly and conspicuously disclose in a single document (i) any exclusions of or limitation on relief such as incidental or consequential damages.

2. Uniform Commercial Code

a) UCC permits agreement respecting the provision of remedies in addition to or in substitution of those provided by UCC (2-719(1)(a)).

b) Can limit remedy to repair, replace or refund of purchase price
c) Limitation must be exclusive and specifically replace UCC remedies.

C. Describe Product Limitations and Risks
a) Buyer's conduct as a basis for affirmative defense.
(i) Voluntary and unreasonable disregard of known and appreciated risks.
(ii) Misuse of the product.
(iii) Failure to follow directions for use.
(iv) Failure to comply with conditions for warranty coverage.

V. Recommendations Respecting New Product Introduction

1. Determine:
a) Type of warranty—"full," "limited."
b) (i) "point in time or event upon which the warranty term commences, if different from the purchase date and (ii) the time period or other measure of warranty duration".
c) Terms of warranty coverage including as set forth in the regulations:
(i) "the identity of the party or parties to whom the written warranty is extended if the enforceability is to the original consumer or is otherwise limited to persons other than every consumer owner during the term of the warranty,
(ii) "a clear description and identification of products or parts or characteristics or components or properties covered by or excluded from the Warranty."
d) Method of providing warranty service.
e) Remedies for breach of warranty, including what will provide and pay for and what won't.
2. Disclaim warranties not intended.
3. Restrict or eliminate potential liability for incidental and consequential damages.
4. Develop Warnings and Cautionary Statements.
a) Describe the product's limitations
b) Stress the dangers of not following the printed procedures and instructions.

  c) Highlight correct methods for assembly, installation, use and maintenance.
  d) Warn against modification of the product and parts substitution.
  e) Warn if misuse and hazard to the user.
  f) Specify maintenance procedures and frequency.
  g) Indicate the useful life of the product.
  h) Ensure that labels and warnings comply with federal, state, local and industry regulations and standards.

5. Review all sales and advertising manuals to ensure that they accurately describe the product.
6. Incorporate disclaimers and limitations of warranties into sales literature and sales agreements whenever possible.

4. Contract Management

4.1 Contract Risk Management

A major area of legal risk for any company is the negotiation, execution, and performance of contracts. Many companies have spent much money creating and/or improving the contract management process. Some companies simply rely on outside counsel to handle its contracts, blissfully unaware that the lack of internal contract risk management controls exposes it in the long run to major legal and business liability—a lawsuit waiting to happen!

A company needs to address many contractual areas prior to drafting contracts as well as managing them. Not only must a company negotiate agreements but it must also manage and comply with the agreements once they have been negotiated and executed.

Some of the areas that need to be addressed include:

- IP
- Warranties
- Indemnities
- Tax
- Sales and marketing issues
- Responsibilities and obligations
- Deliverables
- Payment obligations
- Industry terms and conditions

- Insurance

Obviously, if a proper contract management system is not in place, some or all the issues above may be affected, causing great harm to the company. Pricing could be impacted, or missed contractual obligations could result in the company's indemnity obligations to cover more than expected. Contractual defenses as well may not be implemented due to the lack of appropriate contracts or contractual terms.

4.1.1 Contract Management Issues

In order for a company's contracts to be negotiated, performed, and executed properly, a number of organizations within a company must work together and coordinate efforts. Depending on the kind of contract, its size, and scope, not only should divisions or business units work together, but appropriate policies and processes must be implemented and followed.

For instance, decision makers within a company need to make informed and timely business decisions prior to execution of a contract, but can only do so based on input from internal stakeholders or division heads. A process needs to be in place to ensure timely advice is provided. Depending on the nature of the risks and issues involved (i.e., billing, tax, etc.) appropriate departments will need to be involved.

A proper LRM audit needs to be conducted to ensure the proper contract management process is in place. Such an audit should cover roles and responsibilities of departments within an organization, the kinds of contracts used by the business units, the major legal and business term that must be addressed, the process for informing the relevant decision makers as to the risks faced, and the process for ensuring the contracts are not only signed but also performed. A contract management process can be very detailed, which is why some companies have failed to adopt the process. Of course, when a company fails to implement a contract management process, it opens itself up to potential legal and financial exposure.

A company's contract management process must allow for negotiation and resolution of major business and legal issues while its customers or vendors are satisfied with the process. Therefore, a company's contract management process must not only allow for proper negotiation and resolution of contractual issues, but must also ensure the company is not exposed to undue risk. Though a company may be willing to assume a moderate level of risk, it may not be willing to accept a greater degree of risk without pricing the risk or cost of risk into its pricing calculations. From an accounting standpoint, a company may wish to increase its reserves as well.

4.1.2 Roles and Responsibilities

A company's various business units as well as Legal, Sales, Risk, Finance, Human Resources, Contract Management (if it exists), and other impacted corporate departments or groups must work together to minimize undue risk to the company and ensure how the risk should be managed.

Roles and responsibilities of certain organizations normally include:

- Corporate risk management: The division head or department head responsible for identifying risk and facilitating mitigation by working with Legal, Business Units, and decision makers. Corporate risk management implements policies and procedures to ensure risk mitigation strategies are pursued throughout the life of the contract.
- Legal: The department responsible for identifying legal risks and available legal options and preparation and maintenance of contracts and contract templates. Also responsible for negotiating legal terms.
- Contract management: The department responsible for identifying and documenting legal and business issues raised during negotiation of contract terms (if not done by Legal) and escalation of legal and business terms to the correct decision makers within the company. Usually has to notify Legal of complex legal issues.
- Finance: The department responsible for issues including cash flow, time value of money, and reserve calculations.
- Sales: The division or department responsible for communicating with and maintenance of the customer relationship while helping to mitigate risk to the company. Needs to understand basic risk issues.

- Business Units: The division or various departments responsible for identifying the strategic value of the contract. May want contract managers to stay in their unit.
- Human Resources: The department responsible for issues involving personnel management, secondment if needed, noncompetition issues, and other matters having a direct effect on employees.

Other decision makers or internal stakeholders may also be involved besides the groups listed above. The board of directors, executive committee, CEO, CFO, or controller, etc., may get involved to discuss risk mitigation strategies as is necessary.

4.2 Contract Management Processes

The contract management process, to be effective, must include processes and procedures that identify and resolve certain legal and business issues.

Among those processes and procedure are:

4.2.1 The Escalations Process

This is the process in which certain important legal and business risks get escalated to the proper organization for resolution. Such a process should include:

- Identification of the issues
- Communication to relevant stakeholders
- Business impact analysis
- Resolution of issue
- Communication of resolution and documentation of the resolution

4.2.2 Contract Approvers and Processes

A process has to be implemented to ensure that:

- All Contract Management/Legal comments have been incorporated into the contract or at least considered.
- The contract is ready for execution or signature of the other party.
- The most current version of the contract is ready to be uploaded into the database.
- The correct contact names and billing addresses are in the final version of the contract.
- All terms are final and correct.

4.2.3 Standard Billing and Payment Terms

A company normally has certain standard billing and payment terms in its contracts. Such terms need to be included in the proper agreements. Depending on the kind of contract in question, such terms could include:

- Fixed fee payment
- Time and materials
- Milestone payments
- Maintenance payments
- Payment based on credit

The process should ensure, absent escalation, that the standard billing and payment terms are in the contract as required.

4.2.4 Ownership of Intellectual Property (IP)

One of the most important assets of any company is its IP. It, therefore, stands to reason that IP concerns must be properly reflected in the contract management process. IP concerns include:

- Ownership of IP rights
    - Does the company retain or receive IP rights?
    - Does the contracting party receive right and title to the IP?
- Retention of IP rights

- When does the company retain all right, title, and interest in any and all IP?
- When does the contracting party retain all right, title, and interest in any and all IP?

- Ownership of newly created IP
  - What happens when the company or contracting party creates IP during performance of the contract?
- Similar works
  - What happens when the company performs similar services for third-party customers?

4.2.5 Typical Customer or Vendor Requests

A company's customers or vendors may typically ask for certain terms in a contract. Such terms could impose undue risk on the company or negatively affect its contractual relations with third parties. The contract management process must address and resolve the issues caused by such requests. Terms typically asked for may include:

- Customer retention of IP rights
- Noncompetition provisions
- Customer ownership of deliverables
- Nonstandard payment terms
- Staffing changes
- Broad indemnity provisions
- Limitation of liability

A company's contracts would or should normally address all of the above-mentioned issues. The contract management process must ensure that the issues are escalated to and resolved by the appropriate stakeholders and that all appropriate terms have been negotiated and addressed in a timely manner.

4.2.6 Preliminary Agreements

A well-thought-out contract management process will contain certain company guidelines and preliminary agreement templates to facilitate the deal. A LRM audit should review any and all preliminary guidelines and document templates to ensure the needs of the company are being met and potential legal and business risks are mitigated. Preliminary agreements include:

- Letter of intent (LOI): Normally a document reflecting the understanding between the company and customer or vendor without creating a binding obligation.

  LOI corporate usage guidelines should address subject matter of the LOI, the fact that the parties do not wish to be bound, when a nondisclosure agreement is needed, and under what terms the parties expect to be bound at a later date.

- Memorandum of understanding (MOU): Normally a document for establishing an agreement of critical or major terms between the parties before a full and final contract is negotiated and executed.

  MOU corporate usage guidelines should address what obligations the company is willing to commit to before negotiating a complete contract, as well as a definition of the framework for negotiation of such as the price, milestones, deliverables, etc.

- Letter of authorization (LOA): Normally a document containing a minimum set of key terms and conditions that the parties must agree upon in order to begin work during contract negotiations. Not always used.

  LOA corporate usage guidelines should deal with issues such as IP, liability, price, etc. that may be hard to negotiate after work has started.

Note: A process must be in place requiring the signature and/or sign-off of the appropriate corporate officer or officers prior to execution of any of the preliminary agreements.

4.3 Forms

4.3.1 Confidentiality and Non-Disclosure Agreement

XXXX Corporation.
CONFIDENTIALITY AND NON-DISCLOSURE AGREEMENT

This Confidentiality Agreement (the "Agreement") is entered into and is effective as of _____, 20___ by and between XXXX, INC., ________________________________ (hereinafter "XXXX") and __________________ (hereinafter "Recipient").

1. DEFINITION OF CONFIDENTIAL INFORMATION.

Recipient agrees that information disclosed by XXXX to Recipient regarding XXXX and other trade secrets and details of the business and products of XXXX, including but not limited to information learned by Recipient from XXXX employees, agents or through inspection of XXXX's property, that relates to XXXX's products, designs, know-how, third-party confidential information disclosed to Recipient by XXXX, will be considered and referred to collectively in this Agreement as "Confidential Information." Confidential Information, however, does not include information that 1) is now or subsequently becomes generally available to the public through no fault or breach on the part of Recipient; 2) Recipient can demonstrate to have had rightfully in its possession prior to disclosure to Recipient by XXXX; 3) is independently developed by Recipient without the use of any Confidential Information; or 4) Recipient rightfully obtains from a third party who has the right to transfer or disclose it.

2. NONDISCLOSURE AND NONUSE OF CONFIDENTIAL INFORMATION.

Recipient will not disclose, publish, or disseminate Confidential Information to anyone other than those of its employees with a need to know, and Recipient agrees to take reasonable precautions to prevent any unauthorized use, disclosure, publication, or dissemination of Confidential Information. Recipient agrees to accept Confidential Information for the sole purpose of utilizing the Confidential

Information in connection with its business affairs and relationship with __________. Recipient agrees not to use Confidential Information otherwise for its own or any third party's benefit without the prior written approval of an authorized representative of __________ in each instance.

3. OWNERSHIP OF CONFIDENTIAL INFORMATION.

All Confidential Information, and any Derivatives thereof whether created by XXXX or Recipient, remain the property of XXXX and no license or other rights to Confidential Information is granted or implied hereby. For purposes of this Agreement, "Derivatives" shall mean: (i) for copyrightable or copyrighted material, any translation, abridgment, revision or other form in which an existing work may be recast, transformed or adapted; (ii) for patentable or patented material, any improvement thereon; and (iii) for material which is protected by trade secret, any new material derived from such existing trade secret material, including new material which may be protected by copyright, patent and/or trade secret.

4. NO WARRANTY.

All information is provided "AS IS" and without any warranty, whether expressed or implied, as to its accuracy or completeness.

5. RETURN OF DOCUMENTS.

Within ten business days of receipt of a written request from XXXX, Recipient will return to __________ all documents, records and copies thereof containing Confidential Information. For purposes of this section, the term "documents" includes all information fixed in any tangible medium of expression, in whatever form or format.

6. EQUITABLE RELIEF.

Recipient hereby acknowledges that unauthorized disclosure or use of Confidential Information could cause irreparable harm and significant injury to XXXX that may be difficult to ascertain. Accordingly, Recipient agrees that XXXX will have the right to seek and obtain immediate injunctive relief to enforce obligations under this Agreement in addition to any other rights and remedies it may have.

7. NO EXPORT.

Recipient certified that no Confidential Information, or any portion thereof, will be exported to any county in violation of the United States Export Administration Act and regulations thereunder.

8. ENTIRE AGREEMENT AND GOVERNING LAW.

This Agreement constitutes the entire agreement with respect to the Confidential Information disclosed herein and supersedes all prior or contemporaneous oral or written agreements concerning such Confidential Information. This Agreement may not be amended except by the written agreement signed by authorized representatives of both parties. This Agreement will be governed and construed in accordance with the laws of ____________________.

Understood and agreed to by the duly authorized representatives of the parties:

XXXX, Inc.	Recipient
______________________	______________________
By (Signature) Date	By (Signature) Date
______________________	______________________
Printed Name and Title	Printed Name and Title

4.3.2 Nondisclosure Agreement

_______ a New York corporation, having a principal place of business at ____________ (hereinafter Company) and _____, a corporation, having a principal place of business at (hereinafter XXXXX) agree as follows:

1. In connection with presentations, demonstrations, proposals, meetings and/or discussions relating to each Party's products and services and areas of mutual interest, including, but not limited to, wireless local area network technology, XXXX and Company may, from time to time, disclose to each other (as Owner and Recipient as the case may be) specifications, drawings, data, computer programs, documentation or other technical or business information in written or tangible form which have been marked as being confidential by the Owner (hereinafter Information). Any disclosure made orally shall be identified by Owner as confidential at the time of disclosure thereof, and shall be reduced to a writing and marked confidential and provided to Recipient within fifteen (15) days of such disclosure.
2. With respect to Information provided under this Agreement, Recipient agrees with the Owner to:

    A. Restrict disclosure of the Information solely to those employees of Recipient having a need to know and who have undertaken confidentiality obligations with Recipient, and not disclose Information to any other party;
    B. Advise those employees of Recipient of their obligations with respect to the Information and ensure their compliance with this Agreement;
    C. Use the Information only for internal evaluation to determine the feasibility of entering into a licensing, consulting, teaming or other business arrangement and not, under this Agreement, for any commercial, productive or any other purposes or for the benefit of any third party, except as may otherwise be mutually agreed upon in writing; and

D. Promptly inform the Owner of any requirement or request by any third person that Information be disclosed pursuant to legislation, legal directive, public regulation, court decision or the like or in connection with the pursuit or defense of a claim in order to afford the Owner an opportunity to limit or restrict such disclosure or to obtain appropriate protective/secrecy orders with respect thereto and to obtain its agreement prior to further action.

Restrictions of Paragraph 2a notwithstanding, Recipient may disclose the Information to those of its contract personnel (i.e., individuals performing tasks which are customarily/routinely performed by its employees) involved in the activity to which the Information relates, and who have signed confidentiality agreements with Recipient.

3. Recipient shall have no obligation to preserve the confidential nature of any Information that:

   A. Was previously known to the Recipient free of any obligation to keep confidential and free of any restriction on use and disclosure; or
   B. Is received from third persons without restrictions on use and disclosure and without breach of any agreement with Owner; or
   C. Is disclosed to third persons by the Owner without restrictions on use and disclosure; or
   D. Is or becomes publicly available by authorized disclosure by the Owner and without any restrictions on use and disclosure; or
   E. Is developed by or for the Recipient independently of Information; or
   F. Is approved for release by written authorization of the Owner.

4. The Information shall be deemed the property of the Owner and, upon request, the Recipient will return all Information in tangible form to the Owner or destroy all such Information.

5. Nothing contained in this Agreement shall be construed as granting or conferring any rights by license or otherwise in any Information disclosed to the Recipient or in any intellectual property rights related thereto.
6. Nothing herein shall obligate or otherwise commit any party or any other company in any way, directly or indirectly, to initiate, produce, or complete any observation, study, analysis or report of any product or service, or any aspect thereof, or to take any other action with respect to such product or service; and nothing herein shall obligate or otherwise commit either Party or any other company to license or purchase any product or service from anyone.
7. This Agreement shall not be assignable or transferable by any party, without the written consent of the other parties.
8. OWNER MAKES NO REPRESENTATION IN RESPECT TO AND DOES NOT WARRANT ANY INFORMATION FURNISHED HEREWITH, BUT SHALL FURNISH SUCH IN GOOD FAITH TO THE BEST OF ITS KNOWLEDGE AND ABILITY. WITHOUT RESTRICTING THE GENERALITY OF THE FOREGOING, OWNER MAKES NO REPRESENTATIONS OR WARRANTIES, WHETHER WRITTEN OR ORAL, STATUTORY, EXPRESS OR IMPLIED WITH RESPECT TO THE INFORMATION OR ANY TECHNICAL ASSISTANCE WHICH MAY BE PROVIDED HEREUNDER, INCLUDING WITHOUT LIMITATION, ANY WARRANTY OF MERCHANTABILITY OR OF FITNESS FOR A PARTICULAR PURPOSE.
9. In the event of a breach or a threatened breach or intended breach of this Agreement by Recipient, Owner, in addition to any other rights and remedies available to it at law or in equity (except as otherwise limited by this Agreement), shall be entitled to seek injunctive relief, both preliminary and final, enjoining and restraining such breach or threatened or intended breach.
10. This Agreement shall be governed by and construed under the substantive laws of the State of New Jersey.
11. Facsimile signatures shall be deemed equivalent to original signatures for purposes of this Agreement.

12. This Agreement shall become effective on the later date of signing and shall continue for a period of two (2) years, unless earlier terminated by any party upon ten (10) days written notice to other parties. The obligation to protect the Information shall survive and continue for a period of three (3) years beyond any expiration or termination of this Agreement.

__________XXXX

By: By:

Signature Signature

Name: Name:
Title: Title:
Date: Date:

4.3.3 Letter of Intent—A

[Date]

VIA [INSERT]
[Name]
[Title]
[Company]
[Address]
[Address]

Re: Letter of Intent

Dear [Name]:

This letter, when countersigned by the signatories hereto, will confirm the discussions to date among [name of purchaser], a [state] [type of entity] ("Purchaser"), and [names of stockholders/shareholders] ("Sellers"), the holders of 100% of the outstanding capital stock of [name of target company], a [state] [type of entity] ("Target Company" and together with any subsidiaries, "Target Companies"), regarding the possible acquisition by a newly formed wholly-owned subsidiary of Purchaser

("Purchaser Subsidiary*") of [100%] of the outstanding capital stock of Target Company. Purchaser, Sellers and Target Company are sometimes collectively referred to as the "Parties" and individually as a "Party."

The Parties wish to commence negotiating a definitive written acquisition agreement providing for the transactions contemplated by this letter (the "Definitive Agreement). To facilitate the negotiation of the Definitive Agreement, the Parties request that Purchaser's counsel prepare an initial draft. Each of the paragraphs below contained under the section entitled "Matters in Principal" summarizes certain economic and other terms related to the transactions contemplated by this letter, but are not intended to be binding upon any of us. Each of the paragraphs below contained under the section entitled "Binding Provisions" is intended to bind and be enforceable against each of us whether or not we sign the Definitive Agreement.

I. Matters in Principal

No paragraph set forth in. this section of this letter (the "Non-Binding Provisions' will be legally binding or enforceable against any Party.

1. Transaction.

    (a) Stock Purchase; Closing. Each Seller would sell to Purchaser Subsidiary all of the capital stock of Target Company owned by such Seller, which in the aggregate constitutes 100% of the outstanding equity securities of Target Company, at the aggregate price (the "Purchase Price") set forth in Paragraph 2 below. The closing of the transactions contemplated by this letter (the "Closing") would occur as soon as possible after the termination of the applicable waiting period under the Hart-Scott-Rodino Antitrust Improvements Act of 1976, as amended (the "HSR Acf1), the receipt of any and all required consents and the satisfaction of the other conditions to closing contained in the Definitive Agreement.

(b) Other Material Terms. [Insert other material terms: e.g, Section 338(h)(10) election, leveraged recapitalization accounting, pooling of interests accounting, etc.]

2. Purchase Price: Payment Terms and Escrow: Purchase Price Adjustment.

(a) Purchase Price. The Purchase Price would be $[aggregate amount], plus or minus the purchase price adjustment described in this Paragraph 2.
(b) Payment Terms and Escrow. Purchaser Subsidiary would pay the Purchase Price to Sellers at the Closing in the following manner: (i) payment of $[amount] by wire transfer of immediately available fluids; (ii) delivery of an [unsecured, non-negotiable, subordinated] promissory note in the principal amount of $[amount] accruing interest at a rate of [rate]% per annum, and providing for [number] equal [annual] [quarterly] [monthly] payments of principal and accrued interest; (iii) delivery of [number] restricted shares of [Purchaser] common stock, and (iv) deposit of $ [amount] with a mutually acceptable escrow agent to be held in escrow for a period of [number] [years/months] in order to secure the performance of Sellers' obligations under the Definitive Agreement and related documents.
(c) Purchase Price Adjustment. The-Purchase Price assumes that the Target Companies would have consolidated [stockholders' equity/working capital] of at least $[amount] as of the Closing. The Purchase Price would be increased or decreased, as the case may be, on a dollar-for-dollar basis based on the Target Companies' actual consolidated [stockholders' equity/working capital] as of the Closing, [describe any thresholds]

3. Employment: Non-Competition Agreements.

(a) Employment Agreements. Target Company and each of [Name, Name, Name] would enter into a [number] year employment agreement on mutually agreeable terms, including the following: [describe any preagreed terms].

(b) Non-Competition Agreements. Each of [Name, Name, Name] would execute a [number] year non-competition agreement in favor of Purchaser Subsidiary.

4. Other Terms of the Definitive Agreement.

   (a) Representations and Warranties, Covenants, Indemnities. Sellers and, until the Closing, Target Company would make customary representations and warranties to Purchaser Subsidiary, and would provide comprehensive covenants, indemnities and other protections for the benefit of Purchaser Subsidiary. The representations and warranties in the Definitive Agreement would be without qualification as to knowledge, materiality or otherwise, but no breaches of such representations and warranties would be actionable until all claims for such breaches exceed, in the aggregate, a basket of [percentage]% of the Purchase Price.

   (b) Significant Conditions. The Closing would be subject to the satisfaction of, among other things, the following conditions: (i) the termination of the applicable waiting period under the HSR Act; (ii) obtaining [specify any material consents, releases, etc.]; and (iii) [insert other significant conditions].

II. Binding Provisions

Each paragraph set forth in this section of the letter (collectively, the "Binding Provisions") will be legally binding and enforceable against the Parties.

1. Access. During the period commencing on the date this letter is signed by the Sellers (the "Signing Date") and ending on the date the Binding Provisions are terminated pursuant to Paragraph 14 (the "Termination Date"), Target Company and Sellers will afford Purchaser reasonable access to each of the Target Companies, its

personnel, properties, contracts, books and records, and all other documents and data.

2. Exclusive Dealing. Until the later to occur of the Termination Date or 120 days after the Signing Date: (a) Target Company and each Seller will not, directly or indirectly, through any representative or otherwise, solicit or entertain offers from, negotiate with or in any manner encourage, discuss, accept, or consider any proposal of any other person relating to the acquisition of any stock of any Target Company, its assets or business, in whole or in part, whether directly or indirectly, through purchase, merger, consolidation, or otherwise (other than sales of inventory in the ordinary course consistent with past practice); and (b) Target Company or any Seller, as the case may be, will immediately notify Purchaser in writing of any contact (whether by telephone, personal conversation, fax, e-mail or otherwise) between Target Company, and Seller or their respective representatives and any other person regarding any offer, proposal or inquiry of the nature specified iji subparagraph (a) of this Paragraph.
3. Break-up Fee. If (a) Target Company or any Seller breaches any material term of the Binding Provisions or Target Company or any Seller terminates this letter as provided herein, and (b) within twelve months after the date of such termination, any Target Company or any Seller enters into any agreement relating to the acquisition of a majority of the shares of stock of such Target Company, its assets or business, in whole or in part, whether directly or indirectly, through purchase, merger, consolidation, or otherwise (other than sales of inventory or immaterial portions of such Target Company's assets in the ordinary course) whether or not such transaction is ultimately consummated, then, Sellers and Target Company, jointly and severally, will immediately pay to Purchaser in immediately available funds amount equal to $[amount]. In addition, Purchaser will be entitled to all other rights and remedies provided by law or in equity.
4. Conduct of Business. During the period commencing on the Signing Date and ending on the Termination Date, Target Company will operate its business in the ordinary course of

business consistent with past practices and refrain from any extraordinary transactions.

5. Disclosure. Except as and to the extent required by law, without the prior written consent of the other Party, neither Purchaser, any Seller nor any Target Company will, and each will direct its representatives not to make, directly or indirectly, any public comment, statement, or communication with respect to, or otherwise to disclose or to permit the disclosure of the existence of discussions regarding, a possible transaction between the Parties or any of the terms, conditions, or other aspects of the transactions contemplated by this letter. If a Party is required by law to make any such disclosure, it must first provide to the other Party the content of the proposed disclosure, the reasons that such disclosure is required by law, and the time and place that the disclosure will be made.
6. Costs. In the event the Closing does not occur, each Party will be responsible for and bear all of its own costs and expenses (including any broker's or finder's fees and the expenses of its representatives) incurred at any time in connection with pursuing or consummating the transactions contemplated by this letter. Notwithstanding the preceding sentence, Purchaser will pay one-half and Sellers will pay one-half of the HSR Act filing fee. If, however, the transactions contemplated by this letter are consummated, all of Purchaser's fees and expenses will be paid out of the assets of the acquired entity or entities.
7. HSR Filing. During the period commencing on the Signing Date and ending on the Termination Date, each Party will cooperate with each other and proceed, as promptly as is reasonably practical, to prepare and to file the notifications required by the HSR Act.
8. Entire Agreement. The Binding Provisions constitute the entire agreement between the Parties and, except for that certain Confidentiality Agreement dated [insert date] by and between the Parties, supersede all prior oral or written agreements, understandings, representations and warranties, and courses of conduct and dealing between the Parties on the subject matter hereof. Except as otherwise provided in this letter, the Binding

Provisions may be amended or modified only by a writing executed by each of the Parties.

9. Governing Law. The Binding Provisions will be governed by and construed under the laws of the State of [state] without regard to conflicts of laws principles.
10. Termination. This letter will automatically terminate upon the earlier to occur of: (a) closing of the transactions contemplated by this letter and (b) twenty four months after the Signing Date. In addition, this letter may be terminated earlier upon written notice by any Party to the other Parties unilaterally, for any reason or no reason, with or without cause, at any time; provided, however, that the termination hereof will have no effect on the liability of a Parry for a breach of any of the Binding Provisions, The Binding Provisions will survive any termination of this letter, and will remain in effect for the period specified in such Binding Provision or, if no date is so specified, for the period ending on the date of the second anniversary of the Termination Date.
11. Counterparts. This letter may be executed in one or more counterparts each of which will be deemed to be an original copy of this letter and all of which, when taken together will be deemed to constitute one and the same agreement.

If you are in agreement with the foregoing, please sign and return one copy of this letter agreement to me.

Very truly yours,
[Signature block of Purchaser]

Duly executed and agreed as to the Binding Provisions on [Date]
[Signature block for the Target Company]
[Insert a signature line for each Seller]

4.3.4 Letter of Intent—B

August 12, 2013
Addressee Name
Company Name
Street Address 1
Street Address 2
City, State, Zip
ATTN: ____________________________
Title _______________________

Re: Letter of Intent

Dear ___________,

The purpose of this Letter of Intent is to set forth our mutual interest to engage in negotiations towards reaching agreement and executing one or more acceptable and definitive contracts. This Letter of Intent does not create any contractually binding obligations, and each of our respective companies will be responsible for any costs and expenses which may be incurred during negotiations. It is understood that these negotiations create no fiduciary or confidential relationship, except as may be defined in a separate Non-Disclosure Agreement.

_______ plans to engage in discussions with_______in the areas of ___________. These discussions may lead to technical consulting, licensing or other appropriate agreements acceptable to both parties.

It is understood that any agreement which may be reached is subject to agreement upon all price, warranty, and other commercial terms and conditions. It is also understood that any agreement which may be reached would be subject to all requisite managerial approvals.

This Letter of Intent shall be governed by and construed in accordance with the laws of the State of _________, USA. By entering into this Letter of Intent, _______ is not subjecting itself to the jurisdiction of any court outside the State of _________, and no claim or suit arising out of or related to this Letter of Intent shall be filed against _______ outside the State of _________.

This Letter of Intent contains our entire understanding with regard to this matter, and this Letter may not be amended or changed except in writing signed by both parties.

Very truly yours,

____

Account Executive
Attachment(s)
Copy to:

AGREED BY:

By:
Name:
Title:
Date:

4.3.5 Memorandum of Understanding

Proposed Memorandum of Understanding between __________ and ___________________________________

This Memorandum of Understanding is made as of this __ day of ________, 20_, between __________, [Location] and _________________________, a ________ corporation with its principle place of business located at___________________________.

WHEREAS, the parties have held discussions respecting the establishment of certain potential business relationships which would enhance each party's position in the data communications marketplace and;

WHEREAS the parties desire to set forth the basis for the negotiation of definitive agreements respecting such relationships:

NOW, THEREFORE, the following represents the current intentions and understandings of the parties:

1. Confidentiality—Each party agrees that the provisions of the Reciprocal Nondisclosure Agreement signed by the parties dated , 20 shall remain in full force and effect during the term of this Memorandum of Understanding and for a period thereafter of two (2) years from the return of information to the party that provided it, or for the period described in the Nondisclosure Agreement.
2. Binding Effect—Except for sections 1, 7 and 8 neither the whole nor any part of the content herein is to be deemed to be binding on either party unless and until formal agreements embodying the whole of the agreed terms shall have been drawn up and executed by persons authorized to do so.
3. Agreements—The parties intend to enter into Agreements which:

    3.1. are reciprocal and will provide for the sale of each other's products to fulfill specific customer requirements;
    3.2. will enable ___ to (i) integrate the into several ___ products and (ii) manufacture and sell such integrated products on a world wide basis;
    3.3. provides for collaborative efforts on the development of hardware and software to allow new router based networks to "seamlessly" address the unique problems presented by certain legacy applications;
    3.4. provides for (i) the exchange of technical information respecting each company's network management system and (ii) the development of applications which would extend the capability of each system to manage the local and wide area network without duplication.

5. Interoperability and Certification. The parties agree to commence, within days of the date hereof, interoperability testing and certification of each other's products.
6. Announcements. Neither party shall make any disclosures respecting this Memorandum of Understanding nor the matter contemplated hereby without the prior written consent of an

authorized representative of the other party. The parties intend to be in a position to make a formal announcement respecting the matters proposed herein to the press and their respective customers on , 20 .

7. Expenses. Each party shall bear its own expenses in connection with all activities respecting the subject matters set forth herein.
8. Outside date for completion of negotiation of documents? or set out schedule for negotiations of each/all agreements)
9. New issues. The parties agree that this Memorandum of Understanding is intended to set forth the fundamentals of the proposed relationship but that the foregoing understandings may be revised and new issues presented as the negotiations proceed.

IN WITNESS WHEREOF, the parties hereto have executed this Agreement as of the date first written above.

[Company Name]	[Company Name]
By:______________	By:______________
Title:___________	Title:___________

4.3.6 Letter of Assurance

____

Options:
VIA DHL
VIA FACSIMILE
CERTIFIED MAIL

<Insert Date>

<Insert Customer Name>
<Insert Address>

ATTN: <Insert>

Re: Letter of Authorization for Get-Started Work
Contract No.:

Dear <Insert>:

The purpose of this Letter of Authorization ("LOA") is to authorize __________ to provide services in connection with <INSERT CUSTOMERALIAS'S FULL LEGAL NAME> ("CustomerAlias") <INSERT NAME OF PROJECT>, as described in the attached Schedule A Statement of Work <Insert No.>, which is incorporated by reference into this LOA, ("Ge—Started Work") in anticipation of the negotiation and execution of a master agreement for software licenses and related services ("Master Agreement") and work statement for specific work ("Work Statement") between CustomerAlias and __________.

__________ agrees to perform Get-Started Work on the following basis:

Fees and Expenses. All Get-Started Work performed by __________ pursuant to this LOA shall be performed on a <fixed price> <time and material > basis. __________ shall bill CustomerAlias insert payment terms> Get-Started Work the amount of US$ <XXXX>

Dollars (the "Authorized Amount), which amount excludes __________'s travel and living expenses. After performing the Get-Started Work during the Term of this LOA, __________ may suspend its Get-Started Work until it receives written authorization from CustomerAlias to extend the Term of this LOA and recommence the Get Started Work, with an increased Authorized Amount.

Responsibility for Payment of Taxes. The fees under this LOA are provided exclusive of taxes. CustomerAlias shall pay or reimburse for all value-added, income, withholding, sales or use taxes, customs or import duties, and levies imposed by any authority, government or government agency in connection with the LOA, other than taxes imposed by the United States. If __________ is required to collect a tax to be paid by CustomerAlias, CustomerAlias shall pay this tax on demand. If __________, its subcontractors, or their respective employees are required to pay any non-US taxes in connection with this LOA, including those listed above, and including any penalties and/or interest, then the Authorized Amount of this LOA shall be correspondingly increased.

If, after the effective date of this LOA, there are any changes or developments which may result in an increase in any non-US taxes, and/or any new non-US taxes or assessments are levied by a government other than the United States, or if the methods of administering or the rates of any such taxes or assessments are changed, and such new taxes, assessments or changes result in an increased potential tax liability for __________, its subcontractors or their respective employees, the fees under the LOA shall be correspondingly increased.

If CustomerAlias fails to pay any fee payable under this LOA, or any taxes, duties, levies or assessments, CustomerAlias shall pay all reasonable expenses incurred by __________, including reasonable attorneys' fees, to collect such fees, taxes, duties, levies or assessments.

Payment of __________'s Bills. __________ shall submit bills to CustomerAlias as described above and CustomerAlias shall pay billed amounts within thirty (30) days of the date of the bill. Overdue payments are subject to a late payment charge, calculated and compounded monthly, and calculated at an annual rate of one percent (1%) over the lowest prime rate available in New York City, as published in The Wall Street Journal on the first Monday (or the next bank business day) following the payment due date. If the amount of the late payment charge exceeds the maximum permitted by law, the charge will be reduced to that maximum amount.

Payments to __________ must be in United States dollars and may be either:

a) Wire transferred to:
________________________ Bank
address_____________________
____
ABA No._________________
For Account of __________
Account No._______________
Attention: Account Officer __________, or

b) Mailed to

Confidentiality/Non-Disclosure Obligations. "Confidential Information" means information of a party hereto which is provided or disclosed to the other in a writing, or, if initially disclosed and so designated orally, then within thirty (30) business days thereafter reduced to a writing, which expressly designates in writing such information as being confidential or proprietary to such party; provided, however, that no information of such party shall be considered Confidential Information to the extent that the same:

(a) prior to such disclosure, was, or thereafter becomes, publicly known through no fault of the other; or
(b) prior to such disclosure, was in the possession of the other without an obligation of confidence, or thereafter is independently developed by employees or consultants of the other who have had no prior access to the same; or
(c) after such disclosure, is received from a third party without an obligation of confidence to such third party; or

(d) is required by law, regulation, or court order to be disclosed, provided, however, that the receiving party shall first notify the disclosing party and permit the disclosing party to seek an appropriate protective order.

(e) is disclosed by the owner to a third party without restrictions similar to those contained herein.

Use of Confidential Information. Confidential Information disclosed by Customer Alias (and appropriately marked as being confidential) in connection with the Get Started Work conducted under this LOA shall be used by __________ only for such Get Started Work performed under this LOA. Customer Alias will clearly mark any documents containing proprietary information, as appropriate, before providing them to __________. Confidential Information disclosed (marked as being Proprietary or Confidential) by __________ in connection with the Get Started Work conducted under this LOA, shall be used by Customer Alias solely for the purpose of communicating with __________ and Customer Alias with respect to a potential license of one or more of __________'s software systems. Confidential Information disclosed hereunder by one party to the other shall, for the lesser of (a) the period during which the same continues to be Confidential Information and (b) three (3) years from the date of such disclosure, be protected by the other from further disclosure, publication, and dissemination to the same degree and through the use of the same care and discretion as the other applies to protect its own similar confidential or proprietary information from undesired disclosure, publication, and dissemination and shall be used only for the purpose for which it is provided.

Misuse of Confidential Information. Either party's failure to fulfill the obligations and conditions with respect to any use, disclosure, publication, release, or transfer to any third person of Confidential Information, constitutes a material breach of this LOA. In that event the breached party may, at its option and in addition to any other remedies that it may have, terminate this LOA, its obligations and any rights or licenses granted to the other party upon thirty (30) days written notice. In addition to any other remedies it may have, the breached party has the right to demand the immediate return of any of its Confidential

Information provided to the other party under this LOA, and all copies of the Confidential Information.

No Deliverables. The parties acknowledge and agree that there shall be no deliverables or work products provided by __________ to Customer Alias under this LOA.

__________'s Warranty. __________ warrants that the Get Started Work will be performed in a professionally diligent manner.

Disclaimer of Warranties. EXCEPT AS OTHERWISE EXPRESSLY PROVIDED IN THIS LOA, __________:

A) MAKES NO EXPRESS OR IMPLIED WARRANTIES OF MERCHANTABILITY OR FITNESS FOR A PARTICULAR PURPOSE OR ANY OTHER WARRANTIES OR REPRESENTATIONS INCLUDING ANY WARRANTY OR GUARANTY AGAINST INFRINGEMENT OF ANY INTELLECTUAL PROPERTY RIGHTS; AND
B) NEITHER ASSUMES NOR ACCEPTS ANY LIABILITY TO Customer Alias OR ITS CUSTOMERS WITH RESPECT TO THE QUALITY OR SUFFICIENCY OF ANY RESULTS TO BE ACHIEVED BY THE USE OF THE SERVICES AND ANY DELIVERABLES OR OTHER INFORMATION FURNISHED TO Customer Alias.

Limited Liability. __________ has no liability to Customer Alias, exceeding that specified in the following paragraph, in contract (including warranty and indemnity), or in tort, strict liability or otherwise with respect to any written or oral statement, information, comment or conclusion made by or on behalf of __________ or otherwise in connection with the Get Started Work performed under this LOA including, but not limited to, any materials or any other information made available to Customer Alias under the terms of this LOA. Further, neither party shall be liable to the other party for any indirect, special or consequential damages suffered as a result of any statement, comment, conclusion, or performance or nonperformance hereunder, even if advised of the possibility of damage or loss.

__________'s liability, if any, to Customer Alias or to any third party for claimed loss or damage shall not exceed the amount actually paid by Customer Alias to __________ under this LOA.

Term. The term of this LOA shall commence on <INSERT DATE> and shall expire on <INSERT DATE> (the "Termination Date") unless such Termination Date is extended upon the mutual written agreement of Customer Alias and __________, or the LOA is earlier terminated as provided in the LOA. During the term of this LOA, Customer Alias and __________ shall negotiate in good faith the terms and conditions of the Master Agreement and Addendum. This LOA shall terminate upon the earlier of (i) the Termination Date, (ii) the termination of negotiations of the Master Agreement by either party or (iii) the execution of the Master Agreement and Addendum by Customer Alias and __________. Upon the execution of the Master Agreement and Addendum, the Master Agreement and Addendum shall supersede this LOA, all Get Started Work performed hereunder shall be governed by the Master Agreement and Addendum, and all fees paid by Customer Alias for the Get Started Work performed under this LOA, shall be credited toward the fees due under the Master Agreement and Addendum. If __________ and Customer Alias have not executed the Master Agreement and Addendum by the Termination Date, (i) each party shall forthwith return to the other all papers, reports, documentation, materials and other properties of the disclosing party held by the receiving party in connection with __________'s performance of the Get Started Work or, if requested by the disclosing party, destroy the same and provide a written certification from an authorized officer of the receiving party stating that such destruction is complete, and (ii) Customer Alias shall promptly pay __________ for the Get Started Work under this LOA without further obligation or liability.

Customer's Reexport Obligations. Customer Alias acknowledges that any commodities and/or technical data (including oral disclosures), if any, provided under this LOA shall be subject to the Export Administration Regulations (the "EAR") administered by the United States Commerce Department, and that any export or reexport thereof must be in compliance with the EAR.

This LOA is subject to the receipt of any approvals and/or consents required by United States and foreign government agencies and authorities, including but not limited to the export control laws and regulations of the United States, as may be required for the consummation of the transactions contemplated by this LOA. shall have no liability to Customer Alias for failure to deliver any Get Started Work under this LOA as a result of the refusal of United States or foreign government agencies to issue any necessary approvals and consents for the export of any Service.

Publicity. Nothing contained in this LOA will be construed as conferring upon either party, expressly or by implication, any right or license to use in advertising, publicity, promotion, marketing, or other similar activity, any name, trade name, trademark, or other designation including any abbreviation, contraction, or simulation of the other.

Notices. Any notice or demand which under the terms of this LOA must or may be given or made by __________ or Customer Alias shall be in writing and shall be given or made by facsimile, electronic mail, or similar communication, by hand delivery or by certified or registered mail, addressed to the respective parties identified as the "Contact" identified below.

Such notice or demand shall be deemed to have been given or made twenty-four (24) hours exclusive of weekends and U.S. national holidays after the time when it was sent by facsimile, electronic mail, or similar communication, upon receipt if by hand delivery, or five (5) business days after the day it was deposited, postage prepaid in the U.S. mail.

Compliance with Laws. Each party agrees to comply with all applicable laws and are each responsible, at its sole cost and expense, for obtaining any and all governmental licenses and approvals applicable to such party that may be required in connection with this LOA.

Choice of Law. The LOA must be construed and enforced according to the substantive laws of the State of New Jersey, and Customer Alias agrees to be subject to the jurisdiction of the courts in the State of New Jersey if a suit is commenced in connection with this LOA.

Survival. The terms and conditions of this LOA regarding confidentiality, payment, indemnification, warranties, liability and all others that by their sense and context are intended to survive the execution, delivery, performance, termination or expiration of this LOA survive and continue in effect.

Administrative Contacts.

Customer Alias, Inc.

Tel. No. Tel. No.
Fax No. Fax No.

Entire Agreement. This LOA and the attached Schedule A constitute the entire agreement between the parties about its subject. It incorporates and supersedes all written and oral communications about its subject. It may only be changed or supplemented by a written amendment signed by the authorized representatives of the parties.

If you agree with __________ performing the Get Started Work described in the attached Schedule A according to these terms and those in the attached Schedule A, please have your authorized representative sign and date both copies of this LOA in the spaces provided below and return them to __________. A fully executed original will be forwarded to you for your files.

Very truly yours, ACKNOWLEDGED AND AGREED:

____

<INSERT FULL COMPANY NAME>

By:
Its:
Date:
By:
Its:
Date:

__________ Legal Approval _______

4.3.7 Contract Request Form

Contract Request Form

Attorney-Client Communication:
____________________ Privileged and Confidential

1. Name and address of the other company: (the full name, street address, PO Box if used, city, state and country for the other company)	
2. Person and telephone/fax at other company: (the full name, telephone and fax numbers of the person at the other company who is the contact)	
3. Name of ___ Director/VP who approved: (who authorized the contract)	
4. Describe the project or product this relates to: (such as the marketing program, capital equipment, service plan)	
5. How soon does the contract need to start:	
6. How long does the contract need to last:	
7. What does _____ provide to the other company if the contract is signed: (such as a product or service)	

8. What does the other company provide to _____ if the contract is signed: (such as a product or service)	
9. How much money will _____ pay the other company and when will it be paid:	
10. How much money will the other company pay ______ and when will it be paid:	

11. Will any of this contract involve any other countries?

Yes / No

What countries: __________

12. Relevant Dates:

Contract Needed By	_______	Design is Released	_______
Product ships to Customers	_______	Quotation Due By	_______
Beta Ship Date		Other	

13. Requester: ________

Date: _____ Ext. _____ Fax: _____ M/S: _____

14. Business Unit __________

17. Others who should be kept informed: ______________
(Such as other staff members, supervisors)

Please return to _________ Legal Department.

4.3.8 Confidential Disclosure Agreement (CDA) Request Form

REQUEST FOR CONFIDENTIAL DISCLOSURE AGREEMENT

This form is for use when requesting the preparation of a Confidential Disclosure Agreement (CDA) on behalf of __________, as an individual corporation, and/or as a member or agent of the __________ companies or __________ and/or when __________ has been requested to sign another company's CDA [e.g., Customer, Vendor etc.] (OUTSIDE PARTY).

DATE REQUESTED:__________ DATE NEEDED:__________

1. REQUESTING PARTY for __________ (e.g., SALES REP/AREA):

ADDRESS (if other than Ridgefield Park):____________________

____

____

PHONE NO:____________

2. For requests generated by the Sales Division only, give name of applicable Operations Manager:

NAME:______________ PHONE NO:______________

3. OUTSIDE PARTY (FULL COMPANY NAME):

   ____

   a. ADDRESS:
   b. CONTACT NAME:
   c. PHONE NO. FOR CONTACT:

4. WILL __________ DISCLOSE ANY CONFIDENTIAL INFORMATION TO OUTSIDE PARTY? ([ ] Yes [ ] No [ ] Unknown at this time. IF YES, PLEASE INDICATE THE PURPOSE OF THIS DISCLOSURE. (Please give a complete

justification and attach any additional information you feel is necessary to process this request).

____

____

____

____

5. WILL OUTSIDE PARTY DISCLOSE ANY CONFIDENTIAL INFORMATION TO __________? ([ ] Yes [ ] No [ ] Unknown at this time). IF YES, PLEASE INDICATE THE PURPOSE OF THIS DISCLOSURE. (Please give a complete justification and attach any additional information you feel is necessary to process this request).

____

____

____

____

6. IF A FORMAL PRESENTATION IS PLANNED, WHO WILL BE GIVING THE PRESENTATION AND WHERE? (Name & Title) [See *#1 at end of form, if oral presentation is planned.]

____

7. IS THIS CDA NEEDED FOR AN RFP, RFQ OR RFI? ([ ] Yes [ ] No). IF YES, PLEASE INDICATE RFP, RFQ, RFI NUMBER:

____

8. HAS OUTSIDE PARTY PROVIDED ITS STANDARD CDA FORM? ([ ] YES [ ] NO). IF YES, ATTACH FORM. NOTE: REVIEW AND APPROVAL OF OUTSIDE PARTY'S CDA MAY EXTEND PROCESSING TIME.

9. IS CDA FOR THE RELEASE OF PROPRIETARY DOCUMENTATION SUCH AS: MAINTENANCE MANUALS, SCHEMATICS, PROTOCOL INFORMATION, ENGINEERING SPECS, ETC.? ([ ] Yes [ ] No) IF YES, EXPLAIN AND LIST SPECIFIC DOCUMENTS REQUESTED.

____

____

____

____

10. IS CDA NEEDED FOR OEM/JOINT DEVELOPMENT INFORMATION EXCHANGE? ([ ] Yes [ ] No) IF YES, PLEASE EXPLAIN OR ATTACH INFORMATION.

____

____

____

____

11. DOES THE OUTSIDE PARTY MARKET PRODUCTS OR SERVICES WHICH COMPETE AGAINST PRODUCTS OR SERVICES? ([ ] Yes [ ] No) IF YES, PLEASE EXPLAIN. [See *#2 at end of form, if receipt of competitor's information is contemplated.]

____

____

____

____

AFTER THIS FORM IS COMPLETED, THE REQUESTING PARTY SHOULD FORWARD THE FORM TO THE APPROPRIATE PARTY SET FORTH BELOW TO OBTAIN APPROVAL. AFTER APPROVAL, THE REQUESTING PARTY SHOULD SEND THE APPROVED FORM BY MAIL, CC MAIL, OR FAX TO THE LAW DEPARTMENT AT FAX NO. ________. IF YOU HAVE ANY QUESTIONS, PLEASE CALL ___________.

APPROVAL SUMMARY

The following Table should provide guidance for obtaining the appropriate approval signature(s) required at the end of this form. This Table applies both to CDA's originating inside and outside of and applies whether Confidential Information is received from or given to the other party. In some instances, in particularly sensitive situations, the Law Department may require additional approval before acting on a request.

TYPE OF INFORMATION EXCHANGED	MINIMUM APPROVAL REQUIRED
— Futures presentation information for a current or future customer/ vendor who is not a _______ competitor — CDA for information needed to support a RFP, RFQ or RFI.	Responsible Director and Senior Manager or equivalent
— Any CDA for OEM/Joint Development information. — Any CDA requiring transfer (in or out) of technical documentation. — Any CDA with a _________ competitor for transfer of information (in or out).	Director of Affected Business Unit
— All other information not included above.	Any _________ Manager or Senior Manager reporting directly to a Director

SIGNATURE BLOCKS

I. **FOR REQUESTS FROM SALES (ALL CHANNELS) FOR A FUTURES PRESENTATION TO A CUSTOMER/ VENDOR, NOT A COMPETITOR OF _________, AND FOR REQUESTS TO SUPPORT RFP'S, RFQ'S AND RFI'S:**

APPROVAL: ______________________________
Director or the equivalent

SEE BLOCK #II BELOW FOR POSSIBLE ADDITIONAL APPROVAL.

II. **FOR REQUESTS FOR TECHNICAL DOCUMENTATION OR OEM/JOINT DEVELOPMENT INFORMATION OR FOR A CDA WITH A COMPETITOR (AS INDICATED IN PARAGRAPHS 9-11 ABOVE):**

APPROVAL: ______________________________
Director of Affected Business Unit

III. **FOR ALL OTHER REQUESTS**:

APPROVAL: ______________________________
(Any ______ Manager or Senior Manager reporting to a Director)

SEE BLOCK #II ABOVE FOR POSSIBLE ADDITIONAL APPROVAL

*ALL REQUESTING PARTIES NOTE:

1. Information to be disclosed in unwritten form, for example, as part of an oral presentation, must be identified at the time of disclosure as being confidential, and must be summarized in written form, marked **"CONFIDENTIAL"** (or with a similar

designation) within a specified time period after disclosure (usually 30 days) in order to be considered as "CONFIDENTIAL INFORMATION" protected under a CDA. Information in written form must likewise be marked "Confidential" in order to be protected under a CDA.

2. It is not unusual for __________to receive Confidential Information about another company's product that __________ is OEMing or distributing, while at the same time undertaking an internal development program to replace the other company's product with a __________ product. Normally, __________'s CDA's allow for such independent development of the previously received Confidential Information. However, in any court action brought by such other company, the burden of proof will be on   to prove that its information was in fact actually independently developed and was not derived in part or in whole from the other company's disclosed Confidential Information. To succeed, disclosed Confidential Information must be kept away from the __________ group undertaking independent development, and such independent development must be carefully documented.

5. Credit Risk Management

5.1 Credit Risk

Many companies that sell products to distributors, dealers, and retailers are exposed to credit risk when their customers don't pay for the product prior to or upon taking delivery of the product. This is often seen in purchase or sales contracts in which payment terms are net thirty, net forty-five, or net ninety. Of course, if the parties enter into a consignment arrangement, this is not the case.

Credit risk covers many loss scenarios in which a borrower (normally a buyer or customer) fails to fulfill its payment obligations. Such scenarios involve borrowers regardless of size or scope, including small companies, midsize, or even large companies, and sometimes even governments. Credit risk management is an extremely important piece in the LRM process. However, one of the most important forms of credit risk involves trade credit risk (i.e., the credit risk a company faces when its buyers or customers fail to pay on time or, in some situations, at all). How can a company handle its receivables credit risk or trade credit risk problems?

A company, when calculating the risk of nonpayment, needs to consider ways in which it can transfer or mitigate the risk.

5.2 Credit Risk Processes

Companies that experience credit risks on a regular basis should create a Credit Risk Department. The Credit Risk Department can implement a number of LRM or risk management tools and processes that can mitigate or minimize the impact of credit risk. It is essential that a department or individual continuously monitors the credit risk of customers, as financial circumstances can change very quickly.

Normally, procedures and processes used by a Credit Risk Department in conjunction with Legal, Finance or Risk Management would include the following steps:

- Implementation of credit risk procedures: Normally standardized credit processes including credit terms and conditions of using the terms. The Credit Department should run all terms by Legal.
- Credit acceptance: Usually the first step in the process for credit approval where the company decides whether customers or buyers qualify for extended credit terms and if so under what terms. It is up to the Credit Department in conjunction with Finance to decide what the payment terms would be, such as net forty-five or net sixty.
- Credit collection: Implementation of credit collection processes, including use of credit collection agencies.
- Use of credit risk insurance: Establishment and implementation of a credit risk insurance program to cover all or most customers on extended credit.

It should be noted that credit acceptance decisions are normally based on a number of factors, including:[2]

- Credit history, if any
- The credit application form, if any
- A credit report
- Financial statements
- Corporate guarantees
- Standby letter of credit
- Personal or cross-corporate guarantees
- Personal financial statements of partners or shareholders

[2] See Paul M Collier, *Fundamentals of Risk Management for Accountants and Managers,* Oxford,UK: Elsevier, 2009, p 178

5.3 Credit Risk Insurance

Commercial credit risk insurance, sometimes called "trade" credit risk insurance, can help a company protect its account receivables (A/R) from unexpected losses due to nonpayment or slow payment by the company's buyers. It usually covers nonpayment because of a buyer's insolvency but may also cover nonpayment due to political events that hinder payment or distributors on credit. A/R is the money owed to a company by its customer for products and services sold on credit. Normally, a sale is only treated as an account receivable after the customer has been invoiced for the product or service.

Depending on the industry and size of the company, it may or may not sell many or all of its products via credit. The risk, therefore, of nonpayment or slow payment (90 or 180 days after invoice, etc.) can be quite serious and expose the company to a potential crisis if the A/R is not paid. This is a major concern for any company selling product on credit.

5.3.1 Types of Credit Risks

Credit risk insurance normally covers two kinds of risk: commercial risk and political risk. Commercial risk is of course; the most common risk faced by companies.

- Commercial risk
    - Insolvency or bankruptcy
    - Protracted nonpayment
    - Default of customer

Note: It will not cover nonpayment due to contractual or legal disputes between the company and customer.

5.3.2 Benefits of Credit Insurance

There are numerous benefits for using credit insurance, if applicable. The most obvious benefits are:

- Transfer or mitigation of risk. Credit insurance assures a company that its A/R will be paid if one of its customers declares bankruptcy or is unable to pay. This is subject to the terms and conditions of the insurance policy.
- Improved cash flow. A timely collection of A/R provides much-needed operating cash flow.
- Sales. By using credit insurance, a company is able to extend more credit to its primary customers, promoting increased sales. This can be cyclical, allowing increased turnover of products and, therefore, increased sales.

5.3.3 Insurance Provider

Credit insurance is a very specific insurance product. Usually, only international or specific insurance companies offer such insurance.

It should be noted that as credit risk covers many loss scenarios due to the failure of the borrower to fulfill payment obligations, trade credit risk encompasses the potential loss of a company's A/R due to nonpayment of a customer. Obviously, other credit risk scenarios exist, including project finance risks, but in this chapter we have concentrated on trade credit risk and insurance.

5.4 Forms

There are several basic insurance related forms that cover credit or A/R issues. Credit Risk Insurance, a Put Agreement (specific insurance on a particular account) or Factoring Agreement

5.4.1 Put Agreement—A

CLAIMS PUT AGREEMENT

THIS CLAIMS PUT AGREEMENT (this "Agreement"), dated as of, 2000, is by and between, a corporation, located at (the "Seller"), and, located at (the "Purchaser").

RECITALS

WHEREAS, the Seller is or will be the owner of certain Accounts (as hereinafter defined);

WHEREAS, the Seller considers it desirable to have the right to sell certain Claims (as hereinafter defined) that would result from such Accounts in the event that there should occur a Bankruptcy Event (as hereinafter defined) in respect of the Company; and

WHEREAS, the Purchaser is willing to acquire a limited amount of such Claims on the terms hereinafter set forth.

AGREEMENT

NOW, THEREFORE, in consideration of the promises herein contained and for good and valuable consideration, the receipt and sufficiency of which are hereby acknowledged, the parties hereto agree as follows:

1. Definitions. As used in this Agreement, the following terms shall have the meanings set forth below:

   "Accounts" shall mean all present and future accounts, contract rights, general intangibles, notes, drafts and other forms of obligations, the direct obligor of which is the Company (as hereinafter defined), which are or will be owned by the Seller and which arose from the post-petition sale of goods or the rendition of services to the Company in the ordinary course of the Seller's business, together with all proceeds thereof, all guaranties and security therefor, pursuant to Sections 507(a)(l) and 503(b)(l) of the Bankruptcy Code, and all goods and rights represented thereby or arising therefrom, including, but not limited to, the right of stoppage in transit, replevin and reclamation, provided however, that "Accounts" shall in no event include any of the foregoing arising after the date of a Bankruptcy Event (as hereinafter defined).

"Agreement" shall have the meaning set forth in the first sentence of this Claims Put Agreement. "Assignment Agreement" shall mean the Assignment of Claim, to be entered into between the Purchaser and the Seller, in substantially the form of Exhibit A annexed hereto, pursuant to which the Claims will be conveyed to the Purchaser in the event of the exercise of the Put (as hereinafter defined).

"Bankruptcy Code" shall mean Title 11 of the United States Code, as amended.

"Bankruptcy Court" shall mean any court with jurisdiction over the Bankruptcy Proceeding (as defined herein).

"Bankruptcy Event" shall mean the entry of an Order (as defined below) by the Bankruptcy Court winding down the Company's operations and liquidating its assets under Chapter 11 of the United States Bankruptcy Code, or converting the Company's Chapter 11 case to Chapter 7 pursuant to the United States Bankruptcy Code, or dismissing a Chapter 11 proceeding with respect to the Company or any of its constituent entities.

"Bankruptcy Proceeding" shall mean the case, if any, with respect to the Company commenced in connection with a Bankruptcy Event. "Business Day" shall mean any day other than a Saturday, Sunday or other day on which commercial banks in New York, New York are required or authorized by law to close.

"Claims" shall mean any and all rights, claims (including, but not limited to, "claims" as defined in Section 101(5) of the

Bankruptcy Code, whether constituting administrative, secured or unsecured claims) and causes of action of the Seller that arise under, from, in, to or in connection with Eligible Accounts, together with all proceeds thereof.

"Closing" shall have the meaning set forth in Section 4.

"Closing Date" shall have the meaning set forth in Section 4.

"Company" shall mean Service Merchandise Company, Inc., a Tennessee corporation, as debtor-in-possession.

"Confidential Information" shall have the meaning set forth in Section 15.

"Covered Accounts" are Eligible Accounts which Seller has the ability to put to Purchaser, pursuant to the terms of this Agreement, if a Bankruptcy Event occurs.

"Default Rate" shall mean a fluctuating interest rate per annum as shall be in effect from time to time, which rate shall equal 4% per annum plus the Interest Rate (as hereinafter defined). The Default Rate shall be computed on the basis of the actual number of days elapsed over a year of 365 days.

"Disallowance" shall have the meaning set forth in Section *6(a)*

"Dispute" shall mean (i) any dispute, defense or claim, bona fide or otherwise, that any Put Claim (or any portion thereof) is void or voidable under the Bankruptcy Code, state or federal law or under equitable principles; (ii) any dispute, defense or claim, bona fide or otherwise, as to the amount or validity of any Put Claim or any related Account (or any portion of either thereof) or as to the price, terms, quantity or quality of goods or services represented thereby or any cause or defense to payment whatsoever of any related Account other than the financial inability of the Company to pay; (iii) any dispute, defense or claim, bona fide or otherwise, with respect to any Put Claim (or portion thereof) that any amount received, from any source as or towards payment, by the Seller (or any prior owner of the related Account) is voidable under the Bankruptcy Code; (iv) any dispute, defense or claim, bona fide or otherwise, that any Put Claim (or any portion thereof) is subject to subordination pursuant to Section 510(c) of the Bankruptcy Code; (v) any dispute, defense or claim, bona fide or otherwise, that any Put Claim (or any portion thereof) is subject to offset or reduction; or (vi) the disallowance of the Put Claims under Section 502(b) or 502(d) of the Bankruptcy Code. "Eligible Account" shall mean any Account (i) which is a valid, bona fide account, representing an undisputed indebtedness incurred by the Company for goods actually sold and delivered or for services completely rendered by the Seller, (ii) as to which such goods or services have, or performance has, been accepted by the Company and as to which there exist no setoffs, offsets, defenses or counterclaims, genuine or otherwise, other than customary discounts or allowances; (iii) which does not represent a sale by a parent, subsidiary or affiliate of the Company, or a consignment, sale or return, or bill and hold transaction; (iv) as to which no agreement exists or will be made by the Seller permitting any deduction or discount or allowance which is not stated on the related invoice delivered to the Purchaser as provided herein; (v) which is due and payable on commercially reasonable terms, but in no event more than thirty (30) days after the Closing Date (as defined in Section 3 hereof) and which is not past due as of the date hereof; (vi) which is denominated and payable only in United States dollars; (vii) which is not subject to a Dispute, and (viii) which is treated in the Bankruptcy Proceedings as an allowed administrative expense claim pursuant to Section 503(b)(l)(A) of the Bankruptcy Code.

"Exercise Notice" shall have the meaning set forth in Section 2fc).

"Funding Agent" shall mean __________________________Corp. in its role as broker of the transaction contemplated herein with the understanding that the Funding Agent will incur no liabilities whatsoever for the obligations, representations and warranties made by any other party to this Agreement.

"Indemnitee" shall have the meaning set forth in Section 11.

"Interest Rate" shall mean a fluctuating interest rate per annum as shall be in effect from time to time, which rate shall equal three percent (3%) per annum plus the rate of interest announced publicly by Citibank, N.A. in New York, New York, from time to time as Citibank, N.A.'s base rate, prime rate or equivalent. The Interest Rate shall be computed on the basis of the actual number of days elapsed over a year of 365 days.

"Lien" shall mean any lien (including, but not limited to, "liens" as defined in Section 101(37) of the Bankruptcy Code), security interest or other charge or encumbrance.

"Net Account Value" shall mean, with respect to any Account, the gross invoice amount of the invoice relating to such Account, less (i) any discount, allowance, chargeback or other credit to which the Company is or would be entitled; (ii) any amounts received from any source as or towards payment of such invoice on or prior to the Closing Date; (iii) the invoice amount of any goods that were not shipped or delivered to or not accepted by the Company or are subject to Dispute or services that were not performed or accepted by the Company, or which were returned by or recovered from the Company (by reclamation or otherwise) on or before the Closing Date; (iv) any interest included in such gross invoice amount; (v) any applicable sales tax, value added tax or comparable taxes with respect to the transaction giving rise to such Account; and (vi) any other or similar amount which would reduce the amount of the invoice payable to the Seller.

"Person" shall mean any natural person, corporation, business trust, joint venture, association, company, partnership, limited partnership, limited liability company or government, or any agency or political subdivision thereof.

"Purchaser" shall have the meaning set forth in the first sentence of this Claims Put Agreement.

"Purchase Price" shall have the meaning set forth in Section 2(a).

"Put" shall have the meaning set forth in Section 2(a).

"Put Claim" shall have the meaning set forth in Section 2(c).

"Refund Date" shall have the meaning set forth in Section 6(b).

"Refund Amount" shall have the meaning set forth in Section 6(a).

"Refund Notice" shall have the meaning set forth in Section 6(a).

"Request for Payment of an Administrative Expense" shall have the meaning set forth in Section lOCcD.

"Seller" shall have the meaning set forth in the first sentence of this Claims Put Agreement.

2. Grant of Put, (a) On the terms and subject to the conditions and relying on the representations and warranties herein set forth, the Purchaser hereby grants and issues to the Seller, and the Seller hereby purchases from the Purchaser, the right and option (the "Put") to sell Claims to the Purchaser upon the occurrence of a Bankruptcy Event at a purchase price equal to the Net Account Value of the Covered Accounts relating to the Put Claims multiplied by ninety percent (90%) (the "Purchase Price"). The Put shall expire and be of no further force or effect if not exercised on or prior to the twentieth (20th) day following the occurrence of a Bankruptcy Event, releasing the Purchaser from all obligations hereunder.

(b) Under no circumstances shall the Net Account Value of the Put Claims exceed the aggregate amount of the Covered Accounts detailed in the Invoice Summaries attached hereto as Exhibit A.

(c) The Seller may exercise the Put by irrevocable written notice (the "Exercise Notice") to the Purchaser if a Bankruptcy Event occurs while any of the Covered Accounts are outstanding and not paid by the Company. The Exercise Notice shall specify (i) the Claims being sold in reasonable detail (the "Put Claims"), (ii) the Net Account Value of the Put Claims and (iii) the account to which the Purchaser shall pay the Purchase Price on the Closing Date. The Exercise Notice is effective if received by Purchaser within twenty (20) days from the date of the Bankruptcy Event.

(d) Subject to the provisions of Section 10 on the Closing Date, upon the receipt of an executed Assignment Agreement transferring the Put Claims to the Purchaser, the Purchaser shall pay to the Seller the Purchase Price by wire transfer of immediately available funds to the Seller's account specified in the Exercise Notice.

3. Put Effective Period.

(a) After this Agreement is fully executed, Seller may transfer the credit risk of selling goods to the Company on 30-day terms by submitting to Purchaser a Sales Forecast of Eligible Accounts with a request to assume any credit risk relating thereto ("Credit Risk Transfer Approval"). Credit Risk Transfer Approval may be sought on the third Thursday of the month prior to the month the goods are shipped.

(b) The Put Option is effective each time Purchaser gives Seller written notice that the Eligible Accounts comprising any Invoice Summary submitted by Seller are Covered Accounts, remaining effective while any Covered Accounts are outstanding and unpaid by the Company.

(c) Purchaser retains the right to deny granting Credit Risk Transfer Approval at any time Seller requests it; provided, however, that once Credit Risk Transfer Approval is granted by Purchaser, it may not be withdrawn. For avoidance of doubt, Credit Risk Tranfer Approval is sought and granted on a month-to-month basis, and must be acknowledged in writing by both Seller and Buyer.

4. Closing. The closing of the sale and purchase of the Put Claims (the "Closing") shall take place via telephone, facsimile and federal funds wire transfer within ten (10) business days of the Company's written acknowledgment that the Put Claims are allowed administrative claims of the Purchaser against the Company, the Purchaser having sole legal and beneficial title thereto. The time and date of the Closing are herein referred to as the "Closing Date." In the event the Seller does not satisfy the conditions specified in Section 10, then the Purchaser shall be released from all of its obligations hereunder.

5. Put Premium,

   (a) No later than the last banking day of the month in which Purchaser grants Seller Credit Risk Transfer Approval, Seller shall pay to the Funding Agent a put option premium in immediately available funds in the amount stated in that certain pricing letter between the Seller and the Funding Agent dated ____. Upon receipt of the put option premium by the Funding Agent, the Funding Agent shall pay to the Purchaser a put option premium in immediately available funds in the amount stated in that certain pricing letter between the Purchaser and the Funding Agent dated ____. All payments due to the Funding Agent under this Agreement shall be made by wire transfer of immediately available funds in accordance with the following wire transfer instructions:

   XXX Bank
   ABA#: ____________
   ____
   A/C #: ____________
   Ref: Asset #:

   (b) Excess Put Premium Put Premiums paid on Accounts wherein the comprising goods are not shipped ("Excess Put Premium") will be credited to the Seller's next put premium obligation. If no further put premium obligation exists for whatever reason, the Excess Put Premium will be be fully refunded to Seller, less any offsets taken by Purchaser pursuant to this Agreement.

6. Disallowed Put Claims,

(a) With respect to any Put Claim, upon the occurrence of a breach of any of the representations, warranties or covenants contained herein or in the Assignment Agreement, or in the event all or any part of the Put Claim is disallowed, treated subordinate to other general unsecured trade debt, objected to or otherwise impaired, in whole or in part, in the Bankruptcy Proceedings for any reason whatsoever, including, without limitation, pursuant to an order of the Bankruptcy Court (whether or not such order is appealed) (collectively, a "Disallowance"), other than by reason of the financial inability of the Company to repay the Put Claim, and the Disallowance remains pending and unresolved for a period of thirty (30) days from the date the Disallowance occurred, the Purchaser may, upon written notice to the Seller (each, a "Refund Notice"), require the Seller to refund the Purchase Price paid by the Purchaser for such Put Claim (or portion thereof) subject to a Disallowance, together with interest thereon from the Closing Date up to (but not including) the Refund Date (as hereinafter defined) at the Interest Rate together with any attorney's fees and costs and administrative fees related to the Put Claim (the "Refund Amount"). Each Refund Notice shall specify (i) the Put Claim (or portion thereof) subject to a Disallowance to be refunded, (ii) the Refund Amount of the Put Claim (or portion thereof) subject to a Disallowance to be refunded and (iii) the account to which the Seller shall pay the Refund Amount on the Refund Date.

(b) On the third (3rd) Business Day following receipt of a Refund Notice (the "Refund Date"), the Seller shall pay to the Purchaser the Refund Amount, by wire transfer of immediately available funds to the Purchaser's account specified in the Refund Notice. In the event that the Seller shall not pay the entire

Refund Amount on the Refund Date, the Seller shall on demand from time to time pay interest on such defaulted amount from the Refund Date up to (but not including) the date of actual payment (after as well as before judgment) at a rate per annum equal to the Default Rate.

(c) Upon the Purchaser's receipt of the Refund Amount (together with all accrued and unpaid interest thereon), beneficial ownership in and to the applicable Put Claim (or portion thereof) subject to a Disallowance shall automatically revert to the Seller, and the Purchaser, at the reasonable cost and expense of the Seller, shall deliver to the Seller, all such instruments of sale, transfer, conveyance, assignment and confirmation, and the Purchaser shall take such other action, as the Seller may reasonably deem necessary or desirable in order to transfer, convey and assign to the Seller, and to confirm the Seller's beneficial ownership in and to such Put Claim (or portion thereof) subject to a Disallowance; provided, however, that upon a determination by a court having jurisdiction over the Bankruptcy Proceeding that any Account or portion thereof so transferred to the Seller in accordance with this paragraph is found to be a valid, undisputed, liquidated, and non-contingent obligation of the Company, that the Seller has the right and option to sell and the Purchaser shall have the obligation to buy on a Business Day, Claims related to such Accounts, within five days of the receipt of written notice by the Purchaser, which notice must be mailed within ten (10) days of the entry of such court order and satisfaction by the Seller of the conditions specified in Sections 9(a),(b),(e), and (f), at a price equal to the Net Account Value of the Accounts related to such Put Claims

7. Representations, Warranties and Covenants of the Seller.

The Seller represents, warrants and covenants to the Purchaser as follows:

(a) The execution, delivery and performance by the Seller of this Agreement and the other documents to be delivered hereunder

(i) are within the Seller's organizational powers, (ii) have been duly authorized by all necessary corporate action, and (iii) do not contravene (A) the Seller's organizational documents, (B) any law, rale or regulation applicable to the Seller, (C) any contractual restriction binding on or affecting the Seller or its property or (4) any order, writ, judgment, award, injunction or decree binding on or affecting the Seller or its property.

(b) No authorization or approval or other action by, and no notice to or filing with, any governmental authority or regulatory body is required for the due execution, delivery and performance by the Seller of this Agreement or any other document to be delivered hereunder.

(c) This Agreement has been duly executed and delivered by the Seller and constitutes the legal, valid and binding obligation of the Seller enforceable against the Seller in accordance with its terms.

(d) There is no pending or threatened action or proceeding against or affecting the Seller before any court, governmental agency or arbitrator which may materially adversely affect the ability of the Seller to perform its obligations under this Agreement, or which purports to affect the legality, validity or enforceability of this Agreement or the Assignment Agreement.

(e) No insolvency event has occurred with respect to the Seller.

(f) Each Put Claim will be a legal, valid, non-subordinated, allowed administrative expense claim in an amount at least equal to the Net Account Value of the Account relating thereto and not the subject of any Dispute.

(g) The Seller will be the legal and beneficial owner and holder of the Put Claims on the Closing Date and shall convey to the Purchaser good and marketable title to the Put Claims free and clear of any Liens, Disputes, setoffs, offsets, defenses or counterclaims, genuine or otherwise.

(h) Each Put Claim will relate solely to Eligible Accounts.

(i) It is a sophisticated seller, with such knowledge and experience in financial and business matters so as to be capable of evaluating the merits and risks of consummating the transactions contemplated hereby; it has been solely responsible for its "due diligence" investigation of the Company and its management and business, for the analysis of the merits and risks of entering into this Agreement and of the fairness and desirability of the terms of this Agreement and has not relied on any information provided by the Purchaser or any affiliate or agent of the Purchaser (or the fact that no such information has been provided) in deciding whether or on what terms and conditions to consummate the transactions contemplated hereby; and it understands that the Purchaser (including affiliates and agents of the Purchaser) (x) may have received confidential information from the Company concerning the business and prospects of the Company and the value of obligations of the Company, and (y) may in the future enter into transactions with the Company which could affect the value of the obligations of the Company, and it is entering into this Agreement with full knowledge that the Purchaser may be basing its decision to enter into this Agreement upon material information as to the business or prospects of the Company or on a proposed transaction involving the Company which has not been disclosed to the Seller.

(j) Seller will collect and administer the Covered Accounts in a responsible and timely fashion, consistent with its past practice and ordinary course of business. In the event any of the Covered Accounts are not collected within twenty (20) days after their maturity date, Seller shall give immediate written notice of such to Purchaser.

(k) Seller with provide Purchaser with the names, addresses, and telephone numbers of the Company's accounting personnel responsible for payment of the Covered Accounts and authorizes Purchaser to assist in the timely collection of such Covered Accounts prior to the granting of any further Credit Risk

Transfer Approval. Seller will also provide Purchaser with copies of all correspondence to and from the Company's accounting personnel regarding the collection of the Covered Accounts.

(1) Seller will endorse each invoice forwarded to the Company with a legend which states "In the event this invoice is not paid when due and becomes the subject of an administrative claim filed against the Company, the Company will be charged interest at a rate of 2% monthly from the invoice maturity date, as well as all costs of collection, including attorney's fees and costs and expenses associated with the processing of such administrative claim."

8. Representation.

Warranties and Covenants of the Purchaser. The Purchaser represents, warrants and covenants to the Seller as follows:

(a) The execution, delivery and performance by the Purchaser of this Agreement and the other documents to be delivered by it hereunder (i) are within the Purchaser's corporate powers, (ii) have been duly authorized by all necessary corporate action, and (iii) do not contravene (1) the Purchaser's charter or by-laws, (2) any law, rule or regulation applicable to the Purchaser, (3) any contractual restriction binding on or affecting the Purchaser or its property or (4) any order, writ, judgment, award, injunction or decree binding on or affecting the Purchaser or its property.

(b) No authorization or approval or other action by, and no notice to or filing with, any governmental authority or regulatory body is required for the due execution, delivery and performance by the Purchaser of this Agreement or any other document to be delivered hereunder.

(c) This Agreement has been duly executed and delivered by the Purchaser and constitutes the legal, valid and binding obligation of the Purchaser enforceable against the Purchaser in accordance with its terms.

(d) There is no pending or threatened action or proceeding against or affecting the Purchaser before any court, governmental agency or arbitrator which may materially adversely affect the ability of the Purchaser to perform its obligations under this Agreement, or which purports to affect the legality, validity or enforceability of this Agreement.

(e) No insolvency event has occurred with respect to the Purchaser.

(f) In the event Seller becomes subject to a material change of ownership or management, including without limitation a sale, merger, or acquisition, or becomes subject to any other material corporate governance change, Purchaser has the sole and exclusive right to terminate any of its obligations under this Agreement.

9. Further Assurances.

At any time and from time to time on and after the Closing Date at the request of the Purchaser, and without further consideration, the Seller will execute and deliver such other instruments of sale, transfer, conveyance, assignment and confirmation and take such other action as the Purchaser may reasonably deem necessary or desirable in order to transfer, convey and assign more effectively to the Purchaser, and to confirm to the Purchaser title to all of the Put Claims.

10. Conditions Precedent to Purchase.

The obligation of the Purchaser to purchase the Put Claims hereunder is subject to the satisfaction of the following conditions precedent on or prior to the twentieth (20th) day before the Closing Date or such earlier date as specified below:

(a) The representations and warranties of the Seller set forth in this Agreement shall be true and correct in all material respects as of the Closing Date and the Purchaser shall have been provided with a certificate to such effect, executed by a duly authorized officer of the Seller.

(b) The Seller shall have performed its obligations and complied in all respects with the covenants and requirements contained in this Agreement and has provided to Purchaser a certificate to such effect, executed by a duly authorized officer of the Seller.

(c) The Purchaser shall have received from the Seller a list of each invoice number, invoice date, due date and Net Account Value for each of the Covered Accounts relating to the Put Claims, together with the following documentation for each such Account: (i) an itemized statement of the account balance certified by the Seller; (ii) all invoices, bills of lading and statements and correspondence with the Company relating to such Accounts; (iii) proofs of delivery of the merchandise related to such Accounts signed by the Company; (iv) Company's purchase orders for such Accounts, or electronic equivalent thereof if available; and (v) such additional documentation relating to the Accounts and its assignment to the Seller as the Purchaser may reasonably require.

(d) The Purchaser, at the cost and expense of the Seller, shall have received all such instruments of sale, transfer, conveyance, assignment and confirmation and the Seller shall have taken such other action as the Purchaser may reasonably deem necessary or desirable in order to transfer, convey and assign to the Purchaser, and to confirm the Purchaser's title to, all of the Put Claims. At the request of the Purchaser, the Seller shall prepare, execute and file in the applicable bankruptcy court, a Request for Payment of an Administrative Expense with respect to the Put Claim, in the form and content as reasonably required by the Purchaser, and in an amount equal to the Net Account Value of the Accounts related to the Put Claim (the "Net Account Value of the Put Claims").

(e) The Assignment Agreement shall have been duly executed by the Seller and delivered to the Purchaser.

(f) The Seller shall have delivered to the Purchaser a certificate certifying that it has satisfied the conditions specified in the Section 9.

(g) In the event Seller breaches any of its representations or warranties hereunder or fails to meet any of its obligations or comply with any of its requirements hereunder, all or any of Purchaser's obligations and duties under this Agreement may be terminated at Purchaser's sole discretion.

11. Indemnity.

The Seller agrees to indemnify the Purchaser, the Purchaser's member managers, members and their respective officers, directors, employees, agents and affiliates (each such Person being an "Indemnitee") against, and to hold each Indemnitee harmless from, any and all losses, claims, damages, liabilities and related expenses (including, without limitation, reasonable counsel fees, disbursements and expenses) incurred by or asserted against any Indemnitee arising out of, in any way connected with, or as a result of the breach of any of the Seller's representations, warranties, covenants and agreements set forth in the Agreement; provided, however, that such indemnity shall not, as to any Indemnitee, be available to the extent such losses, claims, damages, liabilities and related expenses have resulted from the gross negligence or willful misconduct of such Indemnitee. The provisions of this Section shall remain operative and in full force and effect regardless of the expiration or termination of this Agreement, the consummation of the transactions contemplated hereby or the invalidity or unenforceability of any provision of this Agreement. All amounts due under this Section shall be payable on written demand therefor.

12. Assignment.

Whenever in this Agreement any of the parties hereto is referred to, such reference shall be deemed to include the successors and permitted assigns of such party and all covenants and agreements by and on behalf of the Seller or the Purchaser that are contained in this Agreement shall bind and inure to the benefit of their respective successors and permitted assigns. The Seller shall not assign or delegate any of its rights, interests, duties or obligations hereunder without the prior written consent of the Purchaser in its sole and absolute discretion and any attempted assignment or delegation without such consent shall be null and void. The Purchaser may at any time assign or delegate all or a portion of any of its rights, interest, duties or obligations hereunder.

13. GOVERNING LAW.

THIS AGREEMENT SHALL BE GOVERNED BY AND CONSTRUED IN ACCORDANCE WITH THE LAW OF THE STATE OF ________________ APPLICABLE TO CONTRACTS MADE AND TO BE PERFORMED ENTIRELY WITHIN SUCH STATE.

14. CONSENT TO JURISDICTION AND WAIVER OF JURY TRIAL.

THE SELLER AND THE PURCHASER HEREBY IRREVOCABLY CONSENT TO THE JURISDICTION OF ANY STATE OR FEDERAL COURT LOCATED WITHIN THE COUNTY AND STATE OF NEW YORK AND IRREVOCABLY AGREE THAT ALL ACTIONS OR PROCEEDINGS RELATING TO THIS AGREEMENT SHALL BE LITIGATED IN SUCH COURTS WAIVING ANY DEFENSE OF FORUM NON CONVENIENS. THE SELLER AND THE PURCHASER EACH WAIVE THEIR RESPECTIVE RIGHTS TO A JURY TRIAL OF ANY CLAIM OR CAUSE OF ACTION ARISING OUT OF OR RELATING TO THIS AGREEMENT, AND FURTHER REPRESENT AND WARRANT THAT IT HAS REVIEWED THIS WAIVER WITH ITS LEGAL COUNSEL.

15. Confidentiality.

Unless otherwise required by applicable law, the parties agree to maintain the confidentiality of this Agreement (and all drafts hereof) and all terms hereof and thereof (the "Confidential Information") in communications with third parties and otherwise; provided, however, that the parties may disclose such Confidential Information to their officers, directors, employees, agents and representatives who need to know such Confidential Information in connection with the transactions contemplated by this Agreement and the administration of this Agreement and who have agreed to be bound by the terms of this Section 14. The provisions of this Section shall remain operative and in full force and effect regardless of the expiration or termination of this Agreement, the consummation of the transactions contemplated hereby or the invalidity or unenforceability of any provision of this Agreement.

16. Notices.

All notices between parties shall be in writing and shall be served either personally, by certified mail, by overnight courier service or by facsimile at the addresses set forth on the signature pages hereto and shall be effective upon receipt.

17. Miscellaneous.

(a) This Agreement together with its exhibits (i) embodies the entire agreement between the parties, supersedes all prior agreements and understandings between such parties, if any, relating to the subject matter hereof and may be amended only by an instrument in writing executed by an authorized signatory of each party hereto, and (ii) may be executed in a number of identical counterparts, each of which shall be deemed an original for all purposes and all of which shall constitute, collectively, one agreement.

(b) No failure on the part of any party to exercise, and no delay in exercising, any right hereunder shall operate as a waiver thereof by such party, nor shall any single or partial exercise of any right hereunder preclude any other or further exercise thereof or the exercise of any other right. The rights and remedies of each party provided herein are cumulative and are in addition to, and not exclusive or in lieu of, any rights or remedies provided by law (except as otherwise expressly set forth herein), and are not conditional or contingent on any attempt by such party to exercise any of its rights against any other party. 10

(c) All representations, warranties, indemnities and covenants made herein shall survive the execution, delivery and performance of this Agreement and all other documents contemplated herein and the purchase and sale of the Put Claims.

(d) The Parties acknowledge that the Funding Agent shall hold and dispose of the put option premium as set forth in Section 4 hereof and shall have no other duties. The Funding Agent shall not be liable for any act or omission of any of the other parties hereto, any loss, liability, injury or damage with respect to, or diminution in the value of, the Accounts or the Put Claims, or the obligations, representations and warranties of any other party hereto. The parties shall indemnify and hold the Funding Agent harmless against any liabilities, damages or expenses incurred by it as a result of acting as such under this Agreement, except liabilities arising from its own gross negligence or willful misconduct. 11

IN WITNESS WHEREOF, the parties have caused this Agreement to be executed, each by its duly authorized officer or representative, all on the day and year first above written.

SELLER:	PURCHASER:
By:	By:
Name:	Name:
Title:	Title:

Address for Notices:	Address for Notices:
Attention:	Attention:
Telecopy No.:	Telecopy No.:

5.4.2 Put Agreement—B

PUT AGREEMENT, dated as of, 2001 by and between [("Assignor") and [ ] ("Assignee").

RECITALS

A. From time to time Assignor holds accounts receivable due from [ ] ("Debtor") arising from the sale, in the ordinary course, of goods or merchandise, or the rendering of services.
B. Assignee desires to sell and grant to Assignor the right and option to sell such accounts receivable to Assignee and Assignor desires to purchase and accept such right and option from Assignee, all on the terms and conditions set forth herein.
C. In consideration of the premises contained herein and other good and valuable consideration, the receipt and sufficiency of which are hereby acknowledged, the parties hereto agree as follows:

AGREEMENT

Section 1. Definitions. As used herein, the following terms have the meanings stated:

Assigned Interest: All of Assignor's right, title and interest in, to and under (i) Receivables in the aggregate principal amount not to exceed $[ ]; (ii) all distributions, and other amounts paid or distributed in respect of the foregoing; (iii) to the extent related to the foregoing, the Merchandise Documents; and (iv) all proceeds of any kind of the foregoing.

Bankruptcy Code: Title 11 of the United States Code, 11 U.S.C. § 101 et sue; as amended.

Bankruptcy Event: The filing of a voluntary or involuntary petition for bankruptcy protection of the Debtor under Chapter 7 or 11 of the

Bankruptcy Code during the Covered Period; provided that, in the case of an involuntary petition, an order for relief has been entered by the bankruptcy court presiding over the Debtor's petition.

Business Day: Any day (other than a Saturday, Sunday or legal holiday in the State of New York) for which banks are open for business in New York City.

Covered Period: The period commencing [ ] through 5:00 p.m. (New York City) [ ].

Disputed: Objected to, disputed, contested, challenged or listed as un liquidated, contingent or disputed on Schedule of Liabilities.

Exercise Period: Any Business Day occurring during the Covered Period, provided however, that the Exercise Period shall terminate [20] days after the occurrence of a Bankruptcy Event.

Final Order: An order under the Bankruptcy Code which has not been reversed, stayed, modified, or amended and as to which (a) any appeal taken, petition for certiorari or motion for rehearing or reconsideration that has been filed, has been finally determined or dismissed in a manner that does not affect the determination of the allowed amount or treatment of the Assigned Interest or (b) the time to appeal, seek certiorari or move for reconsideration or rehearing has expired and no appeal, petition for certiorari or motion for reconsideration or rehearing has been timely filed.

Impaired: Voided, avoided, reduced, expunged, subordinated, disallowed, or subject to any defense, claim, counterclaim, set-off or recoupment. Merchandise Documents: The invoices evidencing each Receivable and all other agreements or documents (or true copies thereof) relating to the creation of, or further evidencing, the Receivables.

Person: Any person, entity, regulatory body or governmental authority.

Purchase Rate: The purchase rate set forth in Schedule A hereto.

Receivables: Certain accounts receivable, arising from merchandise sold or services rendered to Debtor during the period commencing with the first day of the Covered Period through and including the date of a Bankruptcy Event, due from Debtor. As used herein, the term "Receivables" includes without limitation: any and all of Assignor's rights, claims (including "claims" within the meaning of Section 101(5) of the Bankruptcy Code) and causes of action (A) against Debtor arising from, under or in connection with the accounts, contract rights, and other forms of obligations for the payment of money arising out of the sale of goods or the rendering of services and all Merchandise Documents related thereto including, without limitation (i) any and all payments, property or distributions to Assignor from and after the exercise date of the Put Option and (ii) any and all payments, property or distributions resulting from any plan, reorganization, restructuring or liquidation of Debtor; (B) against any Person who may be liable to Assignor under or with respect to the Receivables; (C) all rights in, to and under any collateral, guarantees or performance bonds granted in respect of the Receivables; and (D) all proceeds of any kind of the foregoing. Receivables shall not include accounts (i) which represent a sale to a parent, subsidiary or affiliate of Debtor, (ii) which represent a ill and hold transaction or a claim for the return of goods shipped on consignment, or (iii) which are determined and payable in any currency other than United States dollars.

Schedule of Liabilities: The Schedule of Liabilities required to be prepared by the Debtor pursuant to Section 521 of the Bankruptcy Code in accordance with Rule 1007 of the Bankruptcy Rules.

Section 2. Put Option and Exercise.

(i) Put Option. Assignee hereby irrevocably grants to Assignor the right and option to sell the Assigned Interest to Assignee as provided herein (the "Put Option"). The Put Option is an option in favor of Assignor to sell all or a portion of the Assigned Interest to Assignee, and is not an obligation of Assignor to sell.

(ii) Exercise. The Put Option may be exercised in whole or in part only after the occurrence of a Bankruptcy Event and only once by Assignor delivering to Assignee a Notice of Exercise in the form of Exhibit A (the "Notice") during the Exercise Period. Promptly after delivery of a Notice of Exercise, Assignor and Assignee shall execute and deliver an Assignment Agreement substantially in the form attached hereto as Exhibit B (the "Assignment Agreement").

(iii) Payment. In consideration of the sale and assignment of the Assigned Interest pursuant to the Assignment Agreement, Assignee shall pay to Assignor within five (5) Business Days after Assignee's receipt of that portion of the Schedule of Liabilities indicating Assignor's total unsecured claims (such date of payment is referred to herein as the "Payment Date"). Grantor shall pay on the Payment Date the Purchase Rate multiplied by the amount of claim, if any, listed on the Schedule of Liabilities as liquidated, non-contingent and non-disputed (the "Scheduled Amount") but not in excess of the amount of Assignor's claim as set forth in the Notice and the Assignment Agreement ("Claim Amount"). To the extent the Scheduled Amount is less than the Claim Amount, then within five (5) business days after receipt by Assignee of a final order of the Bankruptcy Court allowing the Assignor's claim in any amount greater than the Scheduled Amount (such excess of claim over the Scheduled Amount but in no event greater than the Claim Amount less the Scheduled Amount, if any, is referred to herein as the "Additional Amount") at the Purchase Rate, multiplied by the Additional Amount.

(iv) Conditions. Assignee's obligation to purchase the Assigned Interest is subject to the following conditions, each of which must be satisfied on or before the Payment Date: (i) Assignor's representations, warranties and covenants contained in this Agreement and the Assignment Agreement shall be true and complete with in all material respects; (ii) a Bankruptcy Event shall have occurred during the Covered Period; (iii) (A) no portion of the Assigned Interest with respect to which the Put Option has been exercised has been Disputed or Impaired and (B) (l) the Schedule of Liabilities lists the Assignor's unsecured claims in the Scheduled Amount as non-disputed, non-contingent and liquidated or (2) the Claim is allowed pursuant to a final order of the Bankruptcy Court, (iv) the Claim Amount does not include any Receivables which arose after any Receivables became more than sixty (60) days past due; (v) Assignor shall have exercised the

Put Option, delivered the Notice to Assignee during the Exercise Period and have delivered to Assignee, if requested by Assignee, the Merchandise Documents; (vi) Assignor shall have executed and delivered to Assignee the Assignment Agreement for the Assigned Interest; and (vii) the Receivables were generated (i.e. invoiced for goods actually shipped or services actually rendered) during the period commencing with the first day of the Covered Period through and including the date of a Bankruptcy Event.

Section 3. Premium. Assignor paid to Assignee the non-refundable payment in the amount of $[ ] upon the execution and delivery of this Put Agreement.

Section 4. Assignor's Representations. Assignor hereby represents and warrants to Assignee as of the date hereof and as of the date of Assignor's exercise of the Put Option that:

(i) it has full power and authority to enter into and perform this Agreement and to assign the Assigned Interest, and this Agreement and such assignment (A) have been duly authorized, (B) are legal, valid and binding and enforceable against Assignor, and (C) are not in contravention of any law, order or agreement by which Assignor is bound;
(ii) it has made no prior assignment of the Assigned Interest or of any interest therein; it is the sole legal and beneficial owner of the Assigned Interest and has good and marketable title thereto, free and clear of all liens, claims and encumbrances of any kind;
(iii) no proceedings relating to the Assigned Interest are pending or, to the knowledge of Assignor, threatened against or affecting Assignor before any court, arbitrator or administrative or governmental body which, in the aggregate, would adversely affect the Assigned Interest or Assignee's rights and remedies hereunder or in respect thereof;
(iv) no consents, notices, filings, approvals or authorizations are required by Assignor to be made to or with or received by the Assignor from any person, entity, or governmental body for the sale hereunder and consummation of the transactions

contemplated by this Agreement, which have not been made or received;

(v) there are no fees, commissions or compensation payable by Assignee to any party engaged or retained by, through or on behalf of Assignor in connection with the consummation of the transactions contemplated hereby; and

(vi) Assignor acknowledges that Assignee may possess material non-public information about Debtor which is not known by Assignor. Notwithstanding Assignee not disclosing such confidential information to Assignor, Assignor desires to enter into this Agreement and Assignee shall have no liability whatsoever to Assignor based on Assignee's use, knowledge, possession or non-disclosure of such information and Assignor releases Assignee from liability therefrom.

Section 5. Assignee's Representations. Assignee hereby represents and warrants to Assignor as of the date hereof that:

(i) Assignee has full power and authority to execute and deliver this Agreement and to consummate the transactions contemplated hereby, and has obtained all consents and approvals, required in connection herewith;

(ii) This Agreement and any documents to be executed and delivered in connection herewith have been duly authorized by Assignee, are valid and enforceable against Assignee in accordance with its terms and are not in contravention of any law, order or agreement by which Assignee is bound;

(iii) Assignee has made such examination, review and investigation of facts and circumstances necessary to evaluate the Assigned Interest as it has deemed necessary or appropriate;

(iv) Assignee has made its credit determination and analysis based upon such information as Assignee deemed sufficient to enter into this Agreement and not based on any statements or representations by Assignor except as expressly set forth herein; and

(v) there are no fees, commissions or compensation payable by Assignor to any party engaged or retained by, through or on behalf of Assignee in connection with the transactions contemplated hereby.

Section 6. Indemnification.

(i) Assignor agrees to indemnify, defend and hold Assignee and its officers, directors, employees, agents, partners and controlling persons (collectively, the "Assignee Indemnitees ") harmless from and against any and all expenses; losses, claims, damages and liabilities which are incurred by or threatened against the Assignee Indemnitees or any of them, including without limitation reasonable attorneys' fees and expenses, caused by, or in any way resulting from or relating to Assignor's breach of any of the representations, warranties, covenants or agreements of Assignor set forth in this Agreement.

(ii) Assignee agrees to indemnify, defend and hold Assignor and its officers, directors, employees, agents, partners and controlling persons (collectively, the "Assignor Indemnitees") harmless from and against any and all expenses, losses, claims, damages and liabilities which are incurred by or threatened against the Assignor Indemnitees or any of them, including without limitation reasonable attorneys' fees and expenses, caused by, or in any way resulting from or relating to Assignee's breach of any of the representations, warranties, covenants or agreement of Assignee set forth in this Agreement.

Section 7. General.

(i) Further Assignments. Assignee shall have the right to sell, assign and transfer this Agreement and its rights hereunder and to delegate its obligations hereunder without the consent of Assignor. Notwithstanding any such sale, assignment or transfer, the obligations of Assignee under this Agreement and the Exhibits hereto shall continue and remain in full force and effect until fully paid, performed and satisfied.

(ii) Costs and Fees. Except as otherwise expressly provided for herein, each party to this Agreement shall bear its own costs and expenses, including but not limited to attorneys' fees and expenses, in connection with the closing of the transactions contemplated hereby.

(iii) Filings and Further Assurances. Each of the parties hereto agrees, at its own cost and expense, to execute and deliver, or to cause to be executed and delivered, all such instruments (including all necessary endorsements) and to take all such action as the other party may reasonably request in order to (i) effectuate the intent and purposes of, and to carry out the terms of this Agreement, and (ii) further effect the transfer of legal, beneficial and record ownership of the Assigned Interest to Assignee.

(iv) Integration. This Agreement, the Notice of Exercise and the Assignment Agreement shall constitute the complete agreement of the parties hereto with respect to the subject matters referred to herein and supersedes all prior or contemporaneous negotiations, promises, covenants, agreements or representations of every nature whatsoever with respect thereto, all of which have become merged and finally integrated into this Agreement. This Agreement cannot be amended, modified or supplemented except by an instrument in writing executed by both parties hereto.

(v) Notices, Payments and Deliveries. Notices shall be given by telecopy (provided confirmation of delivery is obtained), certified or registered mail or personally or by courier at the addresses set forth on Schedule B of this Agreement. Payments and deliveries shall be made as set forth on Schedule B.

(vi) Miscellaneous. The terms of this Agreement shall be binding upon and shall inure to the benefit of the parties and their respective successors and permitted assigns, participants and transferees. All representations, warranties, covenants and agreements made herein shall survive the execution and delivery of this Agreement and the Assignment Agreement. This Agreement shall be governed by and construed in accordance with the laws of the State of New York without regard to any conflicts of laws provisions thereof. Each party to this Agreement hereby irrevocably consents to the jurisdiction of the United States Court for the Southern District of New York and the courts of the State of New York located in the City of New York in any action to enforce, interpret or construe any provision of this Agreement or of any other agreement or document delivered in connection with this Agreement, and also hereby irrevocably waives any defense of improper venue, forum non conveniens or lack of personal jurisdiction to any such action brought in those Courts. Each party further irrevocably agrees that any action to enforce, interpret or construe any provision of this Agreement will be brought only in one of those Courts. Each party hereby waives its right to a trial by jury. No failure on the part of either party to exercise, and no delay in exercising, any right hereunder or under any related document shall operate as a waiver thereof by such party, nor shall any single or partial exercise of any right hereunder or under any other related document preclude any other or further exercise thereof or the exercise of any other right.

(vii) Conflict. If the terms of this Agreement are inconsistent with the terms of the Assignment Agreement" or the Notice of Exercise the terms of this Agreement shall, as between Assignor and Assignee, govern and control.

(viii) Confidentiality. Assignor and Assignee agree to maintain the confidentiality of this Agreement, including but not limited to maintaining such confidentiality with respect to Debtor, except to the extent required by applicable laws or regulations; provided that either party may disclose the Agreement and the transactions contemplated hereby to permitted assignees hereunder; provided further, that from and after a Bankruptcy Event, Assignee shall have the right to disclose this Agreement and the transactions contemplated hereby to the Debtor.

(ix) Counterparts: Telecopies. This Agreement may be executed by telecopy in multiple counterparts and all of such counterparts taken together shall be deemed to constitute one and the same instrument. Transmission by fascimile of an executed counterpart of this Agreement shall be deemed to constitute due and sufficient delivery of such counterpart. Each fully executed counterpart of this Agreement shall be deemed to be a duplicate original.

IN WITNESS WHEREOF, the undersigned have executed and delivered this Agreement as of the date first stated above.

[______________________________]

By: ______________________________

Name: Title:

Tax ID: ______________________________

[______________________________]

By: Name: Title:

5.4.3 Corporate Guarantee Agreement

This Corporate Guarantee Agreement ("Guarantee") is made by and between the corporations, identified on the signature page hereof as Guarantors (""Guarantors") and YYYY Corporation, a ______________corporation ("YYYY").

WITNESSETH

WHEREAS YYYY Corporation ("YYYY") has entered into a Memory Products Agreement (such Memory Products Agreement, and any and all amendments, modifications, supplements, riders, exhibits, and schedules that are attached hereto and may hereafter be attached thereto being hereinafter collectively referred to as "Agreement") with __________ as manufacturer of integrated circuits for YYYY therein, dated, whereby YYYY as licensor agreed to grant __________ a license to manufacture and market YYYY designed integrated circuits as evidenced by the Agreement; and

WHEREAS, as an inducement to YYYY to consent to the Agreement dated, with YYYY, ________ has promised royalty payments as well as service technology payments as part of ________'s obligations; and

WHEREAS ________ will acquire certain proprietary information as well as transfer of technology; and

WHEREAS, the Guarantors of this Agreement are wholly owned subsidiaries of __________ and will receive benefits under this Agreement: as the marketing arm of __________; and

NOW THEREFORE, in order to induce YYYY to consent to this Agreement without demanding other means to insure performance than otherwise agreed hereto, and for other good and valuable consideration, the sufficiency of which is hereby acknowledged, Guarantors hereby covenants and agree with YYYY as follows:

ARTICLE I

Guarantee

1.1 Guarantors unconditionally guarantee the full, prompt, complete and faithful performance, payment, observance and fulfillment ("Performance") by ________ of all the obligations, covenants and conditions of the Agreement, including, but not limited to, the payments of any kind and all sums that may become due pursuant to the Agreement thereunder when due. Guarantors further agree to all expenses (including reasonable attorneys' fees and legal expenses) paid or incurred by YYYY in endeavoring to collect the obligations, or any part thereof, or securing or enforcing the Performance thereof, or in enforcing this Guarantee.

1.2 Guarantors covenant and agree unconditionally that in the event that ________. shall default ("Default") in the Performance of any Obligations, then within 15 days of the receipt of written notice from or on behalf of YYYY to the effect that there exists such a Default and of the amount or Obligations or will provide YYYY with evidence of the Performance of the Obligations or will complete Performance of the Obligation which ________ has failed to perform. In the event that Guarantors should fail or decline to pay any sums due hereunder within 20 days following YYYY's request therefore, then said sums shall bear interest equal to the lesser or (i) the maximum legal rate of interest permitted by applicable law or (ii) 5% per anum above "Prime" the announced base rate of interest charged by Bank America on 90 day; loans to responsible and substantial commercial borrowers in effect from time to time computed on the bases of the actual number of days elapsed using a 360-day year, payable on demand. Further, if Guarantor should fail to pay such amount or perform such Obligation, YYYY may institute and pursue any action or proceeding to judgment or final decree and may enforce any such judgment or final decree against Guarantors and collect in the manner provided by law out of its property, wherever situated, the moneys adjudged or decreed to be payable.

1.3 This Guarantee shall not be limited to any particular period of time, but, rather, shall continue absolutely, unconditionally and irrevocably until full and complete Performance by ________ of all Obligations, or until all Obligations of ________ to YYYY have been paid, discharged, performed or released to the satisfaction of YYYY, and Guarantors shall not be released against YYYY until said Obligations have been completed.

ARTICLE II
Remedies and Rights of YYYY

2.1 YYYY shall give Guarantors notice in writing of any Default or event which might mature into a Default known to it but neither failure to give, nor defect in, any notice shall extinguish or in any way affect the obligations of Guarantors hereunder. Neither demand on, nor the pursuit of any remedies against ________ or any other person, firm or entity shall be required as a condition precedent to, and neither the pendency nor the prior termination of any action, suit or proceeding against any of shall bar or prejudice the making of a demand on the Guarantors by YYYY and the commencement against Guarantors, after such demand, of any action, suit or proceeding, at law or in equity, for the specific performance of any covenant or agreement contained in the Agreement or for the enforcement of any other appropriate legal or equitable remedy.

2.2 The Guarantors' liability hereunder is primary, direct and immediate. Guarantors agree that neither (i) the exercise or the failure to exercise by YYYY of any rights or remedies conferred on them under or derived from the Agreement (ii) the recovery of a judgment at law against ________, (iii) the commencement of an action at law or the recovery of a judgment at law against ________ and the enforcement thereof through levy, execution or otherwise, (iv) the taking, pursuing or exercising any of the foregoing actions, rights, powers, or remedies (even though requested by Guarantors) by YYYY or anyone acting obligations of Guarantors hereunder, but Guarantors shall be and remain liable for and until the Performance of all Obligations notwithstanding the previous discharge (total or partial) from further liability of ________ or the existence of any bar to the pursuit by Guarantors of any right or claim to indemnity against ________ or any right or claim to be subrogated to the rights or claims of YYYY in the licensed products or resulting from any action or failure or omission to act or delay in acting by YYYY, or anyone entitled to act in its or their place.

2.3 In case Guarantors shall be dissolved or shall lose their corporate charter by forfeiture or otherwise or shall become insolvent or admit in writing their inability to pay their debts as the mature, or apply for, consent to or acquiesce in the appointment of a trustee, receiver, liquidator, assignee, sequestrator or other similar official for theirselves or any of their property; or, in the absence of such application, consent or acquiescense, trustee, receiver, liquidator, assignee, sequestrator or other similar is appointed for Guarantors or for a substantial part of their properties and is not discharged within 60 days; or any bankruptcy, reorganization, debt arrangement, or other proceeding under any bankruptcy, or insolvency law or at common law or in equity or any discussion or liquidation proceeding is instituted by or against Guarantors, or remains for 60 days undismissed, then Guarantors shall pay to YYYY forthwith all sums due or to become due pursuant to this Guarantee.

2.4 The benefits, remedies and rights provided or intended to be provided hereby for YYYY are in addition to and without prejudice to any rights, benefits, remedies or security to which YYYY might otherwise be entitled. No delay on the part of YYYY in the exercise of any right or remedy shall preclude other or further exercise thereof or the exercise or any other right or remedy; nor shall any modification or waiver of any of the provisions of this Guarantee be binding on YYYY except as expressly set forth in writing.

2.5 Anything else contained herein to the contrary notwithstanding, YYYY, from time to time, without notice to Guarantors, may take all or any of the following actions without in any manner affecting or impart* ing the liability of Guarantors hereunder : (i) obtain a security interest in any property to secure any of—the Obligations or any obligation hereunder, retain or obtain the primary or secondary liability of ________, in addition to Guarantors, with respect to any of the Obligations, •, (ii) • extend or renew the Agreement for any period, (iii) release or compromise any liability of Guarantors hereunder, (iv)resort to the Guarantors for payment of any Obligation, whether or not YYYY shall proceed against any other party primarily liable on any of the Obligations, or (v) agree to any amendment, modification or alteration of the Agreement.

ARTICLE III
Guarantors' Warranties

Guarantors represent and warrant to YYYY and ________ that :

(i) Guarantors are corporations duly organized and now existing in good standing under the laws of the jurisdictions of incorporation as shown on the signature page hereof and are duly qualified and in good standing and authorized to do business in all jurisdictions wherein the location and nature of the properties used or business, as the same is presently or proposed to be conducted, makes such qualification necessary;

(ii) Guarantors have the corporate power and authority to carry on their business as presently conducted and the execution, delivery and performance by the Guarantors of this Guaran—: tee has been fully authorized by all necessary corporate action; no consent of stockholders is required therefore; and the execution and delivery of, the consummation of the transactions contemplated in, and compliance by Guarantors with any of the terms and provisions of this Guarantee do not and will not conflict with or contravene any law, rule, regulation, judgment, order or decree of any government or court having jurisdiction over the Guarantors.

(iii) Neither the execution and delivery by the Guarantors of this Guarantee nor any of the transactions contemplated hereby requires the consent, approval, order or authorization of, or registration with, or the giving of notice to, any U.S. federal or state authority, except such consents as have been obtained by the Guarantors and are in ftfll force and effect.

(iv) This Guarantee has been duly executed and delivered by Guarantors and constitutes a legal, valid, and binding obligation of said Guarantors enforceable against them in accordance with its terms.

(v) There is no action, litigation or other preceeding pending or threatened against Guarantors before any court, arbitrator or administrative agency which may have a materially adverse affect on the financial condition of the Guarantors which would prevent, hinder or jeopardize the performance under this Guarantee.

(vi) Guarantors are fully familiar with all of the covenants, terms and conditions of the Agreement.

(vii) Guarantors will maintain their respective corporate existence and right to carry on operations and acquire, maintain 10 and renew all rights, contracts, leases and lands necessary in the conduct of its business operations.

ARTICLE IV
Miscellaneous Provisions

4.1 All the covenants, stipulations, promises and agreements contained in this Guarantee by or on behalf of the Guarantors shall bind its successors and assigns. Each and every immediate and successive assignee or transferee of YYYY,. shall have the right to" enforce this Guarantee, by suit or otherwise, for the benefit of such assignee or transferee as fully as if such assignee or transferee were herein by name specifically given such rights, powers or benefits.

4.2 Any notice or demand which by any provision of this Guarantee is required or permitted to be given by YYYY to said Guarantors shall be deemed to have been sufficiently given for all purposes if given by first class mail, postage prepaid, to any Guarantor at its address set forth after its signature below.

4.3 Guarantor hereby expressly waives : (i) notice of the acceptance by YYYY of this Guarantee, (ii) notice of the existence, creation or non-payment of all or any of the Obligations, (iii) presentment, demand, notice or dishonor, protest, or protection of or realization on the Obligations or any thereof.

4.4 This Guarantee shall be governed by and construed and enforced in accordance with the laws of ______________.

4.5 Guarantors, at their sole cost and expense, agree to deliver and supply to YYYY with (i) an opinion of their legal counsel, confirming and substantiating the truth and accuracy of all warranties and representations advanced by the Guarantors" under Article III, and (iii) a certified copy of the Resolutions of the Guarantors' Board of Directors (if needed) authorizing the execution of and performance under this Guarantee.

4.6 Guarantors: (i) hereby, irrevocably submit to the jurisdiction of the State of __________ for purposes of any arbitration action which relates to the transactions contemplated in this Guarantee. Said arbitration shall be conducted in accordance with the rules of the American Arbitration Association.

5.4.4 Individual Guaranty

In consideration of XXXX, Inc referred to as ("XXX") entering into the ______________ Agreement (the Agreement) with (Company name) (Hereinafter referred to as "Seller") for the purchase of goods and services by XXX, the undersigned, (personal guarantor) In (hereinafter referred to as "Guarantor"), hereby unconditionally guarantees prompt and full performance of (company name) to XXX when due of any and all liability of any kind for which Seller may have heretofore become liable to XXX or may hereafter become liable to XXX. Should Seller for any reason fail to deliver any and all goods, products and services or liability to XXX when due under the Agreement, Guarantor hereby unconditionally promises and guarantees the performance of (company name) or guarantees the reimbursement of any amounts paid by XXX minus the purchase price of wine delivered to XXX in accordance with the Agreement, upon demand, to XXX. This guaranty is unconditional and shall not be affected by any release of security, release of other guarantors, renewals, extensions, or substitutions, for any indebtedness or liability of the Seller to XXX. Guarantor hereby waives notice of acceptance, presentment, demand, protest, notice of protest, and notice of dishonor of any obligation guaranteed hereunder. No modification or extension of time or other indulgence granted by XXX to the Seller shall in any way release or effect the obligation of Guarantor hereunder, and no omission or delay on the part of XXX in exercising any rights to collect or enforce payment of any obligation shall constitute a waiver of any such right against the Guarantor hereunder. This guaranty shall include any and all goods and services due XXX as well as any amounts which are due or which may become due from the Seller to XXX, including interest, service charges and costs of collection including reasonable attorney's fees incurred by XXX. This guaranty shall be binding upon the Guarantor and its successors, and assigns, and no assignment hereof shall relieve Guarantor of its obligations hereunder. This guaranty is a continuing guaranty, and shall remain in force until revoked by notice in writing to XXX, and revocation shall not prejudice any claims of XXX with respect to any obligation of Seller arising prior to revocation.

If the obligations of the Seller are also guaranteed by any other person or other entity by Continuing Guaranty or endorsement of any obligation of the Seller or otherwise, the obligation of such other person or entity in this obligation shall be deemed to be several; and the release by you of any other Guarantor, or settlement with him or her, whether by settlement or impairment of his or her Guaranty, shall not operate to prejudice XXX's rights against the Guarantor.

This Agreement shall be construed in accordance with the laws of the State of ________________.

WITNESS:

____________________ ____________________

Notary Public Name

____

Identification Number

6. Compliance

6.1 What Is Compliance?

Many countries now require companies to implement compliance policies for legal reasons. Some companies have implemented compliance policies for brand image and other reasons as well. A compliance program, properly implemented, not only increases a company's brand image but reinforces ethical behavior, which in turn minimizes violation of local laws by upholding compliance of financial and legal rules.

To understand compliance, one needs to review the history of compliance in the United States.

US Compliance History

6.1.1 Background

- In November 1991, an innovative piece of legislation was enacted in the United States that had a profound effect on corporate America. This has reverberated throughout the world.
- The legislation was the US Federal Sentencing Guidelines ("Guidelines").

6.1.2 The Guidelines

- The Guidelines are used by judges to determine the appropriate sentence for corporations convicted of a federal crime.
- According to the Guidelines, a corporation may be sentenced or fined for federal offenses connected with antitrust, securities, bribery, fraud, money laundering, criminal business activities, extortion, embezzlement, conspiracy, etc. As you can see it is quite broad and covers many "illegal" activities.

When deciding on an appropriate sentence, judges were for the first time asked to consider whether the corporation had an "effective compliance program" before the violation took place or, in other words, whether the corporation took appropriate steps to prevent and detect violations of law. Therefore, in order for courts to reduce or mitigate criminal sanctions, companies must now have a compliance program in place. The Guidelines were amended in 2004 (Revised Guidelines).[3]

6.1.3 The Revised Guidelines

- The Revised Guidelines recognize that effective compliance and ethics requires more than policies and procedures, it also entails a focus on organizational culture that promotes law abidance. In other words, a major focus is on compliance and ethics.
- For the first time, a set of laws creates a legal mandate for compliance. It looks at:
    - Incentives
    - Requirements
    - Guidance
    - A focus on ethical behavior

6.1.4 The Revised Guidelines

- The Revised Guidelines recognize seven elements in a proper compliance program.

---

3 Federal Sentencing Guidelines for Organizations (revised and amended as of Nov. 1, 2004).

- The current Guidelines list seven elements of an "effective compliance program" as being:
    - Compliance standards and procedures (a code of conduct should exist)
    - Oversight by high-level personnel (the Board must oversee the program)
    - Due care when delegating authority (due care in hiring employees)
    - Effective communication of standards and procedure (training)
    - Auditing/monitoring/reporting systems must be in place
    - Compliance must be promoted and enforced consistently throughout the organization
    - There must be an appropriate response after violation detected

6.1.5 Failure to Enact Compliance

- In February 1996, in what was the largest criminal fine in US history, a New York federal court, following the Guidelines, sentenced Daiwa Bank (Japan) to pay a $340 million fine.
    - The case involved a bank employee who lost $1.1 billion in unauthorized trades.
    - Prosecution arose out of report of an unauthorized, off-the-books trading scheme—bank officials conspired to conceal the losses from bank regulators for more than two months.
    - The two main reasons for the fine:
        - "Lack of a meaningful compliances program"
        - "Consequent failure to report the employee's wrongdoing"

6.1.6 Lessons

Foreign companies doing business in the United States can learn an especially important lesson from Daiwa Bank. Primarily, foreign companies doing business in the United States must realize they have to comply with US laws and regulations. Daiwa Bank could have avoided the criminal fine had it followed the requirements of the US Sentencing Guidelines.

6.1.7 The United States

In implementing a compliance program in conformity with US law and in compliance with specific laws, a company shows it fully appropriates US laws and regulations. By developing such a compliance program, a company understands in general terms the requirements of US law.

6.2 Establishment of Compliance Program

The establishment of a compliance program anywhere in the world usually consists of adopting a company code of conduct, with perhaps specific policies governing local conditions. However, because of the US requirements, many organizations have adapted compliance policies that conform to US standards. Because of the US sentencing guidelines, specific elements to a valid compliance program are required. They are:

6.2.1 US Compliance Program

- The basics—what is needed?
    - A code of conduct
    - Local codes of business ethics (and other company policies) covering each country in which a company does business
    - Local training on all aspects, such as antitrust, etc.
    - A system to report suspected wrongdoing to the company
    - An anonymous reporting system allowing employees to report wrongdoing anonymously

6.2.2 Code of Conduct

A company's compliance programs' code of conduct should incorporate various principles. Primarily, at least five principles should be followed or reflected in the code. The five principles I suggest a company's compliance code of conduct should incorporate are as follows:

- The company complies with laws and ethical standards.
- The company maintains and promotes an ethical organizational culture.
- The company respects its customers, shareholders, and employees.
- The company cares for the environment.
- The company is a socially responsible corporate citizen.

6.2.3 US Compliance Program Code of Conduct

To establish an "effective compliance program" under the guidelines and other US laws, a foreign company normally goes beyond its local code or domestic code of conduct. Its employees must be familiar with the specific laws that govern their conduct in the jurisdiction in which they work.

If a company has a branch or division in the United States, it must have a US Code of Ethics, which is designed to inform employees in the United States about the specific laws and standards governing their conduct.

6.2.4 The US Compliance Program Local Codes of Business Ethics (and Other Policies)

- A US Compliance and Code of Ethics (and other policies) should cover at a minimum approximately twenty-two different areas. An employee handbook should perhaps cover another forty or more.
- US Code of Conduct
- Principle 1. The company complies with laws and ethical standards:
    - Nondiscrimination, anti-harassment, and anti-retaliation
    - Drugs and alcohol

  - Wage and hour laws
  - Americans with Disabilities Act
  - Employment at will
  - Political contributions and activities
  - Personal political contributions
  - Antitrust law and competitive practices
  - Foreign Corrupt Practices Act
  - Government contracts (if it does government work)
  - Government relations-dealing with government regulators
  - Government reports
- Principle 2. The company maintains an ethical organizational culture:
  - Company property, confidential information
  - Intellectual property and property of others
  - Accurate books and records
  - Computer hardware and software, e-mail
  - Confidentiality of client information
  - Accounting policies
  - Conflicts of interest
  - Nondiscrimination, anti-harassment, and anti-retaliation policies
- Principle 3. The company respects customers, shareholders, and employees.
  - Procurement
- Principle 4. The company cares for the environment.
  - Environments, safety, and health policies
- Principle 5. The company is a responsible corporate citizen.
  - Compliance procedures

6.2.5 Compliance Training

To have an effective compliance program, a company must also hold compliance training after it "launches" the program. Areas of training should be covered and how the training should be given is of major interest.

It is best if the company offers local compliance training covering the relevant laws and practices where people are located. Training can be given in person, online via web-based training, or by other media. It must be given on a regular basis.

6.2.6 Local Training

- Training on the code of conduct can be given by HR, Compliance, or by Legal.
- Local training in antitrust, anti-harassment, antidiscrimination, and anti-retaliation, ethics, illegal business practices, financial integrity, customs, etc.
- The majority of the local training will be in person and online.
- The goal is to equip employees to handle compliance issues.
- Training should help employees to identify potential wrongdoing.
- Training should help employees understand their role in the compliance scheme.
- It should let them know what to report and how to report.

6.2.7 The US Compliance Program: Reporting Wrongdoing

- In the United States, having an effective reporting system has come to mean one that encourages reporting by allowing for a variety of reporting avenues.
- If an employee was limited to one avenue of reporting (i.e., to his supervisor), it is likely he would not report wrongdoing if his supervisor was involved.
- In the United States, a company should allow for employee reporting normally as follows.

6.2.7.1 Employee Reporting

All employees are required to promptly report all known or suspected violations of applicable laws or of the compliance program, including corporate policies. Reports of such violations shall be promptly made to a manager; the compliance officer, if any; HR; or to the Law Department. If any employee wishes, he or she may report violations anonymously via an anonymous e-mail (or by phone) system. All reports will be promptly and thoroughly investigated.

6.3 Training Programs

Training programs may vary depending on the needs of a particular company. Training programs may consist of instructor-led training, Internet-based, or e-learning programs or even a combination of both. It is up to the company to decide which training program fits the needs of its employees as well as suits its budgetary constraints.

6.4 Risk Assessment of Compliance Programs

A risk assessment or LRM audit is vital in the implementation and continued success of any compliance program. Not only do the U.S. Federal Sentencing Guidelines require a periodic risk assessment of a compliance program, but conducting a periodic risk assessment has an upside as well. By conducting a periodic or annual assessment of the compliance program, not only is the company or organization in compliance with the Federal Sentencing Guidelines but it will be able to improve the compliance program.

In order to minimize or avoid many of the legal and financial issues discussed above, a company should:

- Create a basic compliance system
  - For preventing problems
  - For detecting problems
  - For responding and remedying compliance issues
- Create a culture of compliance
  - Foundation for competing with others
  - Priority
  - Instill values of ethics
- The key to implementation
  - Senior management must commit to compliance. Management cannot keep a blind eye to problems.
  - Proper checks and balances must be created in the business processes.
  - Compliance must be built into all business processes.

In the United States, companies must implement a sound compliance system in order for directors of the company to discharge their fiduciary responsibilities.[4]

A well-drafted and implemented compliance policy can go a long way to reduce legal risk before litigation arises. World-class companies are driving compliance throughout their organizations. They understand that besides complying with legal requirements, rigorous financial and legal compliance leads to ethical actions that not only minimize legal risk but benefit the company's reputation and ultimately the bottom line, thereby protecting the company's brand.

6.5 Guidelines and Checklists for Internal Investigation

6.5.1 Sample Code of Conduct

PRINCIPLE #1 WE COMPLY WITH LAWS AND ETHICAL STANDARDS

POLICY NO. 1 NON-DISCRIMINATION, ANTI-HARASSMENT, ANTI-RETALIATION

NON-DISCRIMINATION

PURPOSE:

The Company is committed to working fairly and equitably with each employee. To that end, the Company shall endeavor to provide equal employment opportunities for all individuals without regard to race, color, religion, sex, age, national origin, disability, veteran status, or other classification protected by federal, state, or local laws.

---

4 Carole Basri and Irving Kagan, *Corporate Legal Departments*, 3rd ed., PLI, 2004, 11-4 citing in re Caremark Int'l Inc. Derivative Litig, 698 A.2d. 959 (Del. Ch, 1996).

POLICY:

The Company shall take personnel actions strictly based on each employee's individual ability, performance, experience, and the needs of the Company. Harassment, retaliation, coercion, interference, or intimidation of any employee based on race, religion, color, national origin, sex, age, veteran status, disability, or other classification protected by federal, state, or local laws is strictly prohibited. Any employee who experiences such activity should report it immediately to his or her supervisor or the Human Resources Department. This Policy may be subject to local or State law variances.

The Company shall take all actions reasonably necessary to prevent discrimination or harassment of any individual based on race, color, religion, sex, age, national origin, disability or veteran status and to promptly and thoroughly investigate and resolve any alleged instances of discrimination or harassment involving the terms, conditions and privileges of employment as well as the use of all company facilities and participation in all company-sponsored activities. As such, this policy prohibiting discrimination and harassment shall extend to:

- Recruiting, hiring, training, and promoting persons in all job classifications without regard to race, color, religion, sex, national origin, disability, veteran status, or other classification protected by federal, state, or local laws.
- Ensuring that promotion decisions are in accordance with equal employment opportunity requirements by imposing only valid, job related requirements for promotional opportunities.
- Ensuring that all personnel actions relating to compensation, benefits, transfers, termination, training, and education are administered in a nondiscriminatory manner.

It has been, and will continue to be, the Company's policy to provide equal opportunity to all applicants for employment and to administer all personnel practices, such as recruiting, hiring, promotions, disciplinary actions, and other terms, conditions and privileges of employment in a manner which does not discriminate on the basis of race, color, religion, sex, national origin, age, disability or veteran status

PROCEDURE:

1. **Managerial Responsibility:**

   Managers and supervisors have special responsibilities when it comes to discrimination. Not only must managers and supervisors conduct themselves in a manner consistent with this Policy, they are also responsible for establishing and maintaining a climate in the workplace that allows all associates to do their job effectively. Managers and supervisors must identify and report incidents of discrimination immediately. While managers and supervisors have the reporting options outlined in the applicable Code and this Manual, they must also notify their Human Resources Department of the incident(s), and cooperate in any investigation and corrective action that follows. Managers and supervisors who fail to report discrimination or condone it in the workplace will be subject to disciplinary action up to and including dismissal. (Managers and supervisors of Texas subsidiaries must comply with their respective subsidiary's reporting requirements for all discrimination, harassment and other employment-based concerns).

2. **Reporting and Investigating Discrimination:**

   Discrimination is a violation of the Company's Compliance and Ethics Program and should be reported so that it can be appropriately dealt with. While an associate is free to confront the offender about the alleged discrimination, there is no requirement to do so. While associates have all of the reporting options outlined in the Code and this Manual, they are also encouraged to notify the Company's Human Resources Department of actual or perceived violations of this policy.

Reports of discrimination will be promptly and discreetly investigated, and information regarding such complaints will be restricted to only those who need to know. During an investigation, however, the Company advises that identities of associates may be disclosed. No associate who in good faith complains about or reports discrimination will be retaliated against, nor will any reprisals be allowed. Retaliation in any form is a serious violation of this policy and will result in discipline up to and including termination. Persons filing false, frivolous or malicious complaints will also be subject to discipline up to and including termination. For more details on the system for reporting violations of the Compliance and Ethics Program see the Reporting and Investigating Violations Corporate Policy.

ANTI-HARASSMENT

PURPOSE:

The Company's goal is to promote a workplace environment free of discrimination, which includes freedom from harassment, whether based on sex, age, race, national origin, religion, disability, sexual orientation, marital status, or membership in any other legally protected group. Accordingly, the Company prohibits harassment of its employees whether committed by supervisors, co-workers, customers, or suppliers. This Policy also prohibits retaliation against employees for either complaining about harassment or cooperating with a harassment investigation.

POLICY:

The Company's policy is to treat all employees with respect and courtesy as well as to promote and maintain a working environment free of all forms of harassment. Harassment is defined as verbal or physical conduct or behavior that is unwelcome or unsolicited. Harassment occurs when the conduct or behavior:

- is made either implicitly or explicitly a term or condition of employment;

- has the purpose or effect of creating an intimidating, hostile or offensive work environment;
- has the purpose or effect of unreasonably interfering with an individual's work performance; or
- otherwise adversely affects an individual's employment opportunities.

Harassing conduct includes but is not limited to: epithets, slurs, negative stereotyping or threatening, intimidating or hostile acts (including acts purported to be "jokes" or "pranks"), displaying written or graphic material of an offensive nature (including cartoons, calendars, or pictures), or making verbal comments or gestures that denigrate or show hostility or aversion toward an individual or group. Impermissible conduct also includes harassing an individual because of his or her association with a member of a legally protected group.

Because the Company takes allegations of harassment seriously, it will promptly and thoroughly review all complaints of harassment, and take appropriate action, as warranted under the circumstances. The actions that will be taken, included, but are not limited to, corrective or disciplinary action such as counseling, reprimand, suspension and termination of employment. Managers and supervisors are responsible for taking immediate corrective action to deal effectively with harassment in order to ensure that complaints are investigated promptly, thoroughly and discretely. Managers and supervisors must identify and report incidents of harassment immediately.

Employees are expected to cooperate with the investigation of a harassment complaint. Providing false information during the course of the investigation of a harassment complaint is a serious offense which may result in disciplinary action, up to and including reprimand, suspension or termination of employment.

It is the Company's policy to maintain work environment free of sexual harassment. Unwelcome sexual advances, requests for sexual favors and other forms of verbal or physical conduct of a sexual nature are unacceptable and will not be tolerated.

DEFINITIONS:

Sexual Harassment: Sexual harassment is a violation of law and the Company's harassment policy. Sexual harassment, in any manner or form, whether perpetrated by an employee, supervisor, supplier, or customer is expressly prohibited.

Sexual harassment includes unwelcome sexual advances, requests for sexual favors and other verbal or physical conduct of a sexual nature when:

a. Submission to such conduct is made, either explicitly or implicitly, a term or condition of an individual's employment, or
b. Submission to or rejection of such conduct by an individual is used as the basis for employment decisions affecting such individual, or
c. Such conduct has the purpose or effect of unreasonably interfering with an individual's work performance or creating an intimidating, hostile, humiliating or sexually offensive working environment.

The legal definition of sexual harassment may also include other unwelcome sexually-oriented conduct, whether or not intended as such, which has the effect of creating a workplace environment that is hostile, offensive, intimidating or humiliating to either male or female employees. While it is not possible to list all conduct or behavior that may constitute sexual harassment, the following are some examples of conduct which may constitute sexual harassment

- uninvited physical contact;
- unwelcome or unwanted sexual advances considered unacceptable by the targeted individual;

- requests or demands for sexual favors, including but not limited to, subtle or blatant expectations, pressure or requests for any type of sexual favor accompanied by an implied or stated promise of preferential treatment or negative consequences concerning one's employment status;
- continued suggestions regarding invitations to social events outside the workplace, after it has been made clear that such suggestions are unwelcome;

PROCEDURE:

Each report will be investigated promptly, thoroughly and discretely. The investigation will be conducted in such a way as to maintain confidentiality to the extent practicable under the circumstances. The investigation will include, at a minimum, interviews with the person filing the complaint and the person alleged to have committed the harassment. Both the complainant and the accused will be advised of the findings of the investigation.

Following the investigation, disciplinary action up to and including termination of employment may be taken, as appropriate under the circumstances. The complainant will be notified of any action taken against the person allegedly responsible for the harassment.

POLICY NO. 2 DRUGS AND ALCOHOL

PURPOSE:

The Company's goal is to maintain a work environment that is free from the effects of alcohol and illegal drug use and/or abuse of otherwise legal substances. Illegal drug use or substance abuse may seriously impair judgment, performance and productivity, and may create unsafe working conditions. As well as encouraging voluntary treatment for those employees who may have a problem with drugs or alcohol, the Company has adopted this policy in consideration of the health and safety of all Company employees.

POLICY:

It is the Company's policy to prohibit the unlawful possession, use, sale, manufacture, distribution or dispensation of illegal or controlled substances by any associate while on Company premises; on Company business; or in Company vehicles. Associates are prohibited from reporting to work or conducting Company business while they are affected by or under the influence of illegal drugs and/or alcohol.

PROCEDURE:

Reporting to work or for Company business, or otherwise being on Company premises or in Company vehicles, under the influence of illegal drugs, illegal use of prescription drugs, or alcohol is prohibited. Likewise, the use, possession, sale, distribution, manufacture or purchase of drugs while at work, on Company business anywhere, while on Company premises or in Company vehicles, is prohibited. Certain employees are also subject to state or Federal regulations concerning drug testing or drug and alcohol abuse. Such employees must adhere to any additional requirements imposed by applicable regulations.

CONFIDENTIALITY/PRIVACY:

Employees' rights to privacy are recognized and valued. As such, procedures executed pursuant to this Policy will seek to protect employees' privacy interests. Information obtained through the application and enforcement of the Policy is considered confidential. Any results of testing will be treated in a confidential manner as private medical information and will only be disseminated on a need-to-know basis.

TESTING AND SEARCHES:

To the extent considered necessary for both the safe and productive conduct of Company business and the health and safety of Company employees, or as may be required by law for certain employees in occupations covered by law, drug and alcohol testing and searches may be performed. Such alcohol or drug-related problem affecting job performance, including, but not limited to, safety, productivity, quality of work, health or attendance, in order to determine whether an employee is in possession of or under the influence of alcohol or drugs, or has the presence in his/her system of drugs while performing Company business anywhere, on Company premises, or in Company vehicles.

PRESCRIPTION DRUGS:

Prescription drugs are a cause for concern if they affect the ability of an employee to work safely. It is the responsibility of the employee to review with his/her physician any work restriction(s) that should be observed while taking a prescribed drug. If there is a work restriction, it is also the responsibility of the employee to review that restriction with the Human Resources Department. As long as these procedures are followed, the use of prescription drugs in accordance with the prescription shall not be cause for discipline pursuant to this Policy.

POLICY NO. 3 WAGE AND HOUR LAWS IN THE U.S.

PURPOSE:

The purpose of this Policy is to help ensure that the Company complies with the requirements of law applicable to minimum wages and overtime compensation. These laws provide associates with certain legal protections, and the Company's employment practices should seek to ensure that these protections are preserved. Compliance is also important because violations of the wages and hours laws may subject the Company and its associates to civil and criminal liability.

POLICY:

It is the Company's policy to adhere to the requirements of state and federal law regarding the payment of minimum wages and overtime compensation. In all appropriate cases, the Company will pay its associates the minimum wages mandated by law. The Company will also pay its associates all overtime compensation required by law or by contract.

It is the Company's policy that proper records regarding wages, hours, and overtime compensation will be kept. Company associates must accurately and completely report and record all required wages and hours information. In no circumstances should any associate falsify any record relating to wages or hours worked.

POLICY NO. 4 U.S. AMERICANS WITH DISABILITIES ACT

PURPOSE:

A fundamental part of the Company's commitment to recognizing the contribution and value each employee is the Company's policy of nondiscrimination. Accordingly, the Company shall not discriminate in any of its personnel and employment practices, including, but not limited to: hiring, promoting, transfer, recruitment, advertising, reduction in force or termination, compensation of any kind, selection for training, educational programs, and Company sponsored recreation and social activities. The Company's policy is to comply with all the relevant and applicable provisions of the Americans with Disabilities Act ("ADA"), and other applicable law.

POLICY:

The Company will not discriminate against any qualified Company employee or job applicant with respect to any terms, privileges, or conditions of employment because of that person's physical or mental disability. The Company will make reasonable accommodations, wherever necessary, for all employees or applicants with disabilities, as required by law.

POLICY NO. 5 EMPLOYMENT AT WILL

PURPOSE:

The purpose of this policy is to inform associates that they are employed "at-will," as that term is described below.

POLICY:

In the absence of a written employment contract signed by the Company's President or CEO, Company employees are employed at the will of the Company and are therefore subject to termination at any time, for any or no reason, with or without cause or notice, provided that the termination does not violate any applicable law or regulation. At the same time, such Company employees may terminate their employment at any time and for any or no reason with or without cause or notice. It should also be noted that employment is for no specific duration.

No Company representative is authorized to modify this policy or to enter into any agreement concerning terms or conditions of employment unless the contract is writing and signed by the Company's President or CEO. Supervisory and management personnel are not authorized to make any representations to Company employees or applicants concerning the terms or conditions of employment with the Company which are not consistent with Company policies.

Company employees shall sign an application for employment and/or an offer of employment that contains a statement acknowledging their understanding that they are employed at the will of the Company.

Completion of an introduction period or conferral of regular status shall not change an employee's at-will status, or in any way restrict the Company's right to terminate the employment of such a Company employee, or change his or her terms or conditions of employment.

POLICY NO. 6 GOVERNMENT RELATIONS—POLITICAL CONTRIBUTIONS AND ACTIVITIES

PURPOSE:

The purpose of this Policy is to help ensure compliance with the laws governing Political Contributions.

POLICY:

It is the Company's policy to comply with all federal, state and local laws regarding political contributions and activities. Associates all strictly observe all laws governing political contributions. Associates may not make any political contribution of Company funds, property or services to any political party or committee, or to any candidate for or holder of any office of any government without prior review and approval of the Company's General Counsel. No direct or indirect pressure in any form may be directed toward associates to make any political contribution or participate in the support of a political party, political action committee or the political candidacy of any individual.

DEFINITIONS:

Political Contribution: Any direct or indirect payment, loan, advance, deposit, or gift of money, or any services or anything of more than nominal value to any candidate, campaign committee or political party or organization in connection with any election. Contributions include, among other things, cash, donation of property or services, donation of use of property or facilities, and purchases of tickets to fund-raising events.

PROCEDURE:

1. **Political Contributions from Corporate Assets:**

   The federal government and many state governments do not allow political contributions by corporations, either directly or indirectly. No associate acting for or on behalf of the Company or of any of its subsidiaries, business units or offices shall make any political contribution or expenditure to any candidate, campaign committee, political party or organization in connection with any election to any political office without prior review and approval of the Company's General Counsel, (if a company or business unit does not have a General Counsel, then associates should consult with the Compliance Division or Human Resouces).

2. **Solicitation of Contributions:**

   Associates may not use their position within the Company to solicit political contributions from other associates. No direct or indirect pressure in any form may be directed toward associates to participate in the support of a political party or the political candidacy of any individual.

3. **Personal Political Contributions:**

   The Company supports its associates' participation in the political affairs of their community and country on an individual basis. However, the Company will not reimburse associates for political contributions of any nature.

POLICY NO. 7 ANTITRUST LAW AND COMPETITIVE PRACTICES

PURPOSE:

The purpose of Antitrust laws is to promote competition and to prevent artificial restraints on competition, which actually, or are likely to, reduce output or raise prices. All employees must be aware of applicable antitrust laws and statutory restraints on competitive practices. Price fixing, boycotts, tying arrangements, and discriminatory allowances are almost always illegal. Moreover, under certain circumstances restrictive agreements exclusive or reciprocal dealings monopolization and price inducements may also be deemed anti-competitive, and, thus illegal. Although this policy does not address the topic of state antitrust law, it is important to note that various states have adopted antitrust laws that apply essentially the same standards to intrastate business as the federal antitrust laws apply to business affecting interstate commerce. Employees should avoid any conduct which may be construed as a violation of the antitrust laws.

POLICY:

It is the Company's policy to comply with antitrust laws. Fulfillment of these obligations is of such vital importance to the Company that prescribing a mandatory course of action for all employees with respect to such laws is appropriate. There shall be no exception to the Company's antitrust policy, nor shall it be compromised or qualified by anyone acting for, or on behalf of the Company.

Violation of the antitrust laws can subject both the Company and individual employees to criminal as well as civil liability. Foreign sales and the conduct of our business in foreign countries also require compliance with each country's business competition laws.

PROCEDURE:

1. **Pricing and Other Agreements Affecting Competition:**

   Policies and practices concerning prices and agreements with competitors must be reviewed and approved by the Company's General Counsel in advance, (if a company or business unit does not have a General Counsel, then associates should consult with outside counsel).

2. **Contact with Competitors:**

   It is not illegal or inappropriate for associates of the Company and its competitors to meet and talk from time to time. However, no associate shall at any time, or under any circumstance, enter into an agreement or understanding, written or oral, express or implied, with any competitor concerning prices, discounts, other terms or conditions of sale, profits or profit margins, costs, allocation of service or geographic markets, allocation of customers, limitations on services, boycotts of customers, or bids or the intent to bid. Neither shall an associate even discuss or exchange information with any competitor on these subjects.

3. **Trade or Industry Associations:**

   No associate shall discuss prices, terms or conditions of sale, marketing strategy or any other confidential business information at trade or industry association meetings. If these topics are discussed at such meetings, the Company associate must promptly leave the meeting and notify the Company's General Counsel regarding the situation.

4. **Information About Competitors:**

   As a vigorous competitor in the marketplace, the Company may seek economic knowledge about its competitors. However, the Company will not engage or tolerate associates engaging in illegal or improper acts to acquire a competitor's trade secrets, customer lists, information about another company's facilities, technical developments or operations. In addition, the Company will not hire a competitor's employees for the purpose of obtaining confidential information, or urge competitors' personnel, customers, or suppliers to disclose confidential information.

POLICY NO. 8 U.S. FOREIGN CORRUPT PRACTICES ACT

PURPOSE:

The purpose of this Policy is to help ensure that all associates and agents of the Company are alert to any potential violations of the FCPA and keep the Company within the letter and spirit of the law.

POLICY:

The Foreign Corrupt Practices Act (FCPA) prohibits U.S. companies from making improper payments or gifts to foreign government officials, politicians or political parties. It also requires that companies keep accurate records of transactions and transfers of assets whether domestic or international. All associates and agents of the Company are required to comply strictly with the FCPA and the Company's internal accounting controls.

These principles apply equally to subsidiaries and affiliates globally to the extent they do not conflict with local laws.

REQUIREMENTS and ILLUSTRATIONS:

1. **Improper Payments**:

The FCPA prohibits an offer, promise to pay, or authorization to pay money, gift, promise to give or authorization of giving anything of value to a foreign official, political party or official or any candidate for political office to influence an official act or decision, or to induce an official to use his or her influence to affect or influence a foreign government

2. **Accounting Standards and Record Keeping:**

The FCPA requires the Company to maintain a system of internal accounting controls to ensure that assets are safeguarded, transactions conform to management's authorizations, and accounting records are complete and accurate. FCPA regulations forbid the falsifying of accounting records or making misleading financial statements to auditors or regulatory authorities.

Associates will at all times strictly comply with the accounting standards of the FCPA and the Company internal accounting controls. Questions regarding proper accounting, record keeping or internal controls may be directed to the Company Chief Financial Officer.

POLICY NO. 9 GOVERNMENT CONTRACTS

PURPOSE:

The purpose of this Policy is to help ensure that the Company and its employees comply with all relevant laws and regulations relating to government contracting, and that the Company's relationship government, be strengthened and enhanced. All associates engaged in business with a governmental body or agency must know and abide by the specified rules and regulations governing such business.

POLICY:

Contracting with the government is a unique part of the Company's business. It is absolutely essential that the Company and its associates comply strictly with the laws and regulations which apply to government contracting. It is also necessary that the terms of any contract with the government be adhered to.

DEFINITIONS:

Procurement Official: Any person, including a non-government employee, who has participated personally and substantially in any of the following activities: drafting a specification for a procurement; reviewing and approving a specification for a procurement; preparing or developing a procurement or purchase request; preparing or issuing a solicitation; evaluating a bid or proposal; selecting sources; negotiating a contract; or reviewing and approving a contract award. A non-government employee may be a Procurement Official if he or she has engaged in certain activities on behalf of the government.

PROCEDURE:

1. **Complexity of Government Contracting Regulations:**

Government contracting laws are extremely complex. Because of the complexity of the government contracting requirements, it is impossible for the Company to summarize them in this Corporate Policy. Instead, this Corporate Policy describes several general requirements with respect to government contracting work.

2. **Contract Negotiation:**

Some laws require that businesses engaged in contracting with the government report certain information relating to contract negotiation, and specifically to pricing, sales policies, and administrative practices. This information must be current, accurate and verifiable. It must also be complete up to and including the date of the contract.

During contract negotiations with governments, the Company associates should be accurate and truthful in all statements, correspondence and other communications.

3. **Relations with Government Procurement Officials—Gifts, Meals, Gratuities, and Other Payments or Expenses:**

   Government Procurement Officials are subject to special laws and regulations governing their receipt of gifts and gratuities from organizations with whom they do business. See Policy: Government Relations Dealing With Government Regulators and Employees.

4. **Kickbacks:**

   Associates are prohibited from offering, soliciting, providing, or accepting any gift or other thing of value for the purpose of improperly obtaining or rewarding favorable treatment in connection with government contracting.

5. **Accurate Recording of Costs:**

   It is absolutely essential that the proper procedures are followed in recording costs and charging the government. No person is authorized to permit or require associates to falsify record or otherwise depart from the proper recording procedures.

   All charges and costs must be recorded accurately and faithfully. It is particularly important to make sure that all costs are allocated to the proper account. It is never proper to charge other accounts. If it becomes necessary to transfer a charge, the transfer should be carefully documented and recorded.

6. **Improper Disclosure by Procurement Officials:**

   The law prohibits parties seeking government contracts from soliciting or obtaining from Procurement Officials any "proprietary information" regarding the government contract. This means associates are prohibited both from attempting to obtain the information from the official, as well as receiving the information even when the Procurement Official is willing to disclose it.

POLICY NO. 10 GOVERNMENT RELATIONS—DEALING WITH GOVERNMENT REGULATORS AND EMPLOYEES

PURPOSE:

The purpose of this Policy is to alert associates to the special rules governing business relationships with government employees and help ensure compliance with those rules. Many of the principles that are relevant here are also relevant to the specific area of government contracting.

POLICY:

It is the Company's policy to comply fully with all regulations and laws governing contacts and dealings with government regulators and employees, and adhere to the highest ethical, moral, and legal standards of business conduct.

PROCEDURE:

A. Government Officials and Contractors

i. Gifts and Gratuities

It is a federal crime and violation of this policy for a corporation or other "person" to give or offer, directly or indirectly, anything of value:

- To a U.S. or foreign Government official for the purpose of improperly influencing any act or decision of this individual in his official capacity so that he may assist in obtaining or retaining business for or with such Government;
- To a U.S. or foreign Government official for or because of any official act performed or to be performed by this public official; or
- To a U.S. Government prime contractor or higher-tier subcontractor or its employees for the purpose of

improperly obtaining or rewarding favorable treatment in connection with a prime contract or with a subcontract relating to a prime contract.

It is a federal crime and violation of this policy for any Company employee to solicit or accept anything of value from subcontractors under Government contracts for the purpose of improperly obtaining or rewarding favorable treatment in connection with a subcontract.

1. **Anti-Kickback Act:**

The Anti-Kickback Act forbids prime contractors and subcontractors from offering, soliciting, providing, or accepting any gift of money or other thing of value for the purpose of improperly obtaining or rewarding favorable treatment in connection with Government prime contracts and subcontracts. The Act also requires the Company to report to the government if the Company has reasonable grounds to believe a violation has occurred.

2. **Improper Payments:**

Any offer of a gift or thing of value, to any government regulator or employee, whether federal, state, county, or city, for the purpose of obtaining any improper special treatment is prohibited. The Company will seek the resolution of regulatory or political issues affecting its interests only on the basis of the merits and pursuant to proper procedures and in accordance with all applicable laws.

Solicitation or acceptance of a gift or anything of value from a government employee which is offered for the purpose of obtaining preferential treatment from the Company is also prohibited.

3. **Gifts, Meals, Transportation, and Other Gratuities:**

All associates are expected to maintain proper and cordial relationships with public officials. However, it is necessary to avoid compromising, or even appearing to compromise, the integrity of the Company or public officials. In addition, some jurisdictions strictly prohibit giving gifts, meals and other gratuities to public officials. Therefore, associates must consult with their local General Counsel or if business does not have a local General Counsel, then the HR Department, before offering gifts, meals, or other courtesies to any public official.i
Company employees shall not provide meals, refreshments, transportation, entertainment, gifts, or anything else of value to government employees, except in the following circumstances:

- Working meals and refreshments may be provided in very limited circumstances, as provided in Government regulations. Generally, such meals and refreshments may be provided on Company premises if arrangements have been made for reimbursement to the Company by the Government employee. In addition, coffee, doughnuts, and similar refreshments of nominal value may be provided as a normal courtesy incident to the conduct of business.
- Entertainment may be provided only if the Government employee(s) or the event itself has received advance written approval under applicable Government regulations and a copy of the approval has been provided to the Company.
- Transportation may be provided only when arrangements for Government or commercial transportation are clearly impracticable.
- Other courtesies, such as meals and other amenities provided to those attending a Company-sponsored training or orientation course, may be extended if there is written approval, as set forth under the Government regulations, for the proposal and such proposal has been provided to the Company.

Normal business courtesies in the commercial marketplace can be interpreted as an attempt to improperly influence someone in the government marketplace and may be construed as a bribe, kickback or illegal gratuity. Associates should not extend these courtesies to any government regulators or employees. Government employees are also well aware of these regulations and should automatically decline any gratuity which they feel could jeopardize their compliance.

Associates are responsible for knowing and understanding the laws, rules and codes of conduct of the public officials with whom they interact.

Associates must follow proper disclosure and reporting procedures at all times.

4. **Seminars and Conferences:**

To avoid the appearance of impropriety, associates should not pay the travel expenses or registration fees for a public official to attend a non-Company sponsored seminar or conference.

5. **Outside Business Relationships With Public Officials:**

Associates should not have a business, financial, or other relationship with a public official that affects any judgments they make on behalf of the Company.

6. **Social Contacts:**

The Company respects the privacy of its associates and recognizes that social contacts and interactions with public officials may occur outside the normal conduct of business. These are neither unavoidable nor undesirable. Associates should exercise good judgment and common sense, remembering at all times that these contacts and interactions may be misinterpreted. Actions which could be a conflict of interest must be avoided.

7. **Hiring Former Government Employees:**

The government has enacted specific rules to eliminate even the appearance of a conflict of interest by former government employees who work for government contractors. Different rules pertain to different categories of government personnel (*e.g.*, Department of Defense civilians and uniformed officers, senior government employees, procurement officials, etc.) and generally prohibit such personnel from representing the Company before the government agency or department which employed them for a prescribed time period. For example, the Company may not hire a person who, within his last two years of government service, performed certain procurement functions. Nor may the Company hire a person, who was personally and substantially involved in the award or funding of a federal contract with the Company for two years following his or her involvement as a government employee. Both the Company and the former government employee must comply with these rules.

POLICY NO. 11 GOVERNMENT INVESTIGATIONS AND INTERVIEWS

PURPOSE:

The Company is committed to cooperating with government agencies that are inspecting the Company's facilities or conducting investigations of alleged wrongdoing.

POLICY:

It is the Company's policy that its associates cooperate promptly and fully with appropriate government investigations or interviews regarding possible civil or criminal violations of the law. It is important for the Company to protect its legal rights. To accomplish this, it is Company policy that all government inspections or requests for interviews or documents be referred to the Company's General Counsel for review.

PROCEDURE:

1. **Contact the Company's General Counsel:**

   Any time an associate is approached by someone claiming to be a government inspector or investigator; the associate should immediately inform their manager and the Company's General Counsel. Associates should refer any questions or requests to produce any documents, including documents about customers and suppliers, to the Company's General Counsel.

2. **Documents:**

   Associates do not have the authority to produce documents to government officials, whether Company documents or those of the Company's customers or suppliers, before discussing the production with the Company's General Counsel. Thereafter, associates should cooperate fully in the document production.

3. **Search Warrants:**

   If government agents appear at a Company facility with a search warrant, associates should request and review the agent's credentials and a copy of the warrant and supporting affidavit. The associate should immediately contact his or her manager and the Company's General Counsel.

POLICY NO. 12 U.S. IMMIGRATION LAWS

POLICY:

The Company will fulfill its obligations under applicable immigration laws. In the U.S., managers must consistently follow the same verification procedures for all new hires. When verifying employment eligibility, managers must be aware that some aliens, while legally present in the United States, are not authorized to accept employment. Moreover, students authorized to accept employment pursuant to a practical training program are limited to employment in the field associated with their college major. Company managers shall ensure that each applicant is authorized to do the type of work for which that applicant is being considered.

PROCEDURE:

All employees must provide verification of employment eligibility within three days of the day the individual begins work and must also complete Form 9 in its entirety. *All offers of employment are contingent on the verification of an employee's eligibility in accordance with this law.*

Should a newly hired individual who is currently authorized to accept employment be unable to provide proper documentation, they must present a receipt showing that they have applied for appropriate replacement documents within three business days of employment. They then have 90 days to provide the actual replacement documents. The receipt rule does not apply to initial applications for employment authorization nor does the rule apply to applications for the renewal of already expired employment authorizations.

It is the responsibility of the Human Resources Department to communicate and enforce this policy. The Human Resources Department is responsible for informing each employee of their obligation to provide the necessary documentation

Should any individual be unable to comply with the documentation requirements following their employment by the Company, their employment will be immediately terminated.

PURPOSE:

Federal law requires employers to only hire individuals who are authorized to be employed in the United States. IRCA imposes penalties on employers for knowingly hiring or continuing to employ aliens not authorized to work in the United States. As such, IRCA requires employers to verify employment eligibility of all new employees.

Employers who knowingly hire or continue to employ aliens not authorized to work in the United States are subject to severe civil fines and criminal penalties. Additional, as set forth under Executive Order, federal contracts may be barred for a year to those employers who knowingly hire illegal aliens.

POLICY NO. 13 PRODUCTS LIABILITY

PURPOSE:

To increase customer satisfaction, protect the _________ brand and limit the potential for liability by (a) providing safe and reliable products that comply with all regulatory requirements and (b) appropriately identifying product features and benefits, describing proper use and operation and advising of potential risks in associated product materials and advertising.

POLICY

To ensure customer satisfaction, _________ brand protection and limitation of potential liability, the Company shall implement a Product Liability Program ("Program") that shall include at least the following:

1. **Product Design/Manufacturing:**

Verify product compliance with rules of applicable regulatory agencies, standards bodies and industry best practices. Design product specifications that define acceptable ranges of variation for each product characteristic. Assess likelihood of customer misuse and reduce misuse possibility through design features, safety features and/or labeling. Validate test procedures, test to ensure that products meet specifications and document and maintain test results. Document and maintain records regarding quality assurance and control practices. Monitor industry practices and design changes to keep current on appropriate solutions. Apply best practices solutions across all products in a product category to the extent design platforms will allow.

2. **Product Marketing:**

   Create and provide to customers product user manuals and/or data sheets, as applicable, that detail product technical or functional specifications as appropriate, correct product use, warranties, disclaimers and warnings or contraindications taking into consideration the user's level of expected expertise (such as technical versus non-technical). Use product labels where indicated to warn against risks and educate users on consequences of improper use. Design product packaging to clearly and accurately identify package contents and characteristics. Publish advertising that clearly and accurately reflects product characteristics. All information provided, regardless of form or medium, should be complete, visible and easily understood. Consistency of information should be confirmed to avoid misleading users or creating misunderstandings. Train all in-house sales and marketing teams and customer sales teams on proper product characterization.

3. **Product Complaints:**

   Create and maintain an easily accessible service log that identifies complaints and what solution is provided. Require all third party service providers to document, maintain and provide on request all product repair records. Evaluate all reported failures and malfunctions to determine cause and take corrective action. Document and retain test results and engineering change notices that are issued to correct any problem found.

RESPONSIBILITY:

The Company shall define what group or groups within the organization shall be responsible for each part of the Program.

For Companies that do not manufacture products but import them, it is recognized that the Product Design / Manufacturing responsibilities portion of the Program shall be a cooperative effort with the factory.

PROCEDURE:

Product complaints involving potential safety issues must be reviewed by the group(s) designated by the Company. If a product complaint is made that involves personal injury or property damage, the complaint must also be reported immediately to the Company's General Counsel or Risk Management Department for action. If a lawsuit develops as a result of a product claim, all documentation relative to the product and circumstances must be retained as directed by the General Counsel, or Risk manager even if the Company's records retention guidelines would normally allow record destruction. Reporting to regulatory agencies governing the product/s at issue shall be made consistent with applicable law.

POLICY VIOLATIONS:

Failure to follow the Policy can result in customer dissatisfaction, injury to the _________ brand, regulatory investigations with potentially serious penalties and individual and class action litigation with potentially large damage claims against the Company. Violation of the Policy will result in corrective action and may result in disciplinary action up to and including termination for individual Company employees.

POLICY NO. 14 CUSTOMS COMPLIANCE

PURPOSE:

To deliver product to _________ customers in a cost effective and timely manner by complying with the laws, regulations, and policies enforced by Customs Border and Protection, Bureau of Industry and Security, and other applicable governmental agencies that govern the import and export of products to and from the United States. Compliance will minimize the possibility of lost shipments or delayed deliveries which can result in government or customer imposed fines and reduced sales revenue.

POLICY:

The law requires a Company to exercise reasonable care when filing documentation associated with the import or export of products. This Policy establishes the guidelines for exercising reasonable care and provides the internal controls to achieve that objective. Each Company shall establish and maintain specific Customs Compliance policies and procedures which shall include at least the following:

1. designating an individual to act as the Company's Compliance Manager whose duties include overseeing the import/export process;
2. drafting and implementing a Customs Compliance and Operating Procedures Manual and Export Management System to use as a reference resource;
3. training employees in carrying out their responsibilities under the compliance guidelines on a regular basis (at least once a year for general overview and as needed for special advisories);
4. conducting periodic reviews of the processes; and
5. identifying a notification process for alerting the Compliance Manager of any occurrence that might not be consistent with the Policy or other import/export rules and regulations.

RESPONSIBILITY:

The Compliance Manager shall have responsibility for ensuring that the Company's import/export activities are consistent with the Policy including:

1. supervising and controlling the work of brokers and freight forwarders;
2. ensuring the proper filing and retention of import/export documents;
3. interfacing, when necessary, with government personnel in import/export operations and audit matters
4. maintaining the Compliance Manual in an updated format by amending it with any relevant changes in law, regulations and/or policies and procedures.

PROCEDURE:

The Customs Compliance Manager shall decide which Company employees require knowledge of import/export processes and shall provide a copy of the Compliance Manual to each. Copies shall be distributed to at least the Company General Counsel and the President and Chief Operating Officer.

If any Company employee is contacted by any Government agency which governs import/export practices or if agents from any such agency appear on Company premises, the Customs Compliance Manager is to be notified immediately to handle the matter. In the Customs Compliance Manager's absence, the local General Counsel should be notified.

The Compliance Manager shall identify all Company employees who view and process import/export documentation or otherwise participate in the import/export process and shall provide all with training specific to their job responsibilities on how to identify incorrect documentation and what actions to take in that event.

If any Company employee becomes aware of a violation of the Policy, he/she shall advise the Compliance Manager immediately and the Compliance Manager shall notify the Company General Counsel and senior management with recommendations for corrective action consistent with the Policy and applicable law.

POLICY VIOLATION:

Failure to adhere to the Policy and exercise reasonable care may jeopardize the Company's ability to import/export product on a timely basis and can result in severe monetary penalties both to the Company and to individual employees. Violations of the Policy, including failing to promptly report violations, will result in corrective action and may result in disciplinary action up to and including termination for individual employees.

PRINCIPLE #2 WE MAINTAIN AN ETHICAL CULTURE

POLICY NO. 15 PROTECTION OF COMPANY PROPERTY AND INFORMATION

PURPOSE:

The purpose of this Policy is to establish the accountability and individual responsibilities for protection of Company Property and Confidential Information. Protecting these assets against loss, theft and misuse is an important responsibility of each associate.

POLICY:

It is the Company's policy to ensure that all Company Property and other Confidential Information are protected. All associates, because they are information users, custodians, or stewards, must protect these resources from misuse, theft, fraud, loss, and unauthorized use, disclosure, or disposal. Associates may not use Company Property or Confidential Information for their personal benefit or for any use other than Company business, except, associates may have limited personal use of the Company's e-mail, voicemail and internet systems during non-work hours, only as long as such use does not, in any way, (i) violate the law; (ii) violate a company policy; or (iii) compromise the confidentiality of proprietary or other sensitive information.

DEFINITIONS:

Company Property: All property and information owned, leased, developed or maintained by the Company, including but not limited to Company funds, equipment, supplies, other personal property, real property, intellectual property, computer software, technology databases, Confidential Information and other information about the Company's business.

Confidential Information: Proprietary information, which is the Intellectual Property, confidential data, and any other representation of the Company's knowledge, whether verbal, printed, written, or electronically recorded or transmitted. This includes any technologies, concepts, engineering, sales and financial information and software.

The following are some examples of Confidential Information:

- Business, financial, marketing and service data and plans associated with Company services
- Client names or information
- Internal databases or software documentation
- Materials dealing with potential acquisitions
- Manuals
- Personnel data and salary information

PROCEDURE:

1. **Company Funds:**

Associates are personally responsible for all Company funds over which they exercise control. Associates must take all reasonable steps to ensure that the Company receives good value for Company funds spent and must maintain accurate records of these expenditures. Associates must not use the Company funds for any personal use.

2. **Personal Use of Company Property:**

Use of the Company's property or equipment for personal use is prohibited, except associates may have limited personal use of the Company's e-mail, voicemail and internet systems during non-work hours, only as long as such use does not, in any way, (i) violate the law; (ii) violate a company policy; or (iii) compromise the confidentiality of proprietary or other sensitive information.

3. **Protection of Confidential Information (including Intellectual Property):**

Confidential Information is usually the product of the ideas and hard work of many talented Company associates. The assets are the result of substantial investments in research and development and in planning. Confidential Information of the Company is valuable and must be protected from disclosure. Except for certain legal requirements such as those related to the publication of reports, the Company alone is entitled to determine who may obtain these information assets and how these assets can be used.

Associates may have access to Company-owned Confidential Information and Intellectual Property. Because it is also possible that associates may have contact with someone who would be interested in getting this information, it is important for associates to know that they must not use or disclose Confidential Information or Intellectual Property except when specifically authorized to do so.

4. **Personal Use of Confidential Information:**

Confidential Information is to be used solely for the benefit of the Company. Each associate is responsible for assuring that Confidential Information is used only for valid Company purposes. Associates may not use any non-public information which they have access to in the course of their work for the Company for any personal gain or advantage. This includes sharing information with individuals outside the Company for their personal use as well as sharing with fellow associates whose duties do not require that they have that information. This restriction applies even if the associate developed the information while employed by the Company.

5. **Inadvertent Disclosure:**

Because inadvertent disclosure by loyal associates can seriously harm the Company's interests, associates must exercise caution concerning Confidential Information. Associates entrusted with this information must be careful handling the information. To the extent possible, Confidential Information should be safeguarded and marked "confidential." Confidential Information should not be left in places where persons without authorization have access to it. Associates carrying Confidential Information outside the Company's facilities should take the necessary steps to protect and secure the information.

POLICY NO. 16 INTELLECTUAL PROPERTY AND INFORMATION OF OTHERS

PURPOSE:

The purpose of this Policy is to help maintain the Company's reputation as a fair competitor, ensure the integrity of the competitive marketplace in intellectual property, and comply with the laws regulating intellectual property and industrial espionage.

POLICY:

It is the Company's policy to compete fairly in the marketplace. This commitment to fairness includes respecting the Intellectual Property rights of our suppliers, clients, business partners, competitors and others. No associate should steal or misuse the Intellectual Property owned or maintained by another.

Any associate who comes into possession of a Trade Secret or Confidential Information regarding another company should immediately refer that information to the Company's General Counsel for return to its rightful owner.

DEFINITIONS:

Copyright: An original work of authorship "fixed" in any tangible form of expression. Copyrighted works include periodicals, books, tapes, photographs and software packages and supporting documentation.

Patent: The right, granted by the federal government, to the exclusive production, use, or sale of an invention throughout the United States.

Trademark: Any word name, symbol, device or any combination thereof used by a. manufacturer or retailer of a product, in connection with that product, to help consumers identify that product as different from the products of competitors.

Trade Secret: Any formula, pattern, device, or compilation of information which is used in one's business, and which gives the company an opportunity to obtain an advantage over competitors who do not know or use it. A Trade Secret differs from a Patent in that a Trade Secret is not officially registered with the government and therefore is protected in different ways.

Confidential Information: Business or financial information, compilations or information, scientific data, business and product plans, customer lists, pricing strategies and any other proprietary information that may give the owner of the information a competitive advantage.

Intellectual Property: The Copyrights, Patents, Trademarks, and Trade Secrets owned by an individual or company.

PROCEDURE:

1. **Respecting the Intellectual Property Rights of Others:**

The Company's business depends heavily on the protection of its Intellectual Property. The Company expects its competitors to respect its Intellectual Property rights. Correspondingly, the Company and its associates have an obligation to respect the Intellectual Property rights of suppliers, customers, clients, business partners, and competitors.

The general rule is that the Copyrighted, Trademarked, or Patented property of others should never be used without the explicit and appropriate permission of the owner of the Copyright, Trademark, or Patent.

2. **Software:**

The Company licenses the use of computer software from a variety of third parties. Such software is normally copyrighted by the software developer and, unless expressly authorized to do so, the Company normally has no right to make copies of the software except for backup or archival purposes. It is the Company's policy to respect all computer software copyrights and to adhere to the terms of all software licenses to which the Company is a party.

Associates may not duplicate, transfer, alter, revise, adapt or convert any licensed software or related documentation for use either on Compnay premises or elsewhere unless the Company is expressly authorized to do so by agreement with the licensor. Unauthorized duplication of software may subject associates and/or the Company to civil damages. In cases of willful infringement, criminal penalties under the United States Copyright Act also may apply.

3. **Restrictions on Photocopying:**

Operators of photocopying machines should check all material that is presented for copying for a copyright notice. Any request to copy material that bears a copyright notice should be refused unless the person who requests the copy establishes that he or she is, or has the authority to represent, the copyright owner whose name appears in the notice. Inappropriate photocopying can lead to criminal or civil liability.

4. **Trade Secrets. Confidential Information and Industrial Espionage:**

Trade Secrets and Confidential Information are not protected by the Copyright, Patent, or Trademark laws. While Trade Secret and other Confidential Information may not be protected by the Patent laws, it is still the property of the owner and cannot be used without the appropriate permission. When Trade Secrets are obtained by "improper means," their use is strictly forbidden.

5. **Obtaining Information about Others through Proper Means:**

In the course of the Company's business, associates acquire a great deal of information about competitors. It is not improper to accumulate this information, and it is generally not unethical or illegal to make use of the information as part of our business. Indeed, the Company or any other business could hardly go on without being able to use information it has developed regarding its competitors in order to analyze the marketplace and make informed business decisions. While collecting data on competitors, associates should utilize all legitimate resources, but avoid those actions which are illegal, unethical or which could cause embarrassment to the Company. Company associates are authorized to obtain confidential or proprietary information only in accordance with sound and ethical commercial practices. As such, employees shall only receive such information from other companies pursuant to a signed confidentiality/non-disclosure agreement which has been approved by the Company's General

Counsel. When such information is received, it shall be properly marked indicating that the information is considered to be proprietary and/or confidential and shall be docketed in a manner that allows it to be easily identified and the Company's obligations to be readily ascertained. In addition, such materials shall be circulated only on as-needed basis and shall be properly filed in order to minimize inadvertent disclosure. When a situation is unclear, associates should seek the advice of the Company's General Counsel

6. **Associates with Confidential Information from another Company:**

Associates having Confidential Information from a former employer may be legally or ethically bound by a nondisclosure obligation to the former employer. The Company expects associates to fulfill this obligation. Associates should refrain from giving their fellow associates or from using in the Company's business any Confidential Information belonging to any former employers. The Company does expect its associates to use all information which is generally known and used by persons of their training and experience and all information which is generally known in the industry.

POLICY NO. 17 ACCURATE BOOKS AND RECORDS

POLICY:

It is the Company's policy to prepare accurate and verifiable business Records. False or misleading entries must never be made or concealed in any Company Record. The Company is also committed to maintain complete and accurate Records for the time periods they are needed for business purposes and as required by law.

<u>PURPOSE</u>:

The purpose of this Policy is to help the Company appropriately create, manage and protect its books and records. All associates have a responsibility to create and maintain accurate Records and protect and dispose of them in accordance with rules, regulations, litigation requirements, and business needs. The Company is also required by state and federal statutes and regulations, and by the rules of litigation, to retain certain Records and to follow specific guidelines in managing its Records. Dishonest reporting or failure to disclose information that by law or contract must be disclosed is not only strictly prohibited, but also could lead to civil or criminal liability to individuals and/or the Company. This includes reporting information or organizing the information in a way that is intended to mislead or misinform recipients, whether inside or outside the Company.

<u>DEFINITIONS</u>:

<u>Records</u>: All information that is created, received or recorded either on paper or electronically for or on behalf of the Company. Some examples of Records include:

- Documents or reports submitted to government or regulatory authorities
- Insurance forms, agreements and documents
- Financial accounts and journals
- Time reports
- Expense account documents
- Contract documents

<u>Transaction</u>: This term includes, but is not limited to all payments of money, transfers of property, and furnishing of services.

PROCEDURE:

1. **Applicable laws and Regulations:**

Federal and State law requires that the Company's Records accurately reflect all Transactions, including any payment of money, transfer of property or furnishing of services. Applicable laws and regulations establish specific requirements with regard to record-keeping and communications. All associates are responsible to comply with the following requirements:

- Financial statements and all Records on which they are based must accurately reflect all Transactions
- All disbursements and receipts of funds must be properly and promptly recorded
- No undisclosed or unrecorded fund may be established for any purpose
- No false or artificial statements or entries may be made for any purpose in the Records or in any internal or external correspondence, memoranda, or communication of any type, including telephone, computer or wire communications
- No associate shall intentionally allocate costs to contracts when those costs are contrary to contract provisions or accepted accounting practices

2. **Internal and External Reporting and Penalties:**

Information that associates record and submit to another party, inside or outside the Company, including government or regulatory authorities, must be accurate, verifiable, and complete. False or artificial entries must never be made in any Company Records submitted to government or regulatory authorities for any reason, nor should permanent entries in the Company's Records be altered in any way. Associates must not use any report or Record to mislead those who receive them or to conceal anything that is improper. Information or data must not be reported or organized in a way that is intended to mislead or misinform those who receive it.

Dishonest reporting, both inside and outside the Company, is not only strictly prohibited, it could lead to civil or even criminal liability for associates and the Company. This includes reporting information or organizing it in a way that is intended to mislead or misinform those who receive it. Particularly serious would be the external reporting of false or misleading financial information.

3. **Company Funds:**

Records associated with Company funds must reflect an accurate and verifiable record of all Transactions. No payment or receipt on behalf of the Company may be approved or made with the intention or understanding that any part of the payment or receipt is to be used for a purpose other than that described in the documents supporting the Transaction.

All funds and other assets and all Transactions involving the Company must be reflected in full detail and promptly recorded in the appropriate Books and Records. Accepted accounting principles must be used for all financial recording. "Slush funds" or similar off-book accounts, where there is no accounting for receipts or expenditures on the Company's books, are strictly prohibited. Reserves for contingencies accounted for on the books are not considered slush funds. Questions regarding the recording of Transactions should be directed to the Company's Chief Financial Officer.

4. **"Private" Business Records:**

There is no such thing as a "private" business Record. Notes and documents that associates maintain for their personal use or at home are subject to investigation and disclosure. All Records pertaining to the Company, including any Records kept off-site or on the Company e-mail and computer systems, are subject to the requirements of this Policy.

5. **Retention of Records:**

Disposal or destruction of records is not discretionary with any associate, including the originator of such Records. Legal and regulatory practices require the retention of certain records for various periods of time, particularly in the insurance, tax, personnel and corporate structure areas. In addition, when litigation or a government investigation or audit is pending or imminent, relevant records must not be destroyed until the matter is closed. This program is mandatory and shall be followed by every associate. Destruction of records to avoid disclosure in a legal proceeding may constitute a criminal offense.

The Company has an Information Retention Policy governing Records retention, management, and destruction. Questions on record retention should be directed to General Counsel, particularly if any litigation, investigation or administrative action involving the Company or any of its officers, suppliers or customers is pending.

EXAMPLES OF VIOLATIONS

- Violating procedures concerning contract-signing or negligence in reviewing contract
- Forging signatures when approvers are not present
- Inappropriately using miscellaneous income generated from the disposal of off-balance assets, scrap or waste
- Selling goods without authentic purchase orders
- Creating false transactions without actually shipping the goods
- Manipulating selling prices
- Selling goods to customers knowing that they will take advantage of higher selling prices in their regions (through grey exports)

- Providing inappropriate mass volume discounts or rebates to non-mass volume customers who will disturb _________'s channel balance by reselling the goods
- Recognizing sales in advance
- Manipulating profits by deferring selling, marketing or other expenses

POLICY NO. 18 COMPUTER HARDWARE AND SOFTWARE, E-MAIL, INSTANT MESSENGER, VOICE-MAIL, AND INTERNET POLICY

PURPOSE:

To outline the expectations and proper use of the Company's computer systems, electronic mail (e-mail), voice-mail, internet services and other electronic communication tools and information stored therein. This policy is intended to promote responsible and appropriate use of the Company's computing resources. It addresses issues of privacy, etiquette, permissible and prohibited uses, as well as the Company's disclosure rights.

POLICY:

The Company is committed to providing an environment that encourages the use of computers and electronic information. The Company maintains communication and information technology systems including, but not limited to, e-mail, voice-mail and internet systems utilized to conduct Company business. It is the responsibility of each employee to ensure that this technology is used for proper business purposes and in a manner that does not compromise the confidentiality of proprietary or other sensitive information. The Company permits limited personal use of its computing resources for non-commercial purposes, only if such use does not (i) violate the law (ii) violate the Company policy; or (iii) interfere with the Company's goals, objectives, day-to-day activities, employee job performance, or other employee activities. The Company reserves the right to review such use and inspect all materials on, stored in, or sent over its computer systems. This policy covers all uses of the Company's electronic and telephonic communication tools and all information transmitted by, received from or stored in these systems. Violations of this Policy may subject the employee to disciplinary measures, up to and including dismissal.

CONTENTS:

These policies and procedures consist of four parts:

- Computer Hardware and Software
- E-mail
- Voice-mail, Instant Messenger
- Internet Access

I. COMPUTER HARDWARE AND SOFTWARE:

Ownership

All computer system networks, computer equipment, electronic and telephonic communications systems, and all communications and stored information transmitted by, received from, or contained in the Company's information systems are, and remain at all times, the property of the Company. All voicemail messages created, sent and received are and remain the property of the Company.

Avoiding Viruses, Software Conflicts, and License Violations

To limit exposure to computer viruses, avoid software conflicts and software license violations, and to properly manage our Information Systems, only software approved by the Company may be installed on computing devices. Employees are not authorized to download any software on to their computer or any drives. Unauthorized software installed onto any of the Company's computers will be immediately removed.

Unauthorized software includes, but is not limited to, personal programs such as screen savers, games, etc.

Acquisitions

All hardware and software acquisitions or purchases must be approved in writing by the Company. This includes specialized software for specific practice groups or projects.

Intellectual Property

As a general rule, employees may not copy, use, or transfer materials from others without proper authorization except in certain very limited or "fair use" circumstances. An employee who desires to reproduce or store the contents of a screen or website should contact the Legal Department for advice on whether the intended use is permissible.

Confidential Information

Confidential information shall not be disclosed to unauthorized persons without prior authorization.

Encryption

Only approved encryption tools approved by the Company may be used in connection with the Company's information system.

Troubleshooting

Computer software or hardware problems and questions should only be directed to the Company's IT help desk at __________.

Virus Alert

Unvalidated virus alerts should not be forwarded to other system users. Virus alerts may only be disseminated by the Company. Dissemination of non-verified information by others, regardless of intention, is counter-productive and an unnecessary strain on network resources. Instead, please forward the virus alerts as directed by the Company.

Passwords

While email and voicemail may accommodate the use of passwords for security, the reliability of passwords for maintaining confidentiality cannot be guaranteed. You must assume that someone, other than the intended or designated recipient, may read or hear any and all messages. Moreover, all passwords must be made known to the Company so that the system may be accessed by the company when you are absent. Passwords not known to the company may not be used. Passwords should be guarded and not visibly displayed at the employee's workstation or office.

Access

Employees may access only messages and files or programs that they have permission to enter (whether computerized or not). Unauthorized review, duplication, dissemination, removal, damage, or alteration of files, passwords, computer systems or programs, voice-mail messages, or other property of the company, or improper use of information obtained by unauthorized means, or attempts to engage in any such prohibited conduct, may be grounds for disciplinary action, up to and including termination. The Company will have access to its computer and electronic equipment, including voice-mail, e-mail and internet accounts.

II. E-MAIL

No Expectation of Privacy

The Company's computer and information systems and the data stored on them are and remain, at all times, the property of the company. As such, all information, data, or messages created, stored, sent, or retrieved over the Internet or the company's electronicmail system are the property of the Company. Employees and others should have no expectation that any information transmitted over or stored in the Company's information system is or will remain private. The Company's information systems are accessible at all times by the Company for business and legal purposes. Employees have no right to privacy regarding information, file transmission or storage through the Company's computer systems, voice-mail, e-mail, or other technical resources. The Company reserves the right to retrieve and read any message or file. Employees should be aware that, even when a message is erased or a visit to a Web site is closed; it is still possible to re-create the message or locate the Web site. Accordingly, internet and e-mail messages are considered public communications, not private. Moreover, all communications including text and images may be disclosed to law enforcement or other third parties without prior consent of the sender or the receiver.

E-mail users are advised that the Company may use automated software to perform such monitoring. Nothing that is transmitted via e-mail is confidential or private despite any such designation either by the sender or the recipient.

Certain Messages Prohibited

Employees are strictly prohibited from using the Company's computer and information systems to access, send, save, or print e-mail messages, or other information that (i) may be viewed as inappropriate or offensive to a reasonable person, including but not limited to messages containing obscene, vulgar, or "off color" language, messages that may be discriminatory or harassing to other employees, including racial or sexual harassment, messages that may hold persons up to ridicule or disparagement, false statements or name-calling; (ii) in any manner violates any laws or regulations; or (iii) in any manner that violates any Company policy. Violators will be subject to discipline up to and including discharge.

Limited Distribution

E-mail messages should be distributed only to those individuals who have a business need to receive them.

Limited Access

Each employee has been issued a password to access e-mail. Your password is personal and should not be shared with other employees or third parties. Employees are prohibited from providing e-mail access to an unauthorized user or access another user's e-mail mailbox without prior authorization from the Company IT department.

Be Careful What You Say

Although e-mail may give the appearance of being informal, impersonal and private, it is none of these things. All e-mail messages must be drafted with the same care as a formal memorandum and must not contain any information that might violate the law or otherwise be potentially be harmful or embarrassing to the Company.

Proper Usage and Etiquette

- The best communication strategy to utilize in your work area or division is to speak directly with fellow employees instead of using e-mail. Work relationships may flourish using this approach.
- If there is a matter that requires urgent attention, a telephone call or personal visit is the best approach. Assuming that a co-worker is available and checking e-mails at all times is inappropriate behavior on the sender's part.
- Write concise, specific e-mails. Clearly state the facts or your request.

- E-mail only those that are directly involved in the situation and avoid copying others unnecessarily (reduces productivity for all).
- For matters involving a decision or response from key stakeholders, it may be more appropriate to arrange a meeting.
- Transferring ownership of an issue or a project to another without confirmation is inappropriate. The responsibility resides with the sender until a written or verbal confirmation from the receiving party occurs.
- Do not copy customers when resolving internal work matters with co-workers.

III. VOICE-MAIL, INSTANT MESSENGER

The same policies and procedures that apply to e-mail also apply to voice-mail and instant messenger.

IV. INTERNET ACCESS

Application of Internal E-mail Policies and Procedures to Internet Connections

The Company's policies and procedures concerning internal e-mail also apply to internet connections, including, but not limited to, e-mail sent over the internet and accessing web sites via the internet.

Unauthorized Use

Any unauthorized use of the internet is strictly prohibited. Unauthorized use includes, but is not limited to: violating or attempting to violate any applicable laws or intellectual property rights; connecting, posting, or downloading and e-mailing pornographic material; engaging in computer "hacking" and other related activities; attempting to disable or compromise the security of information contained on the Company's computers.

Confidentiality

Internet messages should be treated as non-confidential. Anything sent through the internet passes through a number of different computer systems, all with different levels of security. The confidentiality of messages may be compromised at any point along the way, unless the messages are encrypted.

Under no circumstances shall information of a confidential, sensitive or otherwise proprietary nature be placed on the internet. Postings placed on the internet may display __________'s logo and address, so make certain before posting information on the internet that the information reflects the standards and policies of the Company.

Downloading from the Internet

Viruses. Downloading programs or other content may introduce viruses into the Company's network. To prevent viruses from being transmitted through the Company's information systems, employees are not authorized to download any software onto their computer or any drive in the Company's information system. If you want to download a program, you must first contact the Company for approval.

Copyrighted Materials. Many of the materials available on the internet, such as articles and software, are protected by copyright. Do not be misled by the ease with which you can acquire or download these materials—you may only have a limited license to view. You are not authorized to download software or any executable files (e.g., games, applications).

Unauthorized Connections

Users may not establish internet or other external network connections that could allow unauthorized persons to gain access to __________'s systems and information without prior approval from the Company. Users may not subscribe to a discussion group, e-mailing list or news service without prior approval from the Company. This is primarily to ensure that the Company's hardware and software can cope with the often voluminous amounts of information which are sent on a daily basis. Employees are responsible and accountable for compliance with the policies and procedures herein. Violations of any guidelines listed above may result in disciplinary action up to and including termination. In addition, the company may advise appropriate legal officials of any legal violations.

POLICY NO. 19 CONFIDENTIALITY OF CLIENT INFORMATION

PURPOSE:

The loyalty that the Company receives from its clients has resulted in the Company's past and present success and will determine the Company's future. The purpose of this Policy is to help ensure continued loyalty by affirming the importance of maintaining the strict confidentiality of client information.

POLICY:

Associates of the Company shall protect client information from misuse, theft, loss, disclosure and unauthorized use. Associates shall not reveal any information whatsoever regarding a Company client without first obtaining the permission of the client.

PROCEDURE:

1. **Protection of Client Information:**

The Company associates will have access to certain client information. Associates should protect this information against loss, theft or misuse. Associates must not use or disclose client information outside the Company, except when specifically authorized to do so.

2. **Regulatory Agencies:**

Client information may be released to regulatory agencies in certain limited circumstances. Associates must be sure that the person requesting client information is a representative of the agency they claim. Associates should insist on official identification. (A business card is not sufficient.)

The Company Legal Department should be notified immediately whenever a regulatory agency representative visits a facility location or contacts an associate for information about the Company or any other company that the company does business with, including clients or suppliers.

3. **Disclosure to Other Company Associates:**

Associates must protect confidential or sensitive client information from disclosure not only to outsiders but also to fellow Company associates whose duties do not require that they be given the information. Special precautions should be used to receive and protect certain client information even within the Company facilities. Associates asked for client information should consider whether the other associate is authorized or has a Company business-related need to receive the information.

POLICY NO. 20 CONFLICTS OF INTEREST

PURPOSE:

A conflict of interest may arise in any situation in which an Associate's loyalties are divided between business interests that to some degree, are incompatible with the interests of the Company. All such conflicts should be avoided. The purpose of this Policy is to prevent conflicts of interest from interfering with the ability of any associate to make decisions solely in the best interests of the Company.

POLICY:

Associates of the Company must avoid activities, interests and associations where their personal interests could conflict, or reasonably appear to conflict, with the interests of the Company. A Conflict of Interest may include any interest, whether financial or otherwise, that would, or would appear to influence a judgment or decision in favor of another person dealing with the Company other than normal passive investment activities. Each associate shall make prompt and full disclosure in writing to the Company Corporate Compliance and Ethics Committee of any situation that may involve a Conflict of Interest. Whether a conflict exists is to be decided by the Company Corporate Compliance and Ethics Committee or Board of Directors, and all such decisions are final.

PROCEDURE:

1. **Personal Financial Gain:**

Associates should avoid any outside financial interest that might influence decisions or actions of the Company, unless approved by the Corporate Compliance and Ethics Committee or Board of Directors. Interests which might influence decisions or actions of the Company include: (i) a Substantial Interest in another business that is a client, market, prospect, supplier, agent or competitor of the Company. A substantial interest is an economic interest that could, or reasonably might be thought to, influence judgment or action; (ii) a personal financial transaction or relationship with a client, market, prospect, supplier, agent, competitor, or other associate of the Company.

No associate may directly or indirectly benefit, or seek to benefit, from his or her position as an associate from any sale, purchase or other activity of the Company. Associates shall not: (i) purchase or lease real estate or other facilities which the associate knows the Company may be interested in, or may need in the future,

(ii) acquire an interest in a firm with which, to the associate's knowledge, the Company is carrying on or contemplating negotiations for merger purchase, joint venture or other business relationship (iii) take personal advantage of an opportunity that properly belongs to the Company.

2. **Outside Employment and Other Conflicting Activities:**

An associate should avoid outside employment or positions that might interfere with his or her position with the company. Outside work that prevents the associate from fully performing work for which he or she is employed by the Company, including overtime assignments; involvement with organizations that are doing or seeking to do business with the Company, including actual or potential vendors or customers; or activities that violate the law or other Company policy that would create a conflict of interest. Associates must obtain prior approval from the Committee before engaging in any activity that might violate this policy. Examples of activities that could present a conflict of interest:

- Self-employment or working for another company while employed by the Company;
- Acting as an outside director of a company.

3. **Public Service and Charitable Activities:**

Associates are encouraged to participate in public service and charitable activities so long as they do not create actual or potential conflicts with associates' duties to the Company.

4. **Financial Transactions between or Among Associates:**

Associates may not engage, or seek to engage, in frequent or significant money transactions with other associates.

5. **Financial Transactions between Associates and Suppliers:**

   Money transactions between associates and suppliers are forbidden.

6. **Determination of Conflicts:**

   Questions regarding a potential conflict of interest should be directed to the Committee. Decisions by the Committee or the Board of Directors regarding whether a situation creates a conflict are final.

   Given the evolving nature of the Company's business, including entering new areas of business, conflicts of interest or even the appearance of a conflict can change over time. The Company will not grandfather any pre-existing conflict situations, and an associate must discontinue any activities that become a violation of this Policy.

POLICY NO. 21 BACKGROUND VERIFICATION OF ASSOCIATES AND ASSOCIATE CANDIDATES

PURPOSE:

The purpose of the Company's Background Verification policy is to: (i) ensure that the Company hiring and internal transfer decisions are made with the best possible information; (ii) safeguard the Company's assets and fiduciary funds the Company maintains on the behalf of others; and (iii) avoid the delegation of substantial discretionary authority to persons with a propensity to violate the law or the Company's Compliance Program.

POLICY:

It is the Company's policy to conduct Background Verification, where appropriate, for all positions that involve substantial authority, in accordance with applicable law. Whether a specific

position for a prospective or existing associate involves substantial authority will be determined on a case-by-case basis.
The Company will disclose the results of Background Verification to an applicant as required by law.

POLICY NO. 22 DISCLOSURE OF INFORMATION TO THE PUBLIC, AND THE MEDIA

PURPOSE:

The Company has a responsibility and an interest in providing accurate and timely disclosure of information. This Policy is also intended to alert associates to their responsibilities under the Company's Media Policy and Guidelines.

POLICY:

It is the Company's policy to provide clear, accurate, complete, timely and consistent Disclosure of Material Information about the Company. This is true for all situations where information is conveyed, no matter how informally. To achieve these goals more fully, the Company has centralized Disclosure by appointing designated spokespersons who are the only personnel authorized to discuss information about the Company with persons outside the Company.

DEFINITIONS:

Disclosure: A Disclosure of previously non-public information can occur any time a corporate director, officer, or associate discusses corporate affairs with outsiders. Typical situations include press releases, interviews, speeches, and discussions with analysts.

Material Information: Material Information is any information that a reasonable investor would consider important when deciding whether to buy, hold or sell a security (*e.g.*, a stock or bond).

PROCEDURE:

1. **Company-Wide Policies:**

   It is the Company's policy to channel the disclosure of information about the company through specifically authorized and designated spokespersons. This means that the number of associates who are authorized to discuss the Company's internal affairs with outsiders is extremely limited. Associates should contact the Corporate Communications Department for dealing with the media.

   However, there are a number of Company-wide policies of which all associates should be aware. These policies include:

   - The Company does not disclose financial or other proprietary information unless legally required to do so;
   - The Company does not discuss contemplated or pending mergers, spin-offs or acquisitions; and
   - The Company does not disclose information about associates other than the fact and dates of employment without the associate's permission, unless required by law.

2. **Designated Spokespersons:**

   In addition to the Company's CEO, the Company has designated the following spokespersons to speak with the public, the media and financial analysts on its behalf:

   - All matters—Vice President of Corporate Communications
   - Financial community (analyst) inquiries—Chief Financial Officer
   - Litigation and legal matters—General Counsel

   The Company may designate certain individuals as district representatives to speak on specific issues. No other associates of the Company are authorized to speak on behalf of the Company. Therefore, unless they have been expressly authorized to make such disclosure, associates that receive any inquiry from a third party (whether a securities analyst, a member of the media or other person) regarding the Company must refer the inquiry to the appropriate spokespersons identified above. If you have any questions you should contact the Company's Communications Department or General Counsel.

<u>POLICY NO. 23</u> GIFTS, GRATUITIES AND ENTERTAINMENT POLICY

<u>PURPOSE</u>:

The purpose of this Policy is to prevent the receipt of gifts, gratuities or favors from interfering with the ability of any associate to make decisions solely in the best interests of the Company.

<u>POLICY</u>:

The Company does not seek to gain any advantage through the improper use of business courtesies or other inducements. Good judgment and moderation must be exercised to avoid misrepresentation and adverse effect on the reputation of the Company or its associates. Offering, giving, soliciting or receiving any form of bribe is prohibited.

Associates and their immediate family may offer or accept only infrequent meals, entertainment or gifts of reasonable value as determined by the CEO of each subsidiary. Gifts in cash are never to be offered or accepted. Associates should not permit suppliers to pay for their entertainment or meal expense and under no circumstances shall an associate solicit any gift, meal or entertainment.

<u>DEFINITIONS</u>:

<u>Client</u>: Client includes clients, prospects, the market and all persons and companies with which the Company has previously

done business, is currently doing business or anticipates doing business with in the near future.

Supplier: Suppliers include not only sellers providing services and material to the Company, but also consultants, financial institutions, advisors and any person or institution which does business or is seeking to do business with the Company.

Immediate Family: The employee's spouse and children (and their spouses), and also the father, mother, sisters and brothers of both the employee and employee's spouse.

PROCEDURE:

1. Client Relations:

The Company does not seek to gain any advantage through the improper use of business courtesies or other inducements. Good judgment and moderation must be exercised to avoid misrepresentation and adverse effect on the Company or its associates' reputation. Offering, giving, soliciting or receiving any form of bribe is prohibited.

Gifts, gratuities, and entertainment may be given if they:

- Are consistent with customary business practices
- Are not excessive in value and cannot reasonably be construed as a bribe or pay-off
- Are not in contravention of applicable law or ethical standards
- Will not embarrass the Company or the associate if publicly disclosed.

2. **Acceptance of Gifts, Entertainment and Services:**

Associates may not encourage or solicit Gifts, entertainment or services from any Supplier or Client. From time to time, associates may accept Gifts, entertainment or services, but only if the Gifts, entertainment or services are reasonable and occur infrequently.

PRINCIPLE #3 WE RESPECT CUSTOMERS, SHAREHOLDERS AND EMPLOYEES

POLICY NO. 24 PROCUREMENT

PURPOSE:

The purpose of this Policy is to assure that the Company gets the best products and services at a fair value, while conducting itself in accord with the highest standards of business practices and with all applicable legal requirements.

POLICY:

The Company purchases and leases millions of dollars worth of goods and services every month. The integrity of the Company's business depends, in part, on proper procurement. It is the policy of the Company to purchase products and services based on merit, regardless of the manufacturer or provider.

DEFINITIONS:

Kickbacks and Rebates: Any agreement pursuant to which the Company's associates, their friends or families receive direct or indirect cash payments, credits or other things of value in consideration for a purchase or sale of goods or services. Some examples of Kickback & Rebates include:

- Placing undue pressure and/or exercising undue powers on suppliers by asking, hinting, insinuating, or eliciting money, goods, services or personal favors in exchange for company business or other company benefit;
- Receiving home renovations/refurbishment services from suppliers without paying due service fees;

- Receiving donations for team building parties from suppliers;
- Making suppliers pay bills or reimburse expenses by giving one's personal receipts;
- Pressuring suppliers to employ acquaintances, book golf courses, or provide funds for charitable causes;
- Taking money by exaggerating rental fees in collusion with landlord.

Group Boycott: Any agreement or concerted effort by the Company and others to refuse to deal with particular supplier or suppliers.

Restrictive Agreements and Exclusive Dealing Agreements: Agreements between the Company and a supplier to limit freedom of decision as to the purchase or procurement of goods and services. These agreements can be express or implied.

Preferential Treatment: Knowingly inducing or accepting a discriminatory preferential price that a supplier would not offer other purchasers where the quantities, specifications and methods of sale would be the same.

PROCEDURE:

1. **Open-Door Policy:**

   The Company will give fair and impartial consideration to every supplier and potential supplier. Current suppliers will be subject to periodic review.

2. **Personal Conflicts of Interest, Favoritism, or Bias:**

   More detail as to the types of situations to avoid is provided in the Conflict of Interest Corporate Policy.

3. **Kickbacks. Rebates and Gifts:**

Purchases of goods and services must not lead to associates or their friends or families receiving personal kickbacks or rebates. Associates and their immediate families may accept only infrequent meals, entertainment or gifts of a reasonable value from vendors or suppliers.

4. **Financial Transaction:**

A money transaction with suppliers is strictly not allowed.

5. **Group Boycotts Prohibited:**

It is Company policy to deal with suppliers on the basis of valid business justifications. Group Boycotts include any concerted effort with other persons or entities to deal only with certain suppliers or to refuse to deal with any supplier. Group Boycotts can come in many forms. Virtually all of these forms are prohibited. Company associates should not attempt to influence the decision of any other company or individual in its decision to do business with any supplier. Associates approached by anyone proposing a group refusal to do business with a particular supplier should immediately reject the proposal and report the incident to the Legal Department.

6. **Restrictive Agreements and Exclusive Dealing Agreements:**

The Company generally discourages any supplier contract provision that restricts the Company's freedom of choice in the selection of a product or service or in choosing to do business with another supplier. Restrictive Agreements and Exclusive Dealing Agreements must be reviewed in advance by the Company's General Counsel, or Contract Manager.

A joint venture with a supplier should generally not contain any non-competition provisions. All contractual provisions that restrict the markets, customers or products/services that may be entered, served or offered by the Company should be reviewed by the Company's General Counsel before an agreement is reached and should only be executed as directed by the Company's General Counsel.

PRINCIPLE #4 ENVIRONMENT LAWS

POLICY NO. 25 ENVIRONMENTAL LAWS AND REGULATIONS

PURPOSE:

The purpose of this Policy is to help ensure that the Company complies with, and that associates are aware of, applicable environmental requirements.

POLICY:

It is the Company's policy to comply with all applicable environmental laws and regulations and to conduct business in a manner which protects the environment, associates, and the general public. It is also the Company's policy to establish and maintain appropriate plans, procedures, and programs to comply with applicable laws and regulations.

PROCEDURE:

1. **Accurate Records and Reporting:**

The Company will prepare, maintain, and file with the appropriate regulatory authority accurate and complete environmental permit applications, reports, plans, records, manifests, certifications, and other documents required under applicable environmental laws and regulations. It is a violation of the Company's policy to alter, destroy, conceal, or fail to file documents required under applicable environmental statutes and regulations. Associates who become aware of false or omitted material information in documents filed with a regulatory authority or the destruction or concealment of environmental documents should contact the Company's General Counsel, or Compliance Manager.

2. **Hazardous Materials:**

It is the Company's policy to handle, treat, store, transport and dispose of hazardous materials in full compliance with all applicable laws. If an associate does not know whether a material is "hazardous," the associate should contact his/her manager, the facility manager or the Company's General Counsel, Risk Manager.

PRINCIPLE #5 WE ARE RESPONSIBLE CORPORATE CITIZENS

POLICY NO. 26 REPORTING AND INVESTIGATING VIOLATIONS AND SEEKING CLARIFICATION OF POLICIES

POLICY:

All associates are required to promptly report all known or suspected violations of applicable laws or of the Compliance and Ethics Program, including violations of the Company's policies. Reports of such violations shall be made promptly to a Compliance manager, the Compliance Committee, the General Counsel, any director or officer of the Company, including the Chief Financial Officer and the Chief Executive Officer, or to the Human Resources Department, if the employee feels more comfortable doing so. All reports, however made, will be promptly and thoroughly investigated.

PURPOSE:

This purpose of this policy is to: (i) encourage associates to report violations; (ii) help ensure prompt and full investigation of violations; and (iii) assure associates that they will be protected from retribution if they make good faith reports of violations or suspected violations of the law or the Compliance and Ethics Program.

PROCEDURE:

1. **Reporting Violations and Suspected Violations:**

   Associates should immediately report violations and suspected violations of the law or the Compliance and Ethics Program. The report will be taken in good faith and further review or investigation will determine the validity of the reported violation.

   Associates may report a violation by approaching, telephoning, emailing or writing to any of the individuals identified in the policy above.

2. **Failing to Report a Violation or Condon in a Violation:**

   Failing to report or condoning a violation of the law or the Compliance and Ethics Program may lead to disciplinary action up to and including dismissal.

3. **Protection Against Reprisal:**

   In order to encourage associates to report violations, associates must be assured that confidentiality will be maintained of all reported incidents to the fullest extent possible. To allay fear of retribution, associates are permitted to make anonymous reports of violations of the law or the Compliance and Ethics Program.

   To the fullest extent possible and permitted by law, the Company will take reasonable precautions to maintain the confidentiality of those individuals who report legal or compliance-related violations. This confidentiality will include both the confidentiality of the person making the report and the person about whom the report is made. It is not possible to guarantee complete confidentiality in every instance because doing so may hinder the Company from fulfilling its obligations to conduct a thorough investigation and in taking appropriate corrective measures.

It is absolutely forbidden for any associate to punish or conduct reprisals against another associate who has reported a suspected violation of the law or of the Compliance Program in good-faith.

4. **Malicious Reporting:**

Associates are encouraged to make good-faith reports of possible violations of the law or of the Compliance and Ethics Program. The Company recognizes, however, that individual associates can abuse the Compliance Program to make unfounded accusations against other associates in order to harass them or to exact revenge for personal disputes. The Company, therefore, reserves the right to investigate persons who make reports when, for example, the Company suspects a person's motives for making a report or when it is necessary to investigate a person's credibility as to a given report.

5. **Investigations:**

Each report of a known or suspected violation will be promptly and thoroughly investigated. In all cases, the Corporate Compliance Division or its designee(s) and any supervisors or managers working on the investigation should carefully document all actions taken and decisions reached. A report should be prepared even if the investigation reveals that no violation occurred. The investigation report should set forth in reasonable detail:

(a) a summary of the incident;
(b) the investigation conducted and the results therefrom; and
(c) the action taken.

6. **Investigations by Associates:**

Unless directed or so charged, associates will not investigate violations of the law or of the Corporate Compliance and Ethics Program. The General Counsel's office or Corporate

Compliance Division will direct the investigation and designate the individuals who will conduct and participate in it.

7. **Responding to Violations:**

If a violation of the law or the Corporate Compliance and Ethics Program has occurred, the Company will determine how and why the offense occurred and will identify and implement steps to prevent similar violations from reoccurring.

POLICY NO. 27 COMPLIANCE AND ETHICS PROGRAM AUDITING AND MONITORING

PURPOSE:

The purpose of this Policy is to ensure the effectiveness of the Corporate Compliance and Ethics Program by establishing procedures for Auditing and Monitoring of the Program.

POLICY:

It is the policy of the Company to maintain an effective Compliance and Ethics Program through the regular Auditing and Monitoring of the Program. The Company has appointed a Compliance and Ethics Committee whose responsibility it is to oversee the administration and enforcement of the Compliance and Ethics Program through a Corporate Compliance Division.

In order to implement its Compliance and Ethics Program, the Company requires that its associates contribute to monitoring the success of the Program. The Company expects its associates to cooperate fully with any and all of its attempts to gather information about how the Compliance and Ethics Program is operating.

It is also the policy of the Company to encourage its associates to express their concerns about the effectiveness of the Compliance and Ethics Program.

DEFINITIONS:

Auditing and Monitoring: Auditing and Monitoring is the systematic review of the Program and the verification that there has in fact been compliance with the Program, including the Compliance and Ethics Policies, and any other Company policies.

PROCEDURE:

1. **Auditing and Monitoring the Compliance and Ethics Program:**

In order to effectively implement its Program, the Company is putting in place a number of procedures for reviewing and evaluating the Program. Auditing and Monitoring may include:

- Verification of the prompt distribution of the relevant portions of the Compliance and Ethics Program to new and existing associates
- Verification of the use of the Compliance and Ethics Program and particularly the Compliance and Ethics Policies in the orientation of new associates.
- Verification of the certification process by which associates affirm that they have read and understood the relevant portions of the Compliance and Ethics Program.
- Verification that requirements included in the Code, Manual and other policies have been consistently implemented and followed.
- Verification of the success of internal investigations, including the confidentiality and thoroughness of the investigations and adequate documentation
- Verification that reprisals are not being made against associates who report violations of the law or the Company's Compliance and Ethics Program
- Verification of the enforcement of the Compliance and Ethics Program Discipline Policy through:
- Review of the adequacy of the documentation of discipline proceedings
- Review of the consistency of sanctions actually imposed

2. **<u>Auditing and Monitoring Regulatory Compliance</u>:**

In addition to Auditing and Monitoring the procedural components of the Program, the Company will periodically review and evaluate compliance with various legal and regulatory requirements.

3. **<u>Cooperation with Auditors and Investigators</u>:**

The Compliance and Ethics Committee may periodically instruct the Corporate Compliance Division to undertake the Auditing and Monitoring of the Company's Program. All associates are expected to assist and fully cooperate with these associates.

From time to time, the Company may also find it necessary to have auditors and investigators from outside the Company involved in the process of reviewing and auditing the effectiveness of the Program. These auditors and investigators may differ from the persons conducting internal investigations—in addition to investigating specific reports of violations; they may be conducting broad reviews of how the Program is operating or specific legal or regulatory compliance.

<u>POLICY NO. 28</u> COMPLIANCE AND ETHICS PROGRAM DISCIPLINE

<u>PURPOSE</u>:

The purpose of this Policy is to alert associates to the discipline which may be imposed for violations of the Compliance and Ethics Program. This Policy and other documents and communications associated with the Compliance and Ethics Program do not limit the Company's right to terminate employment (and any corresponding salary, bonus and associate benefits) of any associate at will at any time, with or without cause or prior notice. Discipline is not limited to violations of the Program, violations of Company policies will still subject an associate to discipline up to and including termination.

POLICY:

It is the Company's policy to enforce its Compliance and Ethics Program (including the Code of Business Ethics and other Company policies), in a consistent manner through appropriate disciplinary mechanisms. Violations of the law are considered a violation of the Compliance and Ethics Program. An associate may, however, violate the Compliance and Ethics Program without violating the law.

When an associate is determined to have engaged in a violation of any Company policy, not only those summarized in the Code or this Manual, he or she may be subject to discipline, up to and including termination. It is the Company's policy to apply its discipline in a reasonable and consistent fashion; however, the form of discipline which is appropriate will be case-specific.

Nothing in this Policy, or any other documents or communications, verbal or written, regarding the Compliance and Ethics Program creates or implies an employment contract or term of employment.

PROCEDURE:

1. **Disciplinary Options:**

   The Company is committed to flexibility in its disciplinary policy. While it is the Company's policy to enforce its Compliance and Ethics Program in a consistent manner, no single set of disciplinary options is appropriate in every case. The Company, therefore, retains the sole discretion to structure disciplinary sanctions as the circumstances warrant.

2. **Relevant Factors to Determining Appropriate Discipline:**

   Associates should be aware that there are a number of factors which may be considered in deciding on the seriousness of a violation and the discipline which is appropriate. Some of these factors "aggravate" (increase) the seriousness of the violation, while others "mitigate" (decrease) the seriousness of the violation. Since these factors are case-specific, similar violations may result in different discipline in different cases. Such a difference does not mean that the discipline is inconsistent.

3. **Determining Whether a Violation Occurred:**

Determining whether a violation of the law or the Program has occurred is perhaps the most important step in the process of enforcing the Program. Given the variety of possible violations, and the range of circumstances in which they can occur, the Company cannot employ a uniform procedure for the investigation and determination of violations.

4. **Documenting Disciplinary Decisions:**

If a violation of the law or the Program has occurred, a disciplinary report should be prepared summarizing the violation and the discipline imposed. The disciplinary report should be included in the associate's personnel file.

POLICY NO. 29 COMPLIANCE AND ETHICS PROGRAM IMPLEMENTATION AND INTERPRETATION

PURPOSE:

This Policy designates the members of the Compliance and Ethics Committee and assigns and communicates the responsibility for overseeing the Program to the Committee.

POLICY:

The responsibility for overseeing the Program is assigned to the Compliance and Ethics Committee.

The Committee has final jurisdiction on questions or interpretations and must approve all changes involving the Program.

Day-to-day responsibility for the operation of the Compliance and Ethics Program shall be assigned to the Corporate Compliance Division.

PROCEDURE:

1. **Responsibilities of the Corporate Compliance and Ethics Committee:**

   The Committee's responsibilities in overseeing and administering the Program include the following elements:

   - Establishing written ethical and compliance standards and procedures;
   - Updating and revising the compliance standards and procedures as necessary;
   - Monitoring compliance with laws, government regulations and the Program;
   - Ensuring the compliance and ethics standards and procedures are disseminated and implemented by management;
   - Maintaining systems to ensure that the Company takes reasonable steps to hire, retain and promote associates that comply with the law, ethical values and Company policies;
   - Maintaining systems to allow associates to report violations of the law or Program without fear of retribution;
   - Ensuring investigations of alleged violations of Company standards and procedures are properly and promptly handled; and
   - Ensuring the Company has taken steps to respond appropriately to misconduct if it occurs and to prevent a recurrence of any such misconduct.

<u>POLICY NO. 30</u> COMPLIANCE AND ETHICS PROGRAM EDUCATION AND CERTIFICATION

<u>PURPOSE</u>:

The purpose of this Policy is to ensure that the mandatory associate training requirements under the Compliance and Ethics Program are implemented. Every associate must understand the ethical and legal standards under which the Company operates and to which he or she must adhere.

<u>POLICY</u>:

The Compliance and Ethics Program will be communicated to all associates. The Code of Business Ethics will be distributed to all associates. This Manual will be available to all associates. Associates who routinely confront certain compliance issues will be provided with copies of applicable policies and will receive additional training relating to their area.

Upon hire, all associates will be required to review the Code of Business Ethics and this Manual. Each associate must certify they have received the pertinent documents, read and understand their contents and agree to abide by the letter and spirit of each.

Management associates are responsible for ensuring that their direct subordinates and have access to and understand the applicable Compliance and Ethics policies and all other Company policies to which they are subject.

<u>PROCEDURE</u>:

1. **<u>Reading the Code of Business Ethics and Manual and Signing the Acknowledgment Form</u>:**

An acknowledgment and certification form will be distributed to all associates. It is imperative that associates sign this form only after reading the Code and Manual. Failure to read and understand the rules contained in the Code and Manual is no excuse for violating those rules.

Certification and understanding of the Program is a condition of employment. All management associates have read and understand the Code and corresponding Manual and returned the acknowledgment form to Human Resources.

2. **Communication and Training Methods:**

At the initial introduction of the Compliance and Ethics Program, the Code of Business Ethics will be distributed to each associate. The following options may be used to inform associates about the Program or to address any subsequent changes:

- Video seminars
- Presentations
- Training programs, including on-line courses
- Posted notices
- Group meetings

Other forms of distribution or instruction may be used from time to time. The fact that any changes made may be in a different format, however, does not mean that the changes are not binding.

3. **Documentation of Compliance Training:**

The Compliance and Ethics Committee is responsible for establishing a training program and for selection of appropriate course materials. The Committee will assign the collection and maintenance of training records to a designee. The designee will be responsible for tracking and preparing reports that should include the training dates, topics and number of hours provided to each employee.

<u>POLICY NO. 31</u> WHISTLE-BLOWERS AND NON-RETALIATION

<u>PURPOSE</u>:

Associates are sometimes concerned that they will be the victim of retaliation or reprisals if they "blow the whistle" by reporting violations of the law or of Company policy. At some companies, fear of reprisal has led some associates to make their concerns known to government officials before they were willing to tell their employer about potential problems. This can lead to government investigations and expensive litigation. It is the Company's policy to encourage its associates to report violations to the Company.

The purpose of this Policy is to assure associates that conscientiously reported violations will be discreetly and thoroughly investigated, and that no reprisals will be taken against associates who report violations in good faith.

<u>POLICY</u>:

It is the Company's policy that reports of suspected violations of the law, the Company's Compliance and Ethics Program or of Company policy will be promptly and thoroughly investigated. It is the policy of the Company that associates who, in good faith, report violations of the law or the Company's Corporate Compliance and Ethics Program will not be the subject of reprisals or other punishment as a consequence of reporting the violation.

<u>PROCEDURE</u>:

1. **<u>Reprisal Strictly Forbidden</u>:**

It is absolutely forbidden for any associate to punish or conduct reprisals against another associate who has reported in good faith a suspected violation of the law or of the Compliance Program.

2. **Malicious Reporting:**

The Company encourages its associates to make good-faith reports of possible violations of the law or of the Compliance and Ethics Program. The Company recognizes, however, that individual associates can abuse the Compliance Program to make unfounded accusations against other associates in order to harass them or to exact revenge for personal disputes. For this reason, the Company must reserve the right to investigate persons who make reports when there is a valid reason to do so. Such reasons may include reasons to suspect a person's motives or when it is necessary to investigate a person's credibility as to a given report.

3. **Federal Whistle-Blowing Laws:**

In addition to the Company's internal policy against reprisals, several laws provide protection for associates who communicate with government officials regarding possible illegal behavior in some contexts. Discrimination against whistle-blowing associates in the terms and conditions of their employment is prohibited. These terms and conditions would include anything affecting the associate's working conditions, including wages, hours, bonuses, and work stations. Discharge of a whistle-blowing associate would also be considered discrimination, and would therefore be prohibited. It is the Company's policy to comply with all applicable whistle-blower laws.

Associates involved in any action being taken against any associate for their disclosure of information to a government official should contact the Company's General Counsel to ensure that no whistle-blower laws are being broken, (if the company or business unit does not have a General Counsel, then notify NAHQ's General Counsel).

POLICY NO. 32 EXIT INTERVIEWS

POLICY:

Associates who terminate their employment with the Company shall complete an exit interview, if appropriate. The interview shall be for the dual purposes of gathering information on why the associate left and on whether the associate is aware of any prior or existing violations of the law or the Company's Compliance and Ethics Program.

PURPOSE:

This Policy has two purposes. First, the exit interviews are part of the Company's quality improvement process and provide information useful in improving the working conditions of all associates. The information provided by a departing associate may be extremely useful in identifying working problems that can then be solved. Second, this Policy will help ensure that the Company becomes aware of all potential and existing violations of the law or the Compliance and Ethics Program. When an associate leaves, he or she may be aware of violations of the law or of the Corporate Compliance and Ethics Program. In fact, those violations may be why that associate is leaving. In such circumstances, it is imperative that the Company be informed of whatever problems may exist.

POLICY NO. 33 INFORMATION RETENTION

POLICY

The Company has created this Information Retention Policy ("Policy") to establish guidelines for identifying, storing, retaining, protecting and disposing of its information and documents.

PURPOSE:

The Company generates valuable information each day in a variety of formats, primarily in electronic formats, and sometimes in paper or "hard" formats. No matter the format, storing information can be costly to the Company. This policy seeks to balance the Company's legal and business-related needs to retain information with their costs, and to keep only the information whose retention is required, and only for as long as necessary.

The following Information Retention Policy and Protocol instructs employees and business partners of the Company's position regarding these issues, and how to comply.

Underlying Principles: This policy is based upon the following principles:

1. The Company must maintain and preserve its business information only as required by law, or as long as it has value to the Company. Conversely, because retaining information causes the Company to incur expenses, information that either has no value to the Company or whose preservation is not required by law, must be discarded.
2. As indicated by the definitions of "information," "document," and "record," information is treated and retained according to its business type. Paper copies and electronic copies of the same document are treated the same for retention purposes.
3. This policy and its retention/destruction schedules may be suspended because legal proceedings or business issues affecting the Company. When the policy needs to be suspended, a "hold instruction" (sometime also referred to as a "litigation hold") will be issued, and will be in effect until formally lifted. ("Hold instructions"/"litigation holds" are described in further detail herein.)

Each employee and partner of the Company is responsible for following this policy. Any employee who believes that an exception should be made to this Policy should immediately consult his supervisor or manager.

DEFINITIONS:

As used herein

1. "*Document*" is the same as "*information*," which is defined below.
2. "*Information*," "*document*," and "*record*" are synonymous, and mean all recorded, retrievable information, regardless of physical form or medium, including all original records and documents, electronic media, electronic mail, letters, memoranda, opinions, reports, books, papers, drawings, business records, contracts, customer and vendor documents, charts, photographs, audio records, microfilm, magnetic tape, and other information created or received in connection with the Company's operations and activities, or related to its legal obligations.

    a. Duplicate copies of records *are* not considered "information" for purposes of this policy, so long as the original record is retained. Duplicate copies of records should be discarded after they have no use or value in connection with a project.
    b. Records that are transitory in nature: These records include those that have no value, or whose value is short-lived, such as certain types of personal notes which are not business-related, telephone messages, or preliminary working papers. These records *are* not considered "information" for purposes of this policy
    c. Drafts: Drafts *are* not considered "information" for purposes of this policy Drafts should not be retained beyond (i) completion of the underlying work project; or (ii) upon notification that the project is not going to be completed, assuming the material is not needed for future reference. In any case, drafts should only be kept in accordance with the retention schedule prescribed for the type of document to which the draft relates.

3. "*Legal proceeding*" is a government or other legal investigation, lawsuit, administrative proceeding, the service of a legal request

or demand for discovery, or some other form of legal process involving the Company.

4. "*Legal requirement*" is a reason based on statutory, regulatory, or substantive law for retaining a record.
5. "*Personal files.*" The law may not distinguish between "personal" work files and the Company's "corporate" or "business" files. As such, "personal files" containing business—or work-related information may be subject to subpoena in case of a legal proceeding, just as would other corporate or business records. Therefore, calendars, diaries, notes, and chronological files, *in electronic and paper forms*, of firm personnel are typically considered "information" or "records" covered by this Policy. Each employee should, at least twice annually, review his "personal files" and dispose of any information or records for which the retention period has passed. (Note that the term "personal files" as used herein, does not cover records relating to employees' personal matters that are unrelated to the Company's business.)
6. "*Record*" is the same as "information," which is defined above.
7. "*Working files*" are the same as "*personal files*," which are defined above.

PROCEDURE: Information Retention Requirements and Responsibilities

A. **Summary of Employees' General Responsibilities:**

As indicated above, each employee of the Company is responsible for adhering to this Policy and satisfying its requirements. At a minimum, each employee must conduct himself/herself as follows:

1. At least semi-annually, employees must discard and destroy information that is older than the applicable retention period outlined in this Policy.
2. Employees must not engage in conduct that is intended to subvert or avoid this Policy.

3. Saving electronic information: Employees are strongly encouraged to save electronic information and records only on shared drives that are hosted backed-up routinely by _________ Data Services America. Information that is saved on other media, including individual computer drives, is subject to accidental loss and destruction, and cannot easily be recovered.

B. **Information Retention Requirements:**

1. The General Counsel will periodically review this Policy and its retention schedules, and will recommend modifications that are necessary to mandate compliance with applicable laws and regulations.
2. Information shall not be destroyed before the applicable retention period has expired. Information shall not be retained for longer than the prescribed period without consulting the General Counsel or the Company's Law Department.

C. **Acceptable Methods of Information Disposal:**

1. Electronic records: Electronic files should be fully deleted and erased from all electronic media, including back-up media.
2. Paper records: Paper records containing business information of any kind should be discarded or disposed in a manner calculated to protect against the unintended distribution of such information. The Company recommends that any sensitive information in paper form be shredded.

D. **Information retention schedule:**

1. Electronic mail: 90 days—Electronic mail will be maintained for a period of ninety (90) days, after which time e-mail messages that have not been separately saved or printed as documents will be permanently deleted.

E-mail older than will be automatically deleted at least weekly. Employees should not save or print an e-mail message unless it has appreciable business value. If an employee saves or prints an e-mail message, then he should retain the saved or printed message in accordance with this Policy and the applicable retention schedule.

- Personal e-mail accounts: The Company employees are discouraged from sending business-related e-mail messages from personal e-mail accounts. Such e-mail messages are not considered "information" covered by this Policy. As such, the Company will not be responsible for preserving such messages.
- Instant messaging: The Company employees are discouraged from sending business-related e-mail messages from instant messaging accounts. Such instant messages are not considered "information" covered by this Policy. As such, the Company will not be responsible for preserving instant messages.

The following schedule pertains to all information and records other than electronic mail, which is covered by item 1 above.

2. Accounting and tax records: 7 years—Accounting and/or tax records include, but are not limited to, records concerning payroll, expenses, profs of deductions, business costs, accounting procedures, and other documents regarding the Company's revenues. Accounting and/or tax records, including back-up documentation, must be maintained for at least 7 years from the date of filing the applicable tax return.

    - *Tax records may not be disposed or discarded without the express written consent of the Senior Manager of Tax.*

3. Marketing and sales documents: 7 years—same as Accounting and Tax Records—The Company must keep final copies of marketing and sales documents for the same length of time that it maintains Accounting and Tax records.

4. Employment and personnel records: Generally, 6 years after employee's termination—Federal and state statutes and regulations require the Company to preserve certain recruitment, employment, and personnel information for specific periods of time. To this end, to the extent that you maintain any documents which may be considered employment or personnel records (e.g., performance evaluations, warning memoranda, completed change of address forms, 401(k) information, etc.), please confer with your Human resources Manager regarding the specific recordkeeping requirements, and prior to destroying any documents.

    - *Please see the attached Employment Record Retention Schedule pertaining to particular employment-related records.*

5. Occupational Safety and Health Documentation: 30 years for exposure and medical records; all others 5 years—These documents, which include occupational injury Reports, OSHA inspection files, and claims documents, must be maintained for five (5) years from the end of the year to which they pertain. However, certain types of medical records must be kept for thirty (30) years, as indicated in the attached Employment Records Retention Schedule.
6. Board of Directors and Board Committee Materials: Minutes permanent; materials for 6 years—Meeting minutes should be retained in perpetuity in the Company's minutes book. A clean copy of all materials pertaining to activities of the Board of Directors and its Committees should be kept for no less than six (6) years.
7. Press Releases and Public Filings: Permanent—The Company should retain permanent copies of all press releases and publicly filed documents under the theory that the Company should have its own copy to test the accuracy of any document a member of the public can theoretically produce against the Company.
8. Legal Files: To be determined by the Company's Legal Department.

- *Legal files may not be disposed without the express written consent of the General Counsel.*

9. Development/Intellectual Property and Trade Secrets: Life of the secret plus 5 years—Development documents are often subject to intellectual property protection in their final form (e.g., patents and copyrights). The documents detailing the development process are often also valuable to the Company, and are protected as trade secrets where the Company:

    - Derives independent economic value from the secrecy of the information; and
    - Has taken affirmative steps to keep the information confidential.

    The Company must keep all documents designated as containing trade secret information for the life of the trade secret plus five (5) years

10. Contracts: 6 years after term—Final executed copies of all contracts entered into by the Company must be retained for at least six (6) years beyond the term of the contracts.

6.5.2 Corporate Compliance Policy—Government Investigations and Interviews

Government Investigations and Government Investigations and Interviews

A. Checklist for Responding to law enforcement requests, government contacts or attempted interviews, and criminal and administrative searches

    1. Preparation

        a. A Senior Manager at each XXX facility shall be designated to coordinate a response to law enforcement requests, government contacts or attempted interviews, and criminal and administrative searches.

b. Written security procedures at each location shall insure that all visitors to non-public areas are identified and that the purpose of their visit is established.

c. Daily visitation log procedures shall be reviewed with appropriate personnel. The procedures shall instruct reception and security personnel to contact immediately the Designated Senior Manager in the event of a visit by law enforcement personnel.

d. The name and contact number for the Designated Senior Manager and the General Counsel shall be posted at the reception area.

2. During a Visit

a. The designated Senior Manager shall immediately notify the General Counsel about the presence of law enforcement officials on the company premises.

b. The designated Senior Manager should ask the lead law enforcement officer executing the search warrant for and verify each agent's identification and agency affiliation and a copy of the warrant and supporting affidavit.

c. A copy of the court order (subpoena or search warrant and the supporting affidavit) should be immediately sent to XXX's General Counsel.

d. If the court order is in the form of a subpoena, the General Counsel will (i) review the subpoena for any legal defect, including the manner in which it was served on the company, the breadth of its' request, its' form and (ii) review the information that is to be provided in response to the subpoena before any information is released.

e. If the court order is in the form of a search warrant, (i) The designated Senior Manager may request that the agents secure the premises but delay the search and seizure until the General Counsel can arrive, review the search warrant, witness the execution of the search warrant and assist in the protection of legally privileged materials.

[Note: Neither The designated Senior Manager nor any other XXX employee shall interfere with execution of the search warrant should the law enforcement agents refuse to delay the beginning of the search until General Counsel can arrive. The designated Senior Manager should make a written note of when the request was made, to whom it was made, when it was rejected and any other relevant circumstances]

f. If the court order is either a subpoena or a search warrant issued under the Foreign Intelligence Surveillance Act (FISA), the general guidelines respecting subpoenas and search warrants set forth below apply. However, subpoenas and search warrants issued by a FISA court also contain a "gag" order. No person or institution served with the search warrant can disclose that the warrant has been served or that records have been produced pursuant to the warrant.

g. If the order is a National Security Letter (NSL) issued under Section 505 of the USA Patriot Act, the general guidelines respecting subpoenas still apply. However, an NSL also contains a "gag" order. No person or institution served with an NSL can disclose that the NSL has been served or that the records have been produced pursuant to the NSL.

h. The Designated Senior Manager should review categories of items or documents subject to seizure and determine during the search which items or documents are critical to the continuing operation of the company's day to day business. A list of the critical items or documents should be provided to the General Counsel.

i. Grand jury subpoenas for documents sometimes contain a "request" that the existence of the subpoena not be disclosed. These request are frequently accompanied by a warning that disclosure could undermine the integrity of an important criminal investigation and a request to contact the prosecutor if the subpoena recipient intends to disclose information about the subpoena. Although the government usually does not have the right to demand secrecy about the existence most grand jury subpoenas, no XXX employee should make any type of disclosure to the subject of the subpoena or to anyone other than The Designated Senior Manager. It is up to the Company's General Counsel or assigned Outside Counsel to decide whether any type of disclosure should be made when there is a "request" for confidentiality by the Government.

j. Law enforcement agents sometimes attempt to interview employees before, during and after the execution of search warrants. The decision to grant or reject a request for a voluntary interview is up to each individual employee. Law enforcement agents cannot demand that an employee answer questions and provide and interview on the spot. However, employees should not be instructed to reject interview requests. Instead, they should be advised that the decision is theirs, that they have a right to seek legal guidance and may want to consult with an attorney before deciding whether or not to provide an interview, that the company might consider providing counsel or paying for counsel of their choice and that the company will respect their decision about whether or not to provide a voluntary interview.

   Because law enforcement agents executing search warrants usually arrive unannounced and because interview requests are frequently made on the spot, The Designated Senior Manager should periodically review all procedures with employees, including this explanation about responding to interview requests.

3. The General Counsel or assigned Outside Counsel will:

   a. Speak to the lead agent and emphasize that the company will do everything it can to make sure that the search proceeds smoothly.
   b. Request a copy of the search warrant and affidavit and confirm the identity of the Magistrate who issued the warrant.

c. Advise the agent that Counsel to the company wishes to observe and monitor the execution of the search warrant.
d. Review the scope of the search warrant
e. If areas other than areas authorized by the warrant are searched, counsel will request that the agents secure the perimeter of the area and segregate documents and items seized from the disputed area until counsel has had time to contact the magistrate who issued the warrant. If the magistrate is unavailable, then counsel may seek to confer with an appropriate supervisor in the United States Attorney's Office or other agency responsible for issuance of the subpoena.
f. Identify for the agents the areas that are known to or likely to contain legally privileged documents.
g. Gather as much information as possible from the agents about the nature of the investigation, potential subjects or targets, relevant statutes, witnesses, theory of prosecution and the purpose of the search.
h. Obtain a back up disk of all computer software that the government seeks to remove from the Company's premises.
i. One individual shall be assigned to follow each search party. The individual shall document the following:

    i) Time the search was instituted;
    ii) Identify of the case or supervisory agent in charge of executing the search warrant and other personnel assisting the agent;
    iii) Rooms, places and areas searched;
    iv) The order in which offices, rooms, or other areas were searched and the times of the respective searches;
    v) The names and job titles of employees interviewed and attempted to be interviewed by agents during the search;
    vi) Questions or comments asked or made by agents during the search and their responses;
    vii) The time the search was concluded;

[NOTE: it is possible that the law enforcement agents conducting the search may not want XXX employees from following them during the search and prevent this type of monitoring. If this happens, XXX employees should not follow the agents during the search. Instead, they should note, in writing, that the request was rejected, and identify the circumstances surrounding the request, including the time and the name or names of the agents who rejected the request.]

4. The General Counsel shall instruct company officers and personnel not to conduct any formal or informal meetings to discuss the investigation or the search warrant without the presence of counsel.
5. The General Counsel shall arrange a privileged meeting of senior management and counsel as soon as possible to review the likely focus of the investigation and to develop a strategy.

   a. The meeting shall address:
   i) the places searched
   ii) the types of documents seized
   iii) names listed in the search warrant
   iv) possible follow up interviews
   v) reminder to management that any informal meetings and conversations among them without the presence of counsel will be deemed to be "non-privileged" and subject to disclosure;

6. All Personnel shall be instructed not to "forcibly resist, oppose, prevent, impede, or interfere with persons executing a search warrant".

6.5.3 *Guidelines and Checklist for Internal Investigation*

I. XXX Inc. (XXX) Actions Following a Report

A. Once a report of a known or suspected violation is received through the Compliance Program reporting system, the Corporate Compliance Officer shall make an initial determination as to whether an internal investigation is warranted and possible, or not, based upon the facts reported to the Corporate Compliance Officer through the Compliance Officer through the Compliance Program reporting system.

B. If an internal investigation is deemed to be required and possible, the Corporate Compliance Officer shall advise XXX's Corporate Compliance Committee (the "Compliance Committee"), in writing, that an internal investigation should be conducted (a form of request to the Compliance Committee is set forth as Exhibit A)
C. The Corporate Compliance Officer shall organize a meeting of the Compliance Committee to explore the steps involved in such an investigation, to gather the facts and analyze their legal consequences.
D. The Compliance Committee shall:

    1. Decide whether or not to conduct an investigation.
    2. If an investigation is deemed to be warranted, advise the Corporate Compliance Officer that an internal investigation is authorized (a form of investigation authorization is set forth as Exhibit B)
    3. Consider the application of the attorney-client privilege and the attorney work product doctrines.
    4. Determine the team required to conduct the investigation in accordance with the following guidelines:

        a. If outside counsel is retained to conduct the internal investigation, XXX's General Counsel shall send a retainer letter to such outside counsel which states that outside counsel is being retained to investigate certain allegations; that the investigation is being conducted to enable both the General Counsel and outside counsel to advise XXX regarding its legal rights, obligations, and potential liabilities; and that all communications with counsel are protected by the attorney-client privilege and thus intended to remain confidential (a form of engagement letter is set forth as Exhibit C).
        b. If an outside consultant is engaged to perform services in connection with the internal investigation, XXX's General

Counsel shall send an engagement letter to such outside consultant (a form of engagement letter is set forth as Exhibit D).

c. It is important to note that best practices dictate that if outside counsel is engaged to conduct the internal investigation, such outside counsel (rather than XXX or XXX's General Counsel) should retain any outside consultants that such outside counsel deem necessary to the investigation.

d. The Compliance Committee or its designee will direct the investigation.

e. The General Counsel's office, or an attorney designated in writing by the General Counsel will act as legal advisor to the Committee and investigators throughout the reporting and investigation processes.

f. Designated investigators must be objective, have a clear understanding of the issues raised by the report, and have the appropriate expertise to investigate the report thoroughly and effectively. For numerous reasons, typically, management will not be designated to conduct or participate in the investigation.

g. The investigator's role is to determine facts. Investigators do not determine what action, if any, XXX should take based on those facts. Making such a determination is the responsibility and function of the Compliance Committee.

h. An investigator's responsibility begins when he or she is notified by the Compliance Committee of a particular concern or allegation and is retained by XXX, if applicable. That responsibility is discharged when the investigator submits the investigation report to the Compliance Committee (described later in this outline).

i. The Corporate Compliance Officer shall send employees who will be interviewed in connection with the internal investigation a letter (a form of internal investigation letter is set forth as Exhibit E).

5. Plan the Investigation as follows:

    a. Assess the purpose of the investigation by determining:

        i) What legal questions will be addressed at the end of the investigation.
        ii) What are the potential uses of the findings and the work product of the investigation.

    b. Categorize the investigation in terms of, among other applicable issues: business issues (e.g. the purpose of the investigation is to guide management decisions) and legal analysis issues.
    c. Consider Legal implications such as formulating a response to civil, criminal, regulatory or other enforcement action.
    d. Schedule an initial organizational meeting intended to:

        i) Review basics of the investigative procedure.
        ii) Discuss scope of the investigation.
        iii) Determine what issues are raised by the report.
        iv) Determine what laws, policies, guidelines, or practices apply to the issues raised by the report and in the organizational meeting.
        v) Conduct preliminary legal research of issues.
        vi) Brief the Compliance Committee with respect to interviews and the document gathering process.
        vii) Obtain copies of all relevant files (including electronic files, voice-mail, email) and other documents relevant to the issues raised, including:

1) a written description of relevant documents broken down into well-defined categories;
2) speak with employees about the request;
3) prepare a search checklist and an index;
4) create numbers for files and/or an on-site index;
5) consider documents stored on an electronic medium; and
6) determine document processing requirements and capabilities including: numbering, copying, reviewing for privilege, indexing,

creating a database, safeguard key documents and electronic data, if electronic data has been erased, determine how it can it be restored and store physical evidence properly to avoid deterioration.

viii) Decide who should be interviewed (note that all individuals with any knowledge that is or may be relevant to the investigation should be interviewed).

ix) Decide the order of the interviews.
x) Outline the questions to be asked/include reminders about confidentiality and anti-retaliation at the outset of each interview.
xi) Take steps to preserve the attorney-client privilege and the attorney work product privilege.

e. XXX should provide warnings and/or advice to employees before each interview (the statement set forth as Exhibit F should be read to each employee prior to each interview).
f. Consider the issue of the company paying for an employee counsel fees in connection with an interview and/or the investigation.
g. Evaluate each issue raised in the report:

i) Is it a request for help, an allegation of wrongdoing, or both?
ii) Is there a simple resolution for the issue?
iii) What resources are needed to investigate the issue thoroughly?

h. If the report was not made anonymously, have an intake meeting with the person raising the issue.

II. General Guidelines for Investigations and Anti-Retaliation

A. Effective internal complaint and investigation processes are a vital part of XXX's goal to provide a workplace where employees feel comfortable and can focus their energies on working together productively. Not only is XXX responsible for investigating the reports it receives, it is committed to doing so. All concerns and allegations reported will be taken seriously and investigated to the extent possible, even if the person who made the report asks that it not be investigated or later withdraws such report. Many times, individuals who report, but do not wish to have the matter investigated, are concerned about retaliation. This concern can make individuals uncomfortable about communicating openly and honestly and thereby interfere with XXX's ability to prevent or uncover wrongdoing and conduct effective investigations. Therefore, it is important to stress to all individuals throughout the investigation process that retaliating against a person who makes a report is against the law, against company policy, and will not be tolerated. Since anti-retaliation is an integral part of the internal complaint and investigation processes, it is discussed later in this section.

B. The issues of attorney-client privilege and attorney work product must be carefully considered. Detailed discussions and analysis of such issues by either the General Counsel or outside counsel may be warranted.

C. The anti-retaliation component of an investigation is critical to success. Protecting individuals against retaliation is critical to achieving XXX's goal of creating a comfortable and productive work environment and in complying with the law. Retaliation is generally described as adverse action taken against an individual for reporting a suspected violation of state or federal law or company policy, or for participating in an investigation of such violation(s)—whether internal or external. Retaliation can take many forms. Some forms may be obvious, others may be subtle. Here are some possible examples of retaliatory actions:

1. Unwarranted discipline or termination.
2. Unsatisfactory performance evaluations.
3. Loss of opportunities for promotion.
4. Disproportionately low pay raises or bonuses.
5. Less desirable work assignments.
6. Excluding or shunning an individual.

Because a widely disseminated, understood and enforced anti-retaliation policy is vital to fostering open and honest communication, the Compliance Committee is responsible for educating XXX's employees about it. In addition, when reports are received, designated investigators must, at the outset of the investigation:

1. Explain XXX's anti-retaliation policy to the individual making the report, and other witnesses and participants in the investigation.
2. Reassure them that XXX will not tolerate retaliation.
3. Remind them that they must report any suspicion of retaliation to a member of the Compliance Committee, the General Counsel's office.

Of course, the ultimate protection against retaliation is the ability to report anonymously. XXX as provided the means to do so through an anonymous email reporting system.

III. The investigation

A. The ultimate goal of an investigation is to enable XXX decision-makers to resolve matters fairly and effectively. The immediate goal of an investigation is to obtain the facts. Therefore, to be effective, an investigation must be:

1. Thorough and accurate.
2. Fair and impartial.
3. In compliance with the requirements of law and of XXX's ethics program.
4. Commenced and competed in a timely manner.

B. The investigators must establish a good rapport with those individuals involved in the investigation (whether it be the individual making the report, an interviewee or other individual). The investigators should:

1. Determine if there is any reason an interviewee thinks the investigator or the investigation cannot be fair or objective.
2. Explain XXX's anti-retaliation policy and reassure the individual that the Company will not tolerate retaliation.

3. Remind the individual that he or she must report any suspicion they have of retaliation.
4. Establish WHO, WHAT, WHEN, WHERE, HOW, WHY, and any other data that might be relevant to the report.
5. Be flexible in the approach to the investigation, interview, meeting or other aspect to the investigation.
6. Follow fact trails to the end and ask follow up questions. For example, if the witness states that her supervisor makes inappropriate remarks, ask: who is the supervisor; what were the remarks; were they said in the presence of anyone, who; when were they said; where were you when the remarks were said; were the remarks made to others, to whom, when; did anyone say anything to the supervisor in response, what was said, who said it, when was it said, was it said in anyone's presence; etc.
7. If the report was made anonymously, attempt to determine the nature of the reporters concern, the division involved, the person against whom the report is made, and any individuals who may have knowledge of relevant facts. In attempting to determine necessary facts, take care not to share the report with others.
8. With each interviewee, determine who else may have knowledge of relevant facts and whether the interviewee is aware of relevant documents, or other relevant information.
9. Keep a record of all steps taken and persons interviewed to obtain facts. Ultimately, in the case of an anonymous report, it may not be possible to obtain enough information to proceed with an investigation. The record you make will help explain why either a limited or no investigation was conducted.
10. XXX must consider the following 1ssues and ensure that it respects employee rights:

    a. Contractual rights.
    b. Protection of whistle-blowing activity (State and Federal laws).
    c. Employee rights of privacy.
    d. Employee rights under the Fair Credit Reporting Act.

11. Below are other important reminders for investigators and a chart of recommended effective interview. techniques when interviewing an individual in connection with an investigation:

DO:

- Ask for guidance, especially form XXX's General Counsel and other designated attorneys.
- Limit discussions about the matter to individuals who need to know.
- Remind all interviewees of the anti-retaliation policy and need for confidentiality.
- Document all interviews and phone conversations.
- Secure all files, reports and other documents.
- Keep XXX's Vice President and General Counsel (or its designated attorneys) updated on all important developments in the investigation.
- Use extreme care in controlling communications related to the investigation.

DON'T

- Leave investigation materials out in the open.
- Discuss disciplinary action with the source, the subject or anyone interviewed.
- Make speculative remarks in your work papers or Investigation Report.
- Allow anyone to tape record an interview.
- Allow anyone (except attorneys assigned to the matter) to make copies of interview notes.

Effective Interview Techniques for All Interviewees
• Draft a preliminary set of question to ask each interviewee; include relevant questions that result from a review of pertinent documents. • Be sure to discuss col1fidentiaility arid anti-retaliation at the outset of every interview. • Have an investigator and an assistant at each interview whenever possible. • Establish a good rapport at the outset of the interview (do not be argumentative, accusatory or rude). • Give a very general purpose for the interview, i.e. "I would like to talk to you about whether you may have heard anyone make inappropriate remarks or jokes" instead of "employee X said supervisor Y is sexually harassing her—have you witnessed that?" • Follow fact trails to the end—use follow-up questions. • Ask questions that will clarify vague or confusing answers. • Ask who, what, where, when, how and why questions. • Start with open-ended questions. • Do not put words in the interviewee's mouth. • Give the interviewee an opportunity to answer the question completely; do not interrupt. • Save tough or embarrassing questions for the end of the interview. • Ask the interviewee if he or she knows of any others with relevant information or can identify relevant documents. • Accurately record all information received from the interviewee. • Observe and record the physical/non-verbal reactions of the interviewee. • Try to avoid drawing conclusions about the interviewee or information received during the interview; doing so will increase your ability to gather all of the facts.

IV. The investigation Report

A. The General Counsel shall determine the form of the investigation report.

B. If a written report is to be made, the report should provide information that is needed to allow XXX decision-makers to resolve matters fairly and effectively. Information contained in the report potentially affects not only XXX and its reputation, but that of individual employees such as the subject of the investigation, witnesses and related individuals. Therefore, it is imperative that the Investigation Report be factual, complete, accurate and understandable so that the decision-making process is not flawed.

C. A well-written Investigation Report has the following characteristics:

1. It is Factual—States the facts, not opinions, suppositions or conclusions.
2. It is Complete—Provides all of the facts relating to the issue(s), even if some facts appear to be inconsistent.
3. It is Accurate—States facts without embellishment or slant. It does not leave out relevant information, no matter the source. An incomplete report cannot be accurate.
4. It is Objective, Fair and Impartial—It should not compromise facts with opinions and conclusions.
5. It is Concise—It contains relevant details and corroborative facts (same or related facts from different sources) are necessary. However, bearing in mind completeness and accuracy, irrelevant details and unnecessary repetition should be avoided.
6. It is Clear and Grammatically Correct—The aim is for simple words and short sentences. However, always apply the rules of spelling, grammar, punctuation and sentence structure.

D. The General Counsel should evaluate the Investigation Report and edit, proofread and revise the Investigation Report when necessary, and when doing so answer these questions:

1. Is the report factual?
2. Is the report complete?
3. Is the report accurate?

4. Is the report objective, fair and impartial?
5. Is the report concise?
6. Is the report clear and grammatically correct?

6.5.4 Internal Investigation Request (Exhibit A)

Corporate Compliance Officer Request for Authorization to Conduct an Internal Investigation

To: Corporate Compliance Committee

From: Corporate Compliance Officer

Re: Request for Authorization for Internal Investigation

XXX has received [outline the communication received e.g. Hotline report, subpoena in detail]

There may be civil litigation involving [describe in detail].

XXX or its officer could be subject to criminal prosecution under [statues].

Litigation could arise over enforcement of the subpoena, and the privileges which XXX or officials or employees may assert.

Corporate officers and employees possess much of the information.

6.5.5 Investigation Authorization Form (Exhibit B)

Investigation Authorization Form

To: General Counsel

From: Corporate Compliance Committee of the Board of Directors

Re: Request for Authorization for Internal Investigation

We have received your request dated [____] for authority to conduct an internal investigation.

You are authorized to conduct an investigation and to advise the Board of the potential civil and/or criminal liability of XXX and its officers and employees.

We request that all communications between your staff, corporate officers and employees and this office be kept in strict confidence (subject to our ultimate discretion). Your communications on this subject will not be disseminated outside our management group.

Please provide us with your legal advice.

6.5.6 Outside Counsel Retainer Letter (Exhibit C)

PRIVILEGED AND CONFIDENTIAL
COMMUNICATION FROM COUNSEL

[NAME]

[ADDRESS]

Re: [BRIEF DESCRIPTION OF MATTER]

Dear [NAME]:

I am general counsel to XXX, Inc. ("XXX"). XXX is in the process of conducting an internal, independent investigation in connection with [______________________________] (the "investigation"). The Investigation involves, among other things, allegations of [______________________________].

On behalf of XXX, I would like to retain you to provide outside legal services relating to the Investigation. As I have advised you, you may be requested to formulate legal theories, opinions and advice in connection with the Investigation. Additionally, the work that you perform will be important in my formation of legal theories, opinions and advice, and I will use your work product in providing legal advice, counsel and representation to XXX in the Investigation. I expect that you will be able to assist in collecting and analyzing facts in the Investigation as well.

The terms of the engagement (this "Agreement") are as follows:

1. You will act under and pursuant to the direction of the undersigned general counsel and will report, periodically as requested by the undersigned, on the progress of your investigation and provide, if requested, a final report of your investigation.

2. Although your specific responsibilities under this Agreement are still to be defined, I currently seek your assistance, fact-gathering, analysis and views with respect to [ ]. In addition, I may require your assistance and views relating to other issues in the Investigation.
3. You agree and understand that all work performed under this engagement is for the undersigned in my capacity as general legal counsel for XXX so that the undersigned may render legal advice to XXX in connection with the Investigation.
4. You are not engaged to represent the individual interests of XXX's shareholders, officers, directors or employees in connection with the Investigation. You are authorized to interview employees of XXX who might have knowledge of relevant facts, and you are given authority to anlyze all relevant documents and data. In this regard, it is understood that the undersigned, on behalf of XXX, will instruct employees of the Company and its attorneys to respond to our inquiry. You are authorized to engage outside accountants, consultants, investigators and other similar professionals, subject to prior approval by XXX and, in conjunction with such professionals, if any, conduct a legal evaluation, draw conclusions regarding actions taken, make legal recommendations and assist the undersigned in developing appropriate legal positions.
5. Unless otherwise specifically directed by the undersigned, you agree to abstain from preparing any reports, work papers or any other documents in connection with this engagement or the Investigation.
6. Any notes, memoranda, schedules, analyses, reports, work papers or other documents that you prepare in connection with this engagement or the Investigation will be and remain the property of XXX and/or the undersigned and will be considered attorney work product, to be used only for the Investigation and subsequent litigation, if any, and for no other purpose whatsoever. Under no circumstances will you disclose to anyone, without the undersigned's permission, this letter, the nature, content, or existence of any documents or other items prepared or reviewed in connection with this engagement, any oral or written communications relating to this engagement, or any information

gained or opinions reached in the course of this engagement. Furthermore, unless authorized by the undersigned, you will not disclose to anyone, other than XXX, even the fact that you have been retained in this matter.

7. To the extent permitted by law, it is intended and agreed that any communications made to you by the undersigned, XXX or any of its agents or employees in connection with the Investigation shall be privileged and that any such communications shall be made to facilitate communications between the undersigned and XXX in rendering privileged legal advice and services to XXX. Therefore, you shall not divulge to anyone any communication or any part thereof received from the undersigned XXX or any of its agents or employees in connection with the Investigation exvept with the prior written consent of the undersigned and/or XXX has raised all legal objections available in good faith opposition to such order and have exhausted all appellate rights with respect to such order.
8. Each and every note, memorandum, schedule, analysis, report, work paper or other document containing substantive information or data that you generate, in connection with the Investigation and/or at the specific request of the undersigned, shall include the following statements prominently displayed on the front page:

"PRIVILEGED AND CONFIDENTIAL DRAFT PREPARED AT THE REQUEST OF COUNSEL"

These statements shall not be included on documents that you are expressly instructed by the undersigned to prepare for submission in the Investigation, or when otherwise expressly instructed by the undersigned.

9. As part of your Agreement to provide services to the undersigned under this engagement, you will notify the undersigned of the following events:

   (a) A request by anyone to examine, inspect or copy the documents or records obtained by you during the course of our engagement; or

(b) Any attempt of service, or the actual service of a court order, subpoena, or summons upon you that requires the production of any such documents or records or testimony about any aspect of the engagement.

10. You have performed an internal search for any potential conflicts of interest based upon the names of the parties we have provided, including the parties to this Investigation, and the issues involved in this matter. You have not found any conflict of interest. Included in your conflict check was a check to determine that you have not served as an expert or consultant to [________________], or any affiliates or employees of these entities. You will avoid any conflicts of interest during the pendency of this engagement, including serving as an expert or consultant to [_____________] or any affiliates or employees of these entities. In addition, to avoid any conflict, during the pendency of this engagement you will not present any papers or reports at any seminar or similar activity, concerning [_________]
11. All documents furnished to you in the course of this engagement shall be returned upon the undersigned's request.
12. Your fees for services rendered pursuant to this Agreement are based upon the hours actually expended by you at your current hourly billing rates of [$ _____] per hour. In addition to your fees, your statements will include any expenses such as photocopying, travel, mileage, vendors, computer charges that you incur. Before you raise your hourly rates, you will seek and obtain approval from the undersigned.
13. You recognize that payment of your fees and expenses is the sole responsibility of XXX and not the responsibility of the undersigned.
14. Your fee is not contingent upon the final results of the Investigation and I understand that you do not warrant or predict results or final developments in this matter.
15. You or I may terminate this Agreement at any time upon written notice. Upon notice of termination, you will stop all work immediately.

16. The provisions of Paragraphs 3, 4, 6, 7, 9, 10, 16 and 17 of this Agreement shall survive indefinitely, even after this Agreement is otherwise terminated.
17. This Agreement will be governed by and construed in accordance with the laws of [_____], without regard to the principles of conflict of laws thereof, and the parties agree to the exclusive venue of the courts located in [___________] County, [___________], for all matters relating hereto. In any controversy relating hereto, the prevailing party shall be entitled to receive from the non-prevailing party the prevailing party's costs and expenses (including reasonable attorneys' fees) relating thereto.
18. The date first written above shall be the effective date of this Agreement. If this letter correctly states our arrangement, please sign the letter below, retain a copy for your records, and return the signed original to me. If you have any questions, please feel free to call me at [_____________].

Very truly yours,

____

[NAME], General Counsel
XXX
Agreed to and Accepted this _______
Day of __________, _________;
[NAME]
[TITLE]

6.5.7 Consultant Engagement Letter (Exhibit D)

PRIVILEGED AND CONFIDENTIAL
COMMUNICATION FROM COUNSEL

[NAME]

[ADDRESS]

Re: [BRIEF DESCRIPTION OF MATTER]

Dear [NAME]:

I am general counsel to XXX, Inc. ("XXX"). XXX is in the process of conducting an internal, independent investigation in connection with [____________________________] (the "investigation"). The Investigation involves, among other things, allegations of [____________________________].

On behalf of XXX, I would like to retain you to provide consulting services relating to the Investigation. As I have advised you, the work that you perform will be important in the formation of the legal theories, opinions and advice and I will use your work product in providing legal advice, counsel and representation to XXX in the Investigation. I expect that you will be able to assist in collecting and analyzing facts in the Investigation as well.

The terms of the engagement (this "Agreement") are as follows:

1. You will act under and pursuant to the direction of the undersigned general counsel and will report, periodically as requested by the undersigned, on the progress of your investigation and provide, if requested, a final report of your investigation.
2. Although your specific responsibilities under this Agreement are still to be defined, I currently seek your

assistance, fact-gathering, analysis and views with respect to [______________________________]. In addition, I may require your assistance and views relating to other issues in the Investigation.

3. You agree and understand that all work performed under this engagement is for the undersigned in my capacity as general legal counsel for XXX so that the undersigned may render legal advice to XXX in connection with the Investigation. You are not engaged to represent the individual interests of XXX's shareholders, officers, directors or employees in connection with the Investigation. You are authorized to interview employees of XXX who might have knowledge of relevant facts, and you are given authority to analyze all relevant documents and data. In this regard, it is understood that the undersigned, on behalf of XXX, will instruct employees of the Company and its attorneys to respond to our inquiry.
4. Unless otherwise specifically directed by the undersigned, you agree to abstain from preparing any reports, work papers or any other documents in connection with this engagement or the Investigation.
5. Any notes, memoranda, schedules, analyses, reports, work papers or other documents that you prepare in connection with this engagement or the Investigation will be and remain the property of XXX and/or the undersigned and will be considered attorney work product, to be used only for the Investigation and subsequent litigation, if any, and for no other purpose whatsoever. Under no circumstances will you disclose to anyone, without the undersigned's permission, this letter, the nature, content, or existence of any documents or other items prepared or reviewed in connection with this engagement, any oral or written communications relating to this engagement, or any information gained or opinions reached in the course of this engagement. Furthermore, unless authorized by the undersigned, you will not disclose to anyone, other than XXX, even the fact that you have been retained in this matter.
6. To the extent permitted by law, it is intended and agreed that any communications made to you by the undersigned, XXX or any of its agents or employees in connection with the Investigation

shall be privileged and that any such communications shall be made to facilitate communications between the undersigned and XXX in rendering privileged legal advice and services to XXX. Therefore, you shall not divulge to anyone any communication or any part thereof received from the undersigned XXX or any of its agents or employees in connection with the Investigation except with the prior written consent of the undersigned and/or XXX has raised all legal objections available in good faith opposition to such order and have exhausted all appellate rights with respect to such order.

7. Each and every note, memorandum, schedule, analysis, report, work paper or other document containing substantive information or data that you generate, in connection with the Investigation and/or at the specific request of the undersigned, shall include the following statements prominently displayed on the front page:

"PRIVILEGED AND CONFIDENTIAL DRAFT PREPARED AT THE REQUEST OF COUNSEL"

These statements shall not be included on documents that you are expressly instructed by the undersigned to prepare for submission in the Investigation, or when otherwise expressly instructed by the undersigned.

8. As part of your Agreement to provide services to the undersigned under this engagement, you will notify the undersigned of the following events:

   (a) A request by anyone to examine, inspect or copy the documents or records obtained by you during the course of our engagement; or
   (b) Any attempt of service, or the actual service of a court order, subpoena, or summons upon you that requires the production of any such documents or records or testimony about any aspect of the engagement.

9. You have performed an internal search for any potential conflicts of interest based upon the names of the parties we have

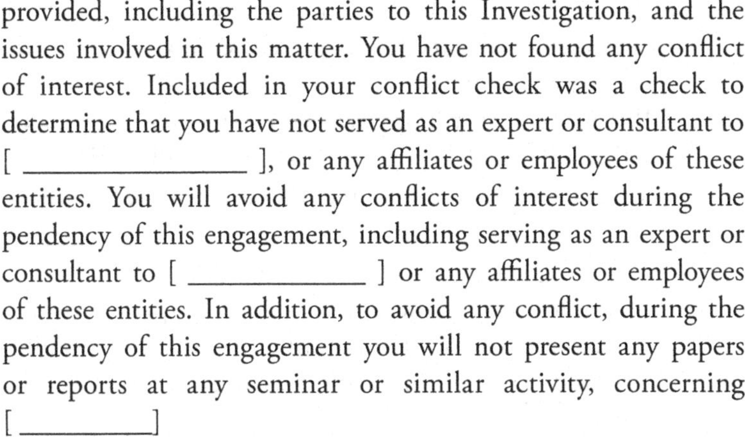

provided, including the parties to this Investigation, and the issues involved in this matter. You have not found any conflict of interest. Included in your conflict check was a check to determine that you have not served as an expert or consultant to [______________], or any affiliates or employees of these entities. You will avoid any conflicts of interest during the pendency of this engagement, including serving as an expert or consultant to [____________] or any affiliates or employees of these entities. In addition, to avoid any conflict, during the pendency of this engagement you will not present any papers or reports at any seminar or similar activity, concerning [________]

10. I understand that you alone will perform the work to be performed pursuant to this Agreement and that you will be prepared to testify as to your work and expert opinion if I decide to request you to act as an expert.
11. You will not subcontract for or use the services of any outside individual, firm, or other entity for any work under the engagement without the prior written approval of the undersigned.
12. All documents furnished to you in the course of this engagement shall be returned upon the undersigned's request.
13. Your fees for services rendered pursuant to this Agreement are based upon the hours actually expended by you at your current hourly billing rates of [$ _____] per hour. In addition to your fees, your statements will include any expenses such as photocopying, travel, mileage, vendors, computer charges that you incur. Before you raise your hourly rates, you will seek and obtain approval from the undersigned.
14. You recognize that payment of your fees and expenses is the sole responsibility of XXX and not the responsibility of the undersigned.
15. Your fee is not contingent upon the final results of the Investigation and I understand that you do not warrant or predict results or final developments in this matter.
16. You or I may terminate this Agreement at any time upon written notice. Upon notice of termination, you will stop all work immediately.

17. The provisions of Paragraphs 3, 5, 6, 8, 9, 17 and 18 of this Agreement shall survive indefinitely, even after this Agreement is otherwise terminated.
18. This Agreement will be governed by and construed in accordance with the laws of [_____], without regard to the principles of conflict of laws thereof, and the parties agree to the exclusive venue of the courts located in [___________] County, [___________], for all matters relating hereto. In any controversy relating hereto, the prevailing party shall be entitled to receive from the non-prevailing party the prevailing party's costs and expenses (including reasonable attorneys' fees) relating thereto.
19. The date first written above shall be the effective date of this Agreement. If this letter correctly states our arrangement, please sign the letter below, retain a copy for your records, and return the signed original to me. If you have any questions, please feel free to call me at [_____________].

Very truly yours,

____

[NAME], General Counsel
XXX
Agreed to and Accepted this _______
Day of __________, _________;
[NAME]
[TITLE]

6.5.8 Employee Investigation Letter (Exhibit E)

PRIVILEGED AND CONFIDENTIAL COMMUNICATION FROM COUNSEL

[NAME]

[ADDRESS]

Re: Conduct of an Internal Investigation

Dear [NAME]:

I am general counsel to XXX, Inc. ("XXX"). XXX is in the process of conducting an internal, independent investigation in connection with [________________________________] (the "investigation"). The Investigation involves, among other things, allegations of [________________________________].

This Investigation is being conducted at the direction of XXX compliance committee of its Board of Directors, under my supervision and control as legal counsel to XXX, and in contemplation of possible future litigation. Accordingly, some or all of the written materials and communications related to the Investigation may be protected from future disclosure to parties adverse to XXX by attorney-client privilege, the attorney work-product rules or both.

Communications between me and an agent XXX such as outside legal counsel or consultants, may be subject to attorney-client privilege. In order to avoid waiving the privilege, the privileged communication must not be disclosed to anyone other than the attorney and the client. In the case of a corporation like, this means that only the corporate agents responsible for seeking legal advice should be privy to our communications.

Second, communications between us, like this letter, should be segregated from other material that may not be privileged or whose attorney-client privilege may later be waived, like questionnaires that may be prepared at some time in the future and distributed to you.

Other material that is developed in the Investigation, because it is being done by me or under my supervision as XXX's lawyer, may enjoy limited protection as attorney's work product. Examples would be your notes of interviews. This information could be obtained later in litigation by order of a judge under certain circumstances.

In order to maintain these privileges, it would be helpful if you segregate any notes or other documents that you generate in the course of this Investigation in a separate file. Mark each document that was prepared specifically for my review "PRIVILEGED AND CONFIDENTIAL, PREPARED AT THE REQUEST OF COUNSEL." Keep communications to me separate from other material, such as your notes, that may enjoy only work product protection.

We should do our best to maintain all applicable privileges. However, it is best to assume that there is some possibility that anything that you write down will eventually fall into the hands of any eventual opponents. Therefore, it is important to make records only of matters that are necessary and pertinent. Please do not record your mental impressions, guesses, opinions, conclusions, and so on.

The goal of the Investigation is to conduct a fair, thorough, and expeditious investigation of [______________________], to determine whether there has been any misconduct or inappropriate conduct, and to determine any additional facts that may be relevant to a determination of what action is necessary or desirable with respect to the Investigation

Please understand that I represent XXX, as a corporate entity, and do not represent you individually. The interests of XXX and your interests may not be identical and my role is that of legal counsel to XXX. If you desire to retain your own legal counsel in connection with the investigation, XXX may consider reimbursing you for the costs of such legal counsel, upon consultation with me and approval of the compliance committee.

All information learned from you in the course of the Investigation, if privileged, is privileged to XXX and not to you individually. XXX alone may make the determination whether to provide such information to a third-party or the government. If you are requested to make such a disclosure, please contact me immediately and I will address the issue on behalf of XXX.

Please call me if you have any questions.

Very truly yours,

____

[NAME], General Counsel
XXX

ACKNOWLEDGEMENT:

I have read and understand the contents of the foregoing letter and agree to comply with the terms, conditions and recommendations contained in such letter.

Dated as of the _____ day of ______________, ______

[NAME]
[TITLE]

7. Records Retention

7.1 Information Retention

Information retention, or "records retention," as it is normally called, is one of the largest sources of potential legal risk (and related financial risk) that companies face. What records a company saves, destroys, or erases may determine the company's fate in litigation. Massive governmental fines have been levied against companies because of records that were improperly kept or that were uncovered in antitrust investigations, antidumping investigations, etc.

A business must consider the risk of keeping documents, especially electronic documents such as e-mail over an extended period of time. Obviously a business wants to protect valuable information as long as it has value. On the other hand, an organization has to be sensitive to the legal risks posed by saving records and documents past legal requirements of a particular situation.

In essence, we have a balancing act. How does a company balance the needs of business with legal requirements? The issue is not really a legal problem per so but a business problem with legal issues. The legal risk, however, of a nonexistent information retention program can be enormous, and, therefore, should be properly addressed in an LRM program.

How does a company handle retention of documents? What legal requirements exist, and how are they implemented? Strict mandatory standards exist in some countries.

In the United States, the law requires an information retention policy (IRP) that

- retains information at least as long as required by law,
- is applied consistently and systematically,
- allows quick retrieval, and
- can be suspended effectively, if required.

What are the risks of noncompliance?

- Huge fines and penalties
    - The act of losing documents that may be considered evidence in litigation or failing to preserve evidence once legal proceedings appear reasonably likely to occur may damage a company financially and/or its reputation. Note what happened to Arthur Andersen and Enron, etc.
- Huge cost of dealing with information in legal proceedings
- Huge expense of keeping too many documents, especially e-mail
- Not properly implemented

Many companies have an IRP, which, unfortunately, is never properly implemented or followed by employees. Thus, the IRP may at least be ineffective or, at worst, not recognized by courts as a legitimate IRP. This opens the door to fines, sanctions, and worse. Make certain if your company has an IRP that it is properly implemented and followed.

7.2 Risk Assessment: A Suggested Action

A company must ensure it has a viable business / legal oriented IRP in place. A risk assessment must be conducted to determine if one exists. Usually, when a company conducts a risk assessment it will find:

- No suspension procedure exists.
- There has been no auditing of documents.
- The retention policy, if it exists, is antiquated and not equated for the current electronic environment.
- E-mail is not handled correctly.
- The IRP has not been properly implemented or communicated.

- Employees not only are unaware of the IRP but are not following it.

7.3 E-mail

E-mail has become a very important concern when implementing an effective information retention policy (IRP). This is primarily due to e-discovery issues of litigation, which will be discussed in the next chapter. The main issue involving e-mail is how long e-mail should be maintained on a computer hard drive before it is deleted. E-mail issues may entail the following:

- No proper archiving of e-mail
- Not properly backed up if needed
- Not properly deleted (i.e., if not accidentally lost, it may be kept forever, resulting in huge costs to review and produce)

An example of e-discovery costs is as follows:

1. Preservation		
Preservation notices		$5,000
2. Collection		
Collection from data sources		$11,000
3. Staging		
Preprocessing		$2,000
Processing		$11,000
4. Review		
Contract attorney review		$50,000
Hosting		$10,000
5. Production		$15,000
	Total	$99,000

- Electronic discovery cost example

In line with the previous chart cost allocation, below is a typical example of costs directly associated with a review of electronic for discovery:

- This cost example is based upon a typical review of electronic content to provide a frame of reference.
- This example is for a review of content collected from twenty-five custodians with thirty gigabytes of data.
- The costs are mainly for the discovery review and production life cycle and exclude legal and consulting fees.

7.4 Action Plan

Once a company has conducted a risk assessment of its IRP, it should implement an action plan to address any risk posed by inadequacies of the IRP. At a minimum the following steps are recommended:

- Draft a comprehensive IRP that addresses all documents, including electronic documents.
- Clean up any old information. Records that are no longer required to be kept legally should be destroyed or deleted unless valid business reasons exist to keep them.
- Upper management should approve of the new IRP.
- Departmental retention coordinators should be appointed to drive the new IRP in each department.
- The new IRP must be rolled out to all employees. This may entail marketing the IRP to each department.
- There should be periodic reminders via e-mail, brochures, or posters reminding all employees of the IRP.
- There should be quarterly status meetings with all department coordinators.
- Annual audit: there should be an annual compliance audit to check on the IRP, especially e-mail.

7.5 Forms

Document Retention Policy

DOCUMENT RETENTION/DESTRUCTION POLICY AND GUIDELINES

CORPORATE POLICY

The XXXX Corporation policy is to protect and retain only those documents and information that have a lasting value to the company, or are required by law to be retained for a certain period of time.

This policy applies to company records and correspondence, on paper of film; information stored in computers or on tape or discs; personal correspondence and files relating to company business; and any other form of permanent recordkeeping.

Personal files of department personnel or company documents may not be maintained by any employee or other persona associated with the company, expect for duplicate working papers which are necessary to transact company business.

This policy and the attached record retention guidelines enable Philips Electronics North America Corporation to comply with legal requirements for record retention while balancing the interests of storage cost, manpower cost of maintaining or purging files and retaining valuable data.

LEGAL PROCEEDINGS AND INVESTIGATIONS

If litigation, a governmental investigation or an administrative proceeding is pending or reasonably anticipated, all existing documents and items reasonably related to the scope of the Iitigation, inquiry or proceeding must be retained. Any such related documents and items which would have been scheduled for document destruction pursuant to the attached record retention periods, must be deferred until destruction clearance is granted by a lawyer representing the company who has responsibility for that proceeding or investigation.

RESPONSIBILITY FOR CARRYING OUT THIS POLICY

Each employee having custody of any company records or information is responsible for protecting them during their retention period, and delivering them at the appropriate time for destruction to the person or organization designated with such responsibility.

The Chief Financial Officer of XXXX Corporation, operating through the financial officers of the various divisions and subsidiaries, and with advice from the Law, Tax and Intellectual Property Departments has responsibility for implementing and enforcing this policy. Compliance by staff and operating organizations will be monitored by the Corporate Audit department and reported to the Chief Financial Officer annually.

Each employee who retains personal files relating to company business is responsible for destroying them or transferring their contents to a regular company file if they should be retained, as soon as the matter to which they relate is completed, or the documents are no longer used regularly by the employee.

RETENTION OF DOCUMENTS

1. Duration

No retention period is forever. Wherever the word permanent' appeals in this Policy, the document retention period is so long that special provisions may be necessary to preserve the documents in question; and destruction requires specific approval by the Tax Counsel or General Counsel or their delegate. Only one copy should be kept as the "permanent" record.

Each department or division must designate a person to be responsible for the daily implementation of this policy. This person shall keep one master list for the business unit or department having any permanent retention documents, specifying their nature and storage location. At least once every 10 years each master list shall be reviewed by members of that business unit or department to determine if any of these documents can be destroyed due to changes in legal requirements or changes in organization status. When any organization is dissolved or merged, its master list shall be incorporated into the-master list of the next higher level or the successor organization. That organization shall ensure that the transferred records are properly described and store.

Certain documents should be kept as long as the company still owns or uses the property to which they relate, and for a certain number of years after the business or property is sold or operations are discontinued. These documents should also be recorded on the master list.

The retention periods for all other business documents and records are fixed pursuant to the attached Record Retention Guidelines,

In addition, a very limited number of documents and items will be retained permanently for the sole purpose of describing the company's history.

2. Manner of Storage

"Vital records," necessary for the continued operation or reconstruction of the business, must be kept safe from toss, and/or have a safely stored back-up. These and all other document and information can be retained in a number of ways: an original paper document, and paper copies: microfilm or microfiche; active computer dab storage; back-up tapes or discs, etc. They can be in active files, or they can be stored off-Ste in a record storage area. Generally, the manner of storage can be chosen according to departmental needs, but the document retention period, including all time in inactive or dead storage for records and backup copies, must follow this policy. However, all computer generated accounting records must be retained in machine sensible data format as well as hard copy (which is required) by agreement that Philips Electronic North America Corporation has entered into with the IRS.

The business unit or department should ensure that the master copy of any permanently retained document must be a good quality paper copy, or be stored on a medium which can be read" for accurate transfer of the information to some future format or medium when apparatus for reading the original becomes obsolescent.

Department or business unit procedures should specify the manner of identifying all things sent to dead storage and their destruction dates.

MULTIPLE COPIES

Only one copy should be defined as the primary copy, to be kept for the entire retention period as the company record, Usually this copy is the one bearing an original signature or maintained by the issuing department, Departments having other copies or backup copies must ensure that these are retained only so long as needed for current operations; this length of time can be shorter than the retention period stated in this policy.

DESTRUCTION OF DOCUMENTS

Documents to be destroyed should be shredded or simply thrown out, depending on the proprietary value of the information they contain. Each department or business unit, depending on its size and the volume of documents stored, should provide guidelines or departmental procedures relating to document destruction, purging of data bases and designate a person responsible for implementing destruction of document.

If the existence of any file or records is itself recorded in a long book, data base or the like, then destruction of the file or records must be noted in some fashion in the log book or data base.

RECORD RETENTION PERIODS:

GUIDELINES

RETENTION PERIODS

The following retention periods must be followed expect where the Chief Financial Officer of XXXX Corporation or the department or business unit lawyer has approved and alternative record retention period. Requirements for longer or special retention will vary from state to state and from industry to industry. Departments and business units should supplement this policy in the form of a more detailed retention/ destruction guide, which includes all necessary special requirements.

ACCOUNTING, PAYROLL, AND FINANCE

ACCOUNTING, PAYROLL, AND FINANCE

Accounts Payable		
Ledgers	10 years	*
Vouchers	5 years	*
Statements	1 year	*
Expenses accounts	4 years	*
Supporting data	4 years	*
Accounts Receivable		
Ledgers	10 years	*
Invoices	6 years	*
Debit and Credit Memorandums	6 years	*
Supporting data	4 years	*
Audit Reports		
Outside	5 years	*
Internal	4 years	*
Bank Statements & Cancelled Checks		
Budgets		
Forecasts	2 years	
Departmental summaries	4 years	
Expense analyses	4 years	

Record	Retention	
Supporting data (Not original documents)	1 year	
Capital Assets Costs	4 years after disposal	*
Cash Books	6 years	*
Letters of Credit	5 years	
Wire Transfers	5 years	
Credit		
Customer History	5 years	*
Resale Certificates	7 years	*
Other	3 years	*
Financial Statements	Permanent	
General Ledgers and Chart of Accounts	Permanent	
Inventory		
LIFO	4 years after closeout	*
Other	4 years	*
Journals		
General	Permanent	
Supporting schedules and tabulations	Permanent	
Supporting Data	6 years	
Notes (Payable or Receivable)	6 years after full payment	*
Payroll Records		
Expect as listed below	6 years	
Account Distribution	2 years	*
Garnishment and Attachments	3 years after satisfaction	
Worksheets	1 year	
Retirement and Pension		
Plans and Agreements	60 years	
Government Approvals	50 years	
Retired Employee Files	6 years after recipient's death	
Vested and deferred rights	60 years	
Rights not vested or deferred	15 years after separation	

Reports to trustee	5 years
Personal information on employees	
60 years or 6 years after employee death	
Savings, Investments, or Stock Plans	
Employee authorizations	Until separation
Payroll deduction reports	3 years
Reports to trustees	6 years
Unemployment Benefits 5 years	
Taxes	
Federal returns	50 years
State & Local	
Income of Franchise Returns	50 years
Sales or Use Returns	10 years
Blanket exemptions	10 years after inapplicable
Property Taxes	10 years
Audit or Appeals	10 years
Ruling	Until inapplicable
Correspondence with taxing authority	10 years
Working papers or detailed support	10 years

ADVERTISING, MARKETING AND SALES

Advertising & promotional documents	3 years
Artwork/mechanicals for printed copy	5 years after use ended
Brochures	10 years
Contracts	4 years after expiration
Customer agreements	4 years after expiration
Customer contest data	5 years
Customer correspondence	2 years
Market data & analysis	2 years
Market share reports	2 years

Performance—incentive bonus records	8 years
Price schedules	7 years
Pricing exception approvals	4 years
Product loading forms	Until product is discontinued
Sales records	10 years
Technical product history & marketing records	10 years

BUSINESS ACQUISITIONS AND SPIN-OFFS

Acquisition studies, no deal resulting	2 years
Acquisition	
Closing documents (bound volume)	Permanent
Contract Life of business plus	6 years
Correspondence	10 years
Spin-off studies, no deal resulting	2 years
Contract for sale of business	
Closing documents (bound volumes)	Permanent
Contract documents	6 years
Correspondence	3 years

CORRESPONDENCE and MEMOS (not otherwise specified)

Form letters not requiring follow-up	1 month
Memos and letters which require no acknowledgement	1 month or follow-up
General inquires and replies which are a cycle having no other than possible reference from the correspondent within a short period of time.	1 month
Requests for specific action and complaints, which have no further value after changes were made or action taken.	1 year
Letter denying our liability	6 years

Quotations where no contract results	2 years
Letters constituting all or part Life of contract plus of a contract, or important in clarifying points in a contract.	4 years
"Chron" files (copies of correspondence)	1 year

DISTRIBUTION AND PURCHASING

Bills of Lading	5 years
Contracts	6 years after expiration
Credit Memoranda	5 years

ETHICS

Confidential files closing of a case	3 years from the

HUMAN RESOURCES

Application, no hire resulting	2 years
INS Form I-9 (Eligibility verification)	3 years after separation
Personnel folder	7 years after separation
Attendance records	3 years
Clock records	3 years
Disability and sick benefits record	6 years
Earnings—SEE ACCOUNTING	
Employee medical & exposure records	30 years
Collective Bargaining (union) and employment agreements	6 years after expirations
Benefits plans (original)	60 years
Health & Safety bulletins	50 years
Injury frequency charts	50 years
Insurance records: group, employee	11 years
Accident reports, injury claims, settlements	30 years
Occupational injury & illness records	10 years
Worker's Compensation reports	10 years

INSURANCE

Policies	
Aircraft Product Liability	25 years
Automotive Liability	25 years
Comprehensive General Liability	Permanent
Environmental Impairment Liability	Permanent
Executive Liability	10 years
Fire, Business Interruption and related property	Permanent
Surety bonds	2 years after expiration
Worker's Compensation	50 years

INTELLECTUAL PROPERTY

Copyright	Useful life of work
Invention disclosures	20 years
Licenses negotiations (no license)	3 years after negotiation
Licenses	3 years after expiration
Patent application files	3 years after patent issues
Patent validity studies	Life of patent
Trademark	
Search, no application	2 years
Application	Life of trademark plus 5 years
Infringement accusations against us	5 years
Enforcement against others (no lawsuit)	
Major marks	Life of trademark
Minor marks	5 years

LAW

Abandoned Property/Escheat Reports	Permanent
Agreements and other Legal Instruments and Documents (original)	25 years after expiration or end of subject matter

Applications Filed with Regulatory Agencies	Permanent
Articles of Incorporation and Amendments	Permanent
Bank Account Files (inactive)	4 years
Claims/Litigation (including pleadings, discovery attorney work-products, transcripts, exhibits, etc.)	6 years after action terminated
Claims/Litigation Final Judgments/ Settlement	Permanent
Compliance Orders—Agencies/Court	3 years after activity ceases
Compliance Permits—Federal/State Leases	10 years after activity ceases
Corporate By-laws	Permanent
Corporate Policies and Directives (copies)	Until superseded or obsolete
Corporate Policies and Directives (originals)	Life of entity
Corporation Qualification (foreign) plus 10 years	Life of legal activity
Corporate Seals (predecessor companies)	1 year after dissolution
Corporate Secretary Records (predecessor companies)	25 years
Delegation of Authority Records	Life of legal entry
Dividend Checks (unclaimed)	10 years
Financing Agreements, Loans Documents, Promissory Notes, Mortgages and Other Documents evidencing company debt.	Permanent
Government Regulatory Agency Investigations	20 years
Legal Projects (including determining legal requirements and providing legal advice within company)	10 years after activity ceases
Legal Projects—Legal Opinion/Briefs	Permanent
License and Property Rights Agreements—other than PC Software License	Permanent

Listing Applications and Agreements and	1 year after listing is removed Support Papers or cancelled
Management Survey and Reports	10 years
Minutes of Board of Directors Meeting (including Committee Meetings).	Permanent
Minutes of Shareholder Meetings	Permanent
Miscellaneous Shareholder Correspondence	3 years
Opinions of Counsel	Permanent
Outside Counsel bills—maintained within department	2 years
Performance Appraisals—maintained within department	3 years
Permits and Registrations	10 years after expiration
Product Warranty and Product Integrity Related Cases (other than litigation)	5 years after claim has been resolved or settled or closed
Proxy and Proxy Statements (historical files)	Life of legal entity
Reception Desk (sign-in log)	2 years
Records Destruction Notices (originals)	Life of legal entity
Records Retention Schedules	Life of legal entity
Records Storage Requests	2 years after records have been destroyed
Routine SEC Reports (10-K, 10-Q, 8-K, etc.)	Permanent
Security and Exchange Commission Filings and Support Papers	25 years
Shareholders' Share Ledger Accounts (closed)	50 years after closing
Stock Certificates—cancelled	Permanent
Stock Transfer Sheets	50 years

PERSONAL NOTES AND DRAFTS

Time periods given are the maximum. Shorter retention is desirable.

Bound diaries and calendars	3 years
Meeting notes	1 month

Miscellaneous plans and notes	3 months
Negotiation notes	1 month after negotiation ended
Speeches	1 year

PUBLIC RELATIONS

Press releases—minor matters	1 year
Press releases—major or stock impact	5 years

8. IT Issues

8.1 Computer Hardware, Software, E-mail and Internet Policy

COMPUTER HARDWARE AND SOFTWARE, E-MAIL, INSTANT MESSENGER, VOICE-MAIL, AND INTERNET POLICY

PURPOSE:

To outline the expectations and proper use of the Company's computer systems, electronic mail (e-mail), voice-mail, internet services and other electronic communication tools and information stored therein. This policy is intended to promote responsible and appropriate use of the Company's computing resources. It addresses issues of privacy, etiquette, permissible and prohibited uses, as well as the Company's disclosure rights.

POLICY:

The Company is committed to providing an environment that encourages the use of computers and electronic information. The Company maintains communication and information technology systems including, but not limited to, e-mail, voice-mail and internet systems utilized to conduct Company business. It is the responsibility of each employee to ensure that this technology is used for proper business purposes and in a manner that does not compromise the confidentiality of proprietary or other sensitive information. The Company permits limited personal use of its computing resources for non-commercial purposes, only if such use does not (i) violate the law (ii) violate the Company policy; or (iii) interfere with the Company's goals, objectives, day-to-day activities, employee job performance, or other employee activities. The Company reserves the right to review such use and inspect all materials on, stored in, or sent over its computer systems. This policy covers all uses of the Company's electronic and telephonic communication tools and all information transmitted by, received from or stored in these systems. Violations of this Policy may subject the employee to disciplinary measures, up to and including dismissal.

CONTENTS:

These policies and procedures consist of four parts:

- Computer Hardware and Software
- E-mail
- Voice-mail, Instant Messenger
- Internet Access

1. COMPUTER HARDWARE AND SOFTWARE:

Ownership

All computer system networks, computer equipment, electronic and telephonic communications systems, and all communications and stored information transmitted by, received from, or contained in the Company's information systems are, and remain at all times, the property of the Company. All voicemail messages created, sent and received are and remain the property of the Company.

Avoiding Viruses, Software Conflicts, and License Violations

To limit exposure to computer viruses, avoid software conflicts and software license violations, and to properly manage our Information Systems, only software approved by the Company may be installed on computing devices. Employees are not authorized to download any software on to their computer or any drives. Unauthorized software installed onto any of the Company's computers will be immediately removed. Unauthorized software includes, but is not limited to, personal programs such as screen savers, games, etc.

Acquisitions

All hardware and software acquisitions or purchases must be approved in writing by the Company. This includes specialized software for specific practice groups or projects.

Intellectual Property

As a general rule, employees may not copy, use, or transfer materials from others without proper authorization except in certain very limited or "fair use" circumstances. An employee who desires to reproduce or store the contents of a screen or website should contact the Legal Department for advice on whether the intended use is permissible.

Confidential Information

Confidential information shall not be disclosed to unauthorized persons without prior authorization.

Encryption

Only approved encryption tools approved by the Company may be used in connection with the Company's information system.

Troubleshooting

Computer software or hardware problems and questions should only be directed to the Company's IT help desk at _________.

Virus Alert

Unvalidated virus alerts should not be forwarded to other system users. Virus alerts may only be disseminated by the Company. Dissemination of non-verified information by others, regardless of intention, is counter-productive and an unnecessary strain on network resources. Instead, please forward the virus alerts as directed by the Company.

Passwords

While email and voicemail may accommodate the use of passwords for security, the reliability of passwords for maintaining confidentiality cannot be guaranteed. You must assume that someone, other than the intended or designated recipient, may read or hear any and all messages. Moreover, all passwords must be made known to the Company so that the system may be accessed by the company when you are absent. Passwords not known to the company may not be used. Passwords should be guarded and not visibly displayed at the employee's workstation or office.

Access

Employees may access only messages and files or programs that they have permission to enter (whether computerized or not). Unauthorized review, duplication, dissemination, removal, damage, or alteration of files, passwords, computer systems or programs, voice-mail messages, or other property of the company, or improper use of information obtained by unauthorized means, or attempts to engage in any such prohibited conduct, may be grounds for disciplinary action, up to and including termination.

The Company will have access to its computer and electronic equipment, including voice-mail, e-mail and internet accounts.

2. <u>E-MAIL</u>

No Expectation of Privacy

The Company's computer and information systems and the data stored on them are and remain, at all times, the property of the company. As such, all information, data, or messages created, stored, sent, or retrieved over the Internet or the company's electronicmail system are the property of the Company. Employees and others should have no expectation that any information transmitted over or stored in the Company's information system is or will remain private. The Company's information systems are accessible at all times by the Company for business and legal purposes. Employees have no right to privacy regarding information, file transmission or storage through the Company's computer systems, voice-mail, e-mail, or other technical resources. The Company reserves the right to retrieve and read any message or file. Employees should be aware that, even when a message is erased or a visit to a Web site is closed; it is still possible to re-create the message or locate the Web site. Accordingly, internet and e-mail messages are considered public communications, not private. Moreover, all communications including text and images may be disclosed to law enforcement or other third parties without prior consent of the sender or the receiver.

E-mail users are advised that the Company may use automated software to perform such monitoring. Nothing that is transmitted via e-mail is confidential or private despite any such designation either by the sender or the recipient.

Certain Messages Prohibited

Employees are strictly prohibited from using the Company's computer and information systems to access, send, save, or print e-mail messages, or other information that (i) may be viewed as inappropriate or offensive to a reasonable person, including but not limited to messages containing obscene, vulgar, or "off color" language, messages that may be discriminatory or harassing to other employees, including racial or sexual harassment, messages that may hold persons up to ridicule or disparagement, false statements or name-calling; (ii) in any manner violates any laws or regulations; or (iii) in any manner that violates any Company policy. Violators will be subject to discipline up to and including discharge.

Limited Distribution

E-mail messages should be distributed only to those individuals who have a business need to receive them.

Limited Access

Each employee has been issued a password to access e-mail. Your password is personal and should not be shared with other employees or third parties. Employees are prohibited from providing e-mail access to an unauthorized user or access another user's e-mail mailbox without prior authorization from the Company IT department.

Be Careful What You Say

Although e-mail may give the appearance of being informal, impersonal and private, it is none of these things. All e-mail messages must be drafted with the same care as a formal memorandum and must not contain any information that might violate the law or otherwise be potentially be harmful or embarrassing to the Company.

Currently only "Microsoft Outlook" and ________ Electronics' "mySingle" e-mail software are permissible.

Proper Usage and Etiquette

- The best communication strategy to utilize in your work area or division is to speak directly with fellow employees instead of using e-mail. Work relationships may flourish using this approach.
- If there is a matter that requires urgent attention, a telephone call or personal visit is the best approach. Assuming that a co-worker is available and checking e-mails at all times is inappropriate behavior on the sender's part.
- Write concise, specific e-mails. Clearly state the facts or your request.
- E-mail only those that are directly involved in the situation and avoid copying others unnecessarily (reduces productivity for all).
- For matters involving a decision or response from key stakeholders, it may be more appropriate to arrange a meeting.
- Transferring ownership of an issue or a project to another without confirmation is inappropriate. The responsibility resides with the sender until a written or verbal confirmation from the receiving party occurs.
- Do not copy customers when resolving internal work matters with co-workers.

3. <u>VOICE-MAIL, INSTANT MESSENGER</u>

The same policies and procedures that apply to e-mail also apply to voice-mail and instant messenger.

4. <u>INTERNET ACCESS</u>

Application of Internal E-mail Policies and Procedures to Internet Connections

The Company's policies and procedures concerning internal e-mail also apply to internet connections, including, but not limited to, e-mail sent over the internet and accessing web sites via the internet.

Unauthorized Use

Any unauthorized use of the internet is strictly prohibited. Unauthorized use includes, but is not limited to: violating or attempting to violate any applicable laws or intellectual property rights; connecting, posting, or downloading and e-mailing pornographic material; engaging in computer "hacking" and other related activities; attempting to disable or compromise the security of information contained on the Company's computers.

Confidentiality

Internet messages should be treated as non-confidential. Anything sent through the internet passes through a number of different computer systems, all with different levels of security. The confidentiality of messages may be compromised at any point along the way, unless the messages are encrypted.

Under no circumstances shall information of a confidential, sensitive or otherwise proprietary nature be placed on the internet. Postings placed on the internet may display _________'s logo and address, so make certain before posting information on the internet that the information reflects the standards and policies of the Company.

Downloading from the Internet

Viruses. Downloading programs or other content may introduce viruses into the Company's network. To prevent viruses from being transmitted through the Company's information systems, employees are not authorized to download any software onto their computer or any drive in the Company's information system. If you want to download a program, you must first contact the Company for approval.

Copyrighted Materials. Many of the materials available on the internet, such as articles and software, are protected by copyright. Do not be misled by the ease with which you can acquire or download these materials—you may only have a limited license to view. You are not authorized to download software or any executable files (e.g., games, applications).

Unauthorized Connections

Users may not establish internet or other external network connections that could allow unauthorized persons to gain access to __________'s systems and information without prior approval from the Company. Users may not subscribe to a discussion group, e-mailing list or news service without prior approval from the Company. This is primarily to ensure that the Company's hardware and software can cope with the often voluminous amounts of information which are sent on a daily basis. Employees are responsible and accountable for compliance with the policies and procedures herein. Violations of any guidelines listed above may result in disciplinary action up to and including termination. In addition, the company may advise appropriate legal officials of any legal violations.

8.2 E-discovery Action Plan

A. Form Task Force ("E-discovery Preparedness and Response Team") to assess current status of the Group's efforts to address E-discovery issues;

1. Assemble the task force with representatives from:

    a. Subsidiary and division legal teams, Patent Counsel, if applicable and parent organization
    b. E-Discovery Counsel

2. Arrange Task Force Meeting

    a. Review new Rules and recent case law;

b. Review status of group company's past, present and likely future litigation;
c. Select in-house counsel a-discovery coordinators from each company;

   i) Review each company's:

      1) IT systems
      2) Network topology and content maps.
      3) General characteristics of the data.
      4) Applicable policy retention protocols, and the actual current practices.
      5) Focus on data storage and destruction systems and practices.

   ii) Perform inventory of each company's ESI and paper records:
   iii) Identify types of ESI
   iv) Identify all apparently obsolete, unneeded records, which are for reasons unknown still being preserved;
   v) Identify locations of all data repositories, including distributed data;
   vi) Identify all custodians of the ESI, including records and IT managers, and data user/creators;
   vii) Prepare Computer systems & ESI location map;
   viii) Prepare outline on computer systems, data and procedures;
   ix) Consider current IT architecture and systems to facilitate ESI retrieval and litigation holds;
   x) Review & Rewrite Records Management Policy Manual;
   xi) Consider establishing and training a Data Compliance Officer;
   xii) Consider and Implement Automated Procedures;
   xiii) Create and implement an employee training program for document creation and retention;
   xiv) Select at least two technical IT a-discovery coordinators from each company;

1) 30 (b) ()witness on IT a-discovery
2) Other witnesses if needed

xv) Prepare a Project Budget;
(company specific & task specific)

xvi) Identify and retain outside experts and e-discovery vendors;

1) Determine what outside services, if any, may be required immediately, or in the foreseeable future;
2) Review experts previously used by the company;
3) Consider additional or replacement vendors that can assist in the preparation activities and response to litigation;
4) Request, negotiate and conclude written agreements;
5) Integrate experts and vendors into various tasks of the Team.

xvii) Prepare and assist in the implementation of customized E-discovery litigation response plan and procedures to identify, preserve, collect, process, review, analyze and product ESI; to defend the ESI productions; and prepare and prosecute counter E-discovery requests.

3. Role of National e-Counsel

i) National e-Counsel attorney files appearance with local counsel in proceedings to handle all technical e-discovery issues only as further specified herein;
ii) National e-Counsel is responsible for all internal communications with the company's IT department and E-discovery Team and thus assumes the Zubulake imposed responsibilities;

1) Local counsel is thus relieved of the court imposed duty to speak directly with IT,

and understand the complexities of the ESI technologies.

iii) National e-Counsel conducts and supervises the Team's Identification, Preservation and Collection stages of the Company's E-discovery response;
iv) Local counsel conducts and supervises the subsequent Review and Production stages of the response to E-discovery, and all other aspects of the case, including trial;
v) Conduct audits at the end of cases to consider revisions to plan and learn from all mistakes made.

9. Crisis Management

Any discussion of LRM would not be complete without a brief discussion of crisis management. Crisis risk management (CRM) itself would be a topic for a book. Nonetheless, it is a fitting topic to discuss. Without effective management of a corporate crisis, a company's future would be in doubt. Any LRM program should consider the development of a crisis management strategy and the implementation of crisis risk management within the organization.

9.1 Crisis Defined

What is a crisis? A crisis can be considered to be a major unpredictable or catastrophic event that has potentially negative results. A crisis, in other words, is a major unpredictable event that may significantly damage or impact a company or organization by harming its brand, reputation, or public image. The problem with a "crisis" is that not only can't it always be forecast or predicted, a crisis can and will affect stakeholders, which can determine the fate of the company.

The past decade can be considered the decade of the "mega crisis." Many people have been affected (some have died) because of the "mega-crises" that have happened. Examples include:

- Coke and Pepsi were implicated in tainted products in India.
- Enron, Worldcom, and Tyco were accused of financial scandals.

- The World Trade Center towers in New York were destroyed.
- The financial and housing collapse and major recession of 2008.
- Toyota implicated in recalls because of brake issues.
- Major tsunami affecting Thailand and Indonesia, resulting in deaths of approximately 250,000 people.
- The Fukushima Daiichi nuclear disaster

There are numerous kinds of crises that a company should be prepared to handle, especially in an international context. Among them are financial crises, natural disasters, product failures, workplace violence, cyber-attack, or hacking, and, of course, terrorism.

It is undisputable that a major crisis can pose serious threats to a company, and, therefore, the crisis must be managed. Crises can result in (a) government fines, (b) loss of retailer confidence, (c) loss of investor confidence, (d) loss of employee confidence, and (e) massive litigation, including class actions.[5] In other words, the end of the company!

The problem facing any risk manager or general counsel is that the media in today's society has become very anti-business. As this anti-business culture of attack has gotten worse over the last twenty years, a crisis can no longer be handled by a simple PR or marketing statement. A full-fledged crisis management operation must be put in place. Damage control is now a very serious matter for any potential crisis, no matter how small.

It has been said that a company has twenty-four hours to put a strategy into place to handle a crisis. Some now say that because of the Internet, a company only has a few hours to address the situation. The impact of a company's strategy or lack thereof will probably be felt in ten to twenty days—or even less. Companies without an adequate strategy have failed to recover from the crisis. So what should a crisis management strategy consist of?

---

5 Robert W. Littleton and Thomas R. Cherry, *"International Crisis Management," International Corporate Practice*, Carle Basri, editor, New York: PLI 2011, 8-3.

9.2 Crisis Management Strategy

Companies that successfully manage crises have used four or five basic steps to prepare for a crisis to the extent possible. They include the following steps:

- Identify areas of vulnerability of the company.
- Develop a plan for dealing with potential threats.
- Form a crisis management team to handle threats.
- Simulate crisis scenarios of potential threats.
- Learn from experience of managing the crisis.

Other companies have used a variety of steps to handle crises, including:

- Avoiding the crisis
- Preparing for the crisis
- Properly reacting as soon as the crisis exists, and
- Resolving the crisis

To help put everything into context, a company should realize that crises, including international crises, occur in stages. The crisis management strategy should be prepared to deal with the stages as they unfold. Each stage requires certain responses from the company, and each stage has a certain impact upon a company.[6] Typically, however, a company does not have a crisis management strategy in place, especially one that can handle the various stages of a crisis. Many times a company is caught sleeping without a strategy and fails to adequately manage or resolve the crisis, which may severely impact the company. Usually, a poorly managed crisis follows a similar pattern:

- Early indications of a crisis brewing—perhaps reports from the Service Department indicating product failure.
- Warnings of the upcoming crisis are ignored by company management.
- The crisis explodes, overwhelming management.

---

6 Ibid, 8:4.

- Management tries to resolve the crisis quickly without success.
- The company fails to provide adequate information or take adequate measures to handle the crisis.
- The company suffers the consequences of an outraged media, public, and even stakeholders.
- The company's existence is threatened or put into jeopardy as its stock plummets.

9.3 International Crisis

In today's world, many companies do business internationally. Because of international considerations, an international crisis is harder to manage than a domestic crisis. As it is more complex, companies caught up in an international crisis have to pay more attention to international, cultural, and communication issues than they would in a purely domestic scenario. Cross-border crisis management has become very important. Therefore, an international crisis requires a number of steps, including:

- Planning for an international crisis
- Appointing a crisis manager
- Establishment of a crisis management team
- Knowledge of foreign situation as impact
- Communications
- Cross-border management of the crisis

The principle focus of any crisis management strategy, especially in an international contest, is communications. All crisis management plans call for effective crisis communications, which many times are not always executed. Inadequate or failed communications lead to bad publicity, unhappy stakeholders, and potential disaster. An effective crisis communication strategy is necessary for any international crisis.

A number of processes are need to implement an effective crisis communication strategy to manage an international crisis, including:

- Creation of the crisis communication team.
- Identify key spokespersons who will speak for the organization. Who are they? What are their roles?
- Training cultural issues, if the crisis involves other cultures.

- Establishment of communication procedures and protocols. Who communicates to whom and why?
- Identify key messages to communicate to key stakeholders and groups.
- Decide on communication methods to be used. Do they involve the Internet, TV, radio, etc? May be decided by the geographic location of the crisis.
- Be ready to handle the crisis.

9.4 Communication Components of a Crisis Management Plan

As stated above, communications is important. Therefore, a communications plan must take into consideration proper communication to numerous entities, including:

- The media
- Employees
- Crisis Management Team
- Government
- Websites
- The public
- The stakeholders (internal and external)

9.5 Considerations

When establishing a crisis management strategy, a number of questions must be asked.

- How many disputes or potential disputes are involved?
- How many participants are involved?
- How many stakeholders are involved?
- How is the best way to communicate effectively to the media and stakeholders?
- Who should the spokesperson be?
- Should there be more than one spokesperson?
- What are the facts surrounding the crisis?
- How many cultures are involved?

A company that has an effective crisis management strategy in place will be able to handle a crisis when it happens. Those companies who are not ready to handle crises or who fail to handle them properly not only will fail to prosper but may also fail.

9.6 Checklists

1. Has the Crisis Management Committee been formed? Who is on it?
2. Is there a Crisis Manager? What are his or her duties?
3. Has a crisis management strategy?
4. What are the communication protocols in place?
5. Who will be the spokesperson for the company?
6. Has a budget been approved for the crisis?
7. Have the facts surrounding the crisis been established?
8. How will the company use social media?
9. Has a war room been created for the crisis?
10. If a government recall is necessary, who will handle it?
11. What are corporate policies for handling recalls?
12. Will an outside crisis management expert be used?
13. Who will handle internal communications?

10. Corporate Structure Issues

10.1 Corporate Governance Considerations

10.1.1 Corporate Governance Issues

A. Corporate Form

1. Corporation, partnership
2. Tax considerations

B. Jurisdiction of Formation

1. Shareholders' rights
2. Dividends
3. Corporate actions

C. Corporate Management

1. Directors and Officers

    a. Appointment and removal
    b. Standards of conduct
    c. Limiting liability
    d. Committees

2. Formation documents, articles of incorporation, articles of organization
3. Corporate management oversight and control

    a. Articles of incorporation
    b. Bylaws
    c. Operating Agreement

10.2 Corporate Organization and General Compliance Issues

10.2.1 Corporate Organization Issues

A. Operations in U.S. or elsewhere

1. State or Jurisdiction of Incorporation

    a. List of states or countries where entities are incorporated
    b. Formation
    c. Dissolution

        i. Voluntary dissolution
        ii. Involuntary dissolution
        iii. Judicial dissolution

2. Foreign Corporation

    a. "Doing business"
    b. Qualification

        i. Access to courts
        ii. Monetary penalty or fine
        iii. Taxation and reporting requirements

    c. Registered agent

        i. Most states in U.S. require
        ii. Receive service of process

iii. Failure to have registered agent can result in revocation of authority to transact business

d. Fees, reporting, service of process
e. Cessation of business in a state

i. Withdrawal, clearance from state finance, labor departments, payment of all taxes and fees, filing of all reports
ii. Revocation of authority to transact business
iii. Failure to withdraw-accrual of tax and fees

3. Tax and Reporting requirements

a. Corporate taxes

i. Federal income tax
ii. Franchise tax, excise tax
iii. State corporate income tax
iv. Property tax

a) Real property
b) Tangible personal property
c) Intangible personal property
d) Sales and use tax

b. Annual corporate report

10.3 Intercompany Activities

A. Employee Benefits

1. Subsidiaries and "Control Group", service providers, fiduciary responsibilities

B. Intellectual property

1. Creation and ownership of IP, royalties, licensing

2. Technology transfer
3. Coordination and management of disputes

C. Inter-company transactions

1. Service Agreements

    a. Advertising and marketing
    b. IT related services
    c. Manufacturing
    d. HR
    e. Legal

2. Distribution Arrangements
3. Import/Export
4. Financial

    a. Loans
    b. Royalty payments
    c. Sales of accounts receivables

5. Regulatory
6. Insurance
7. Immigration
8. Litigation

11. Outside Legal Fees & Tools for Reducing

A company, wherever situated, will eventually be subject to litigation, government investigations, fines, employee actions, etc. To properly defend itself will require the use of law firms, especially in the United States. However, as explained in the preceding chapter, legal fees and costs can be excessive. The financial well-being of a company may depend upon how well it is able to manage outside legal fees and costs.

As part of an overall LRM program, a company's Law Department must implement processes to control, reduce, and manage outside legal fees and costs. By utilizing legal risk management tools, a Law Department or Risk Management Department can proactively reduce legal fees and costs.

11.1 Tools for Reducing Legal Fees

- Processes that can measure the performance of outside counsel
- Processes that track legal costs and expenses
- Use of KPIs that measure the Law Departments metrics
- Creation of a contract management system, which standardizes contracts and forms
- Negotiation of legal fee agreements with outside counsel
- Use of outside billing guidelines, which prevent excessive billing by law firms

11.1.1 *KPIs*

Key performance indexes (KPIs) are an effective way to measure a Law Department's metrics as well as use and effectiveness of outside counsel. I recommend a corporate Law Department to establish at least ten to twenty KPI metrics to get a good picture of the effectiveness of not only the Law Department but outside counsel. This can be reflected in the dashboard on your computer monitor. Typical examples would be:

- Law Department's total expense
- Law Department's total expense as a percentage of revenue
- Number of active litigation matters
- Number of new litigation matters
- Number of closed litigation matters
- Law Department's fees for outside counsel
- Total external spending on litigation matter
- Cycle time to resolve claims
- Estimated dollar savings through use of legal risk management tools
- Percentage of legal matters that receive a management—specific post-mortem review

There are other KPIs to use, but the above metrics can be used to help quantify the number of litigation matters, average time to resolve matters, total legal costs, and savings through LRM processes. The more processes put in place to measure performance from a risk management point of view the better. KPIs not only measure the effectiveness and efficiency of a law department but can be used as a tool to improve the effectiveness of the Law Department.

11.2 Forms

11.2.1 KPI's

Sample Summary of XXX Law Dept. Top 15 KPIs

General law Department Metrics for XXX

1. Law department's total expense

2. Law department's total expenses as percentage of total revenue
3. Expense of temporary staffing (for internal positions) Litigation Matters
4. Number of active litigation matters
5. Number of new litigation matters
6. Number of closed litigation matters
7. Average cycle time to resolve matters Non-Litigation Matters
8. Number of active non-litigation matters
9. Number of new non-litigation matters
10. Number of closed non-litigation matters External Legal Spending
11. Law department's total fees for outside counsel
12. Law department's total fees for outside legal vendors and suppliers (excluding law firms)
13. Law department's total fees for legal research
14. Total external spending on litigation matters
15. Total external spending on non-litigation matters (other than intellectual property)

1. Law department's total expense

< $1,000,000
$ 1,000,001 to $ 10,000,000
$ 10,000,001 to $ 20,000,000

<u>Purpose for this KPI</u>

- KPI Metric Category: General Law Department Metrics
- Measure Description: Measure of law department's total expenses, including outside legal spending and excluding settlements, awards and overhead
- Type of Performance Measure: Cost
- Suggested Use/Purpose: This KPI records total spending of Law department over a period of time.

2. Law department's total expenses as percentage of total revenue

0 to 0.25 percent
0.26 to 0.50 percent

0.51 to 0.75 percent
0. 76 to 1 percent

<u>Purpose for this KPI</u>

- KPI Metric Category: General Law Department Metrics
- Measure Description: Measure of law department's total expenses, including outside legal spending and excluding settlements, awards and overhead
- Type of Performance Measure: Cost
- Suggested Use/Purpose: This KPI records total spending of Law department over a penod of time.

3. Expense of temporary staffing (for internal positions) Litigation Matters

< $250,000
$ 250,001 to $ 500,000
$ 500,001 to $ 750,000
$ 750,001 to $ 1,000,000

<u>Purpose for this KPI</u>

- KPI Metric Category: General Law Department Metrics
- Measure Description: Measures amount spent on temporary staffing to handle overflow work
- Type of Performance Measure: Cost
- Suggested Use/Purpose: This KPI helps law departments determine how to budget for additional staff positions on a temporary or permanent basis.

4. Number of active litigation matters

< 500
500 to 2,500
2,501 to 5,000

Purpose for this KPI

- KPI Metric Category: Litigation Matters
- Measure Description: Measures active litigation case load
- Type of Performance Measure: Process efficiency
- Suggested Use/Purpose: This KPI helps law departments track the number of active litigation matters to assist with staffing, budgeting and other operational planning.

5. Number of new litigation matters

< 100
101 to 500
501 to 1,000

Purpose for this KPI

- KPI Metric Category: Litigation Matters
- Measure Description: Measures number of new litigation matters each year (provide numbers for the year preceding the date of the OLSI Survey)
- Type of Performance Measure: Process Efficiency
- Suggested Use/Purpose: This KPI helps law departments track the number of new litigation matters to assist with staffing, budgeting and other operational planning.

6. Number of closed litigation matters

< 100
101 to 500
501 to 1,000

Purpose for this KPI

- KPI Metric Category: Litigation Matters
- Measure Description: Measures number of closed litigation matters each year
- Type of Performance Measure: Process Efficiency

- Suggested Use/Purpose: This KPI helps law departments track the number of closed litigation matters to assist with staffing, budgeting and other operational planning.

7. Average cycle time to resolve matters Non-Litigation Matters

< 6 months
6 months to 12 months
12 months to 18 months

Purpose for this KPI

- KPI Metric Category: Litigation Matters
- Measure Description: Measures the average amount of time to resolve active litigation matters for matters closed in a particular year
- Type of Performance Measure: Cycle Time
- Suggested Use/Purpose: This KPI helps law departments track how quickly they resolve active litigation matters to assist with staffing, budgeting and other operational planning.

8. Number of active non-litigation matters

<50
551 to 600
601 to 650

Purpose for this KPI

- KPI Metric Category: Non-Litigation Matters
- Measure Description: Measures active non-litigation case load
- Type of Performance Measure: Process efficiency
- Suggested Use/Purpose: This KPI helps law departments track the number of active non-litigation matters to assist with staffing, budgeting and other operational planning.

9. Number of new non-litigation matters

<10
11 to 50
51 to 100

<u>Purpose of the KPI</u>

KPI Metric Category Non-Litigation Matters

- Measure Description Measures number of new non-litigation matters each year
- Type of Performance Measure Process Efficiency
- Suggested Use/Purpose This KPI helps law departments track the number of new non-litigation matters to assist with staffing, budgeting and other operational planning.

10. Number of closed non-litigation matters External Legal Spending

551 to 650
651 to 700
701 to 750

<u>Purpose of this KPI</u>

- KPI Metric Category: Non-Litigation Matters
- Measure Description: Measures number of closed non-litigation matters each year
- Type of Performance Measure: Process Efficiency
- Suggested Use/Purpose: This KPI will help the XXX law department track the number of closed non-litigation matters to assist with staffing, budgeting and other operational planning.

11. Law department's total fees for outside counsel

< $ 1,000,000
$ 1,000,001 to $ 25,000,000

$ 25,000,001 to $ 50,000,000

Purpose of this KPI

- KPI Metric Category: External Legal Spending
- Measure Description: Measures the amount XXX Legal spend on outside counsel
- Type of Performance Measure: Cost
- Suggested Use/Purpose: This KPI helps XXX Legal track the amount spent on outside counsel in order to assist with staffing, budgeting and other operational planning.

12. Law department's total fees for outside legal vendors and suppliers (excluding law firms)

< $ 100,000
$ 150,000 to $ 200,000
$ 250,000 to $ 300,000

Purpose of this KPI

- KPI Metric Category: External Legal Spending
- Measure Description: Measures the amount law departments spend on outside counsel
- Type of Performance Measure: Cost
- Suggested Use/Purpose: This KPI will help the XXX Law Department track the amount spent on outside vendors and suppliers in order to assist with staffing, budgeting and other operational planning.

13. Law department's total fees for legal research

<$ 10,000
$ 10,001 to $ 20,000
$ 20,001 to $ 30,000

Purpose of this KPI

- KPI Metric Category: External Legal Spending
- Measure Description: Measures the amount law departments spend on outside legal research
- Type of Performance Measure: Cost
- Suggested Use/Purpose: This KPI will help the XXX Law Department track the amount spent on outside legal research services in order to assist with staffing, budgeting and other operational planning.

14. Total external spending on litigation matters

< $ 100,000
$ 100,001 to $ 10,000,000
$ 10,000,001 to $ 25,000,000

Purpose of this KPI

- KPI Metric Category: External Legal Spending
- Measure Description: Measures the amount XXX Legal spends on outside law firms, vendors, suppliers and legal research to handle their litigation matters
- Type of Performance Measure: Cost
- Suggested Use/Purpose: This KPI helps law departments track the amount spent on outside law firms, vendors and suppliers and legal research to handle litigation matters. This KPI assists with staffing, budgeting and other operational planning.

15. Total external spending on non-litigation matters

< $ 100,000
$ 100,001 to $ 2,500,000
$ 2,500,001 to $ 5,000,000

Purpose of this KPI

- KPI Metric Category: External Legal Spending
- Measure Description: Measures the amount law departments spend on outside law firms, vendors, suppliers and legal research to handle their non-litigation matters
- Type of Performance Measure: Cost
- Suggested Use/Purpose: This KPI will help the XXX Law Department track the amount spent on outside law firms, vendors and suppliers and legal research to handle non-litigation matters. This KPI assists with staffing, budgeting and other operational planning.

11.2.2 Outside Billing Guidelines

Requirements for Legal Counsel Retained by or on Behalf of XYZ Co., LTD

NOTE: THIS IS A SAMPLE OUTSIDE BILLING GUIDELINE FORM. YOU ARE FREE TO ADD MORE RESTRICTIONS AND QUALIFICATIONS OR DELETE AS MANY AS YOU WANT

Outside Counsel Billing Guidelines

The following guidelines and rules are designed to guide outside counsel (hereinafter, "Counsel") retained to represent XYZ, Co.,Ltd. ("_XYZ_") and/or its subsidiaries and affiliates (collectively, "XYZ"), in assisting XYZ to manage its legal affairs. These guidelines intend to help Counsel produce effective and efficient results for XYZ, in a fair and cost-effective manner.

XYZ_ may find it necessary to amend these guidelines or add others during the course of an engagement as appropriate to manage legal matters properly. Prior notice will be given and the matter discussed with Counsel if such action is deemed necessary by XYZ. Questions regarding these rules and guidelines should be directed to XYZ.

NOTE: YOU CAN ADD MORE POLICY GUIDELINES IF NEEDED

I. General Guidelines

A. Media communication policy: Counsel will not communicate with any media outlet, or respond to any inquiries for information from any media outlets regarding XYZ and/or its customers, claims or other legal matters, without prior approval from XYZ. Media inquiries should be directed to Attn GC, XYZ Law Department.

B. Outside Coordinating Counsel—Products Liability Matters: XYZ has selected outside coordinating litigation counsel for certain products liability matters. XYZ expects that other Counsel assigned to matters managed by coordinating counsel will:

1. Provide copies of reports and other communications to coordinating counsel.
2. Respond to requests for information and document from coordinating counsel.
3. Work with coordinating counsel to develop XYZ's claims and defense, including, but not limited to, the following: discovery responses prepared on behalf of XYZ; depositions of XYZ personnel; discovery and investigation of claims; selection of defense experts; and challenges to adverse experts. XYZ believes that cooperation in this regard is critical to ensuring that strategies undertaken on XYZ's behalf are consistently undertaken in the various cases in which XYZ is involved.

II. Initial Requirements for New Engagements.

C. Engagement Letters: Unless instructed otherwise, within seven (7) days of Counsel's receipt of an assignment from XYZ, Counsel must provide SAE with an engagement letter. XYZ expects that Counsel will not charge XYZ for the time and expenses associated with preparing engagement letters. Engagement letters must set forth the following information:

1. Confirmation of the assignment and scope of work.

2. Counsel's agreement to follow and abide by the within Guidelines, as well as other applicable corporate policies and procedures.
3. Counsel's personnel who are proposed for the assignment and their billing rates, consistent with the within Guidelines pertaining to "Staffing of Matters."
4. Counsel's verification that it has not identified any actual or potential conflicts of interest arising from the engagement or that such conflicts have been resolved in accordance with the within rules and guidelines and applicable rules of professional conduct.

D. Case Plan and Budget: Within fourteen (14) days of Counsel's receipt of an assignment from XYZ, Counsel must submit to XYZ a Case Plan and Budget that sets forth the following data, which XYZ will review with Counsel on a timely basis after the engagement is made:

1. Counsel's assessment of XYZ's potential liability, including a discussion of the relative liabilities of XYZ ands or its subsidiaries.
2. Counsel's knowledge about adverse counsel and the local jurisdiction.
3. A proposed strategy for defending or prosecuting the case.
4. Identification of significant activity anticipated by Counsel, including removal to federal court, factual investigation, motions and discovery, and an estimated completion date for each significant activity.
5. Identification and assessment of prospects for early resolution of the case, including settlement and dispositive motion practice.
6. For litigation matters, a discovery end date and an anticipated trial date.
7. A budget for the anticipated work during the engagement, with apportionment of the budget to anticipated tasks.

III Reporting to XYZ. In addition to the initial case reporting described above, XYZ expects that Counsel will communicate with XYZ on a regular basis, at least quarterly, to apprise XYZ of significant developments which occur during a case. Counsel shall also be responsible for updating the case plan and budget quarterly. During the case, XYZ may request monthly updates on significant events or milestones identified by XYZ.

E. Significant events about which Counsel should report to XYZ include depositions (summaries should be provided), and summaries of expert reports, opinions, testimony, and other important events. In particular, before filing any dispositive motions, Counsel must advise XYZ of Counsel's intent to file any such motions, and provide draft motion papers for XYZ's review at least two (2) weeks prior to the anticipated filing date.
F. Pre-trial reports: For litigation matters, unless otherwise specified by XYZ, at least ninety (90) days prior to a scheduled trial date, Counsel must submit to XYZ a detailed pre-trial report which includes a description of the important issues for trial, the relative strengths and weaknesses of the positions of parties regarding those issues. Thereafter, Counsel will provide monthly written status reports up to the trial date.
G. Copies of documents:

    1. Copies of the following documents, when generated, should be sent to XYZ: pleadings; orders; research memoranda (where authorized); legal briefs and motion papers; expert reports; and medical reports.
    2. In addition, Counsel should send transcripts of depositions of XYZ personnel to XYZ.
    3. Deposition transcripts should be sent to XYZ in ".txt" or ASCII format, with copies of any exhibits in Adobe PDF or ".tif" format, via electronic mail.
    4. Counsel should send such documents other than deposition transcripts to XYZ electronically (in Adobe PDF or ".tif" formats, via electronic mail or otherwise) wherever possible, to minimize the costs of transmission and to accommodate __________'s electronic record keeping systems.

H. Budgetary matters: Counsel must contact XYZ to advise that Counsel's fees or expenses are expected to exceed the case budget or an approved updated case budget, at least fourteen (14) days prior to the rendering of an invoice containing the fees or expenses that exceed the case budget. Counsel's communication to XYZ in this regard must include the amount of the expected overage, and a detailed explanation of the reason(s) why the case budget or an approved updated case budget would be exceeded, if the overage is approved by XYZ. XYZ will review such communications from Counsel, and will determine whether or not to permit the reported overage.

I. Counsel will respond to all other requests from XYZ for information and documents in a timely manner.

II. Staffing of Matters.

A. XYZ reserves the right to review and modify Counsel's proposed staffing of matters handled on behalf of XYZ. For the sake of efficiency, Counsel should make every effort to limit the number of professionals performing work on matters for XYZ to the lowest levels consistent with Counsel's professional responsibilities.

B. Changes to and Continuity of Personnel: Counsel must first seek and receive __________'s permission to modify (additions and substitutions) the case staffing outlined in the initial case report. If __________ approves such staffing changes, then XYZ will not reimburse Counsel for time associated with educating new staff members to the facts and background of the matters, unless the staffing changes are occasioned solely by substantive developments in the matters which call for the addition of personnel.

C. Experience levels of attorneys assigned to XYZ matters: Counsel may not assign lawyers who have less than three (3) years of experience in the field of practice relevant to a matter, without prior approval from XYZ.

D. Summer Associates/Interns/Clerks: The tasks performed by such personnel will not be paid for by XYZ, absent special circumstances and prior approval by XYZ.

E. Paralegals: Counsel will not assign paraprofessionals, paralegals, or legal assistants to matters assigned by XYZ without prior approval from XYZ.
F. Administrative/clerical tasks: XYZ firmly believes that administrative/clerical tasks are part of Counsel's overhead and costs of doing business, and will not be paid for by XYZ. "Administrative/clerical tasks" include, but are not limited to, filing, date-stamping, indexing, copying, or scanning documents, and/or making travel arrangements.
G. Intraoffice conferences: XYZ will compensate Counsel only for the cost of the most senior person's participation in the conference. Please note that Counsel who spend more than ten percent (10%) of their billable time annually on intra-office conferences will be closely reviewed by XYZ.
H. Multiple counsel at particular billable events: Counsel should consult with XYZ regarding anticipated needs for attendance of multiple billers at particular events. Without prior approval, XYZ will compensate Counsel only for the cost of the most senior person's participation in the event.
I. Depositions: Counsel should consult with XYZ before scheduling, noticing or otherwise initiating any depositions other than those already approved in the initial litigation plan. Similarly, Counsel should consult with XYZ prior to attending any depositions initiated by other parties.

NOTE: PLACE OTHER RESTRICTIONS HERE

IV Billing: Rendering Billing Statements/Invoices, and Billing Rates.

J. General: XYZ reserves the right to review all charges for services and disbursements for legal work conducted on its behalf, without limitation. XYZ reserves the right to conduct on-site audits and to review Counsel's files and/or billing statements/invoices. Counsel agrees to comply with all reasonable requests for information and documents. XYZ further reserves its right to decline to pay charges which violate these Guidelines, and which are not fully explained, approved or documented by Counsel after inquiry by XYZ.

K. Timing of rendering invoices: Invoices must be submitted not more than ninety (90) days after the month in which the time was accrued. The timing of the invoices is necessary for XYZ's budgeting and matter management. Counsel are advised that any time entries or invoices which are rendered outside this period will not be paid by XYZ without approval by the General Counsel.

L. Billing rates:

   1. Counsel agrees that billing rates set at the beginning of a matter will remain in effect unless Counsel submitts a written request for a change or revision, and the written request is approved by XYZ. Such written requests must be submitted to XYZ at least sixty (60) days in advance of the effective date of the proposed change or revision.
   2. If Counsel's firm is comprised of multiple offices whose lawyers' (and other approved personnel's) billing rates vary by office, then for XYZ's matters, Counsel agrees to charge XYZ the lowest of the firm's rates for lawyers of the same level experience as those assigned to XYZ's matters, regardless of where the lawyers assigned to XYZ's matters are stationed.

M. Any other requests by Counsel for increases in compensation rates must be made to XYZ in writing, and XYZ must agree to such increases before such increases may appear in Counsel's billing statements. XYZ will not agree to such increases more often than biannually.

V Billing Entries and Descriptions.

N. All billing statements/invoices shall be supported with details of the work performed. The details to be included are:

   1. A narrative description of the work performed for each specific task by the attorney or other professional performing it. The descriptions should set forth clearly the task performed and why it was necessary. For example, the

following billing description, "Conference with ABC re: status," is not sufficient.

2. Name or initials of the person who performed the task
3. The time spent on the task, in tenths of an hour increments
4. A summary by each attorney or other professional who performed work for XYZ during that month, showing the total number of hours billed by that person, his/her billing rate, and total charges for that person.

O. Single entry timekeeping is required: Each activity performed by a timekeeper must be set forth separately from other time entries. "Block billing" entries, and entries which otherwise combine multiple tasks into single entries, are not acceptable to, and will not be paid by _________.

P. Use of standardized forms and pleadings: XYZ encourages Counsel to rely upon standardized forms for the creation of documents, where appropriate. XYZ may only be charged for Counsel's time to revise and modify such documents for the particular task for XYZ, and not for time spent to create the original forms.

Q. Travel time: XYZ will reimburse Counsel for the reasonable cost of Counsel's actual time to travel to an appropriate case-related event.

VI Invoice format.

R. Please address invoices to XYZ at ____________________ and send a hard copy of each invoice, with all documentation of disbursements made on XYZ 's behalf to ________________.

VII Expenses/Disbursements.

S. Each disbursement shall be billed at Counsel's actual out-of-pocket costs. No mark-ups or administrative fees may be added.

T. Approval by XYZ: Counsel shall not make any single disbursement of $500 or more without procuring prior approval from _________.

U. Documentation of Disbursements: Counsel must provide documentation for each disbursement made on XYZ's behalf, including receipts and invoices. Such documentation must be provided to XYZ with the hard copy of Counsel's invoice sent to XYZ.

V. Interstate and long distance travel: XYZ defines "interstate and long distance travel" as travel between and among more than one State and/or intrastate travel outside a seventy-five (75) mile radius from Counsel's office. Counsel may not travel interstate or long distance without prior approval from XYZ.

NOTE: YOU CAN PLACE MORE RESTRICTIONS ON TRAVEL HERE

1. XYZ expects that Counsel will undertake reasonable efforts to secure the most cost-effective fares possible. XYZ encourages Counsel to book travel arrangements as early as possible to take advantage of discounts for early reservations.
2. Airfares: XYZ will reimburse Counsel only for economy or coach—fare for approved flights within the continental USA, ASIA, within Europe, and within Latin America; business-class airfare may be reimbursed with pre-approval for overseas travel.
3. Rental cars: XYZ will reimburse the charges for rental cars of mid-size class or lower only.
4. Meals and hotels: Counsel should use his/her professional judgment in selecting hotel accommodations and incurring expenses.
5. XYZ will not reimburse counsel for the costs of travel agents.

W. Local and intrastate travel: XYZ defines "local and intrastate travel" as travel within Counsel's State of domicile, and other travel within a seventy-five (75) mile radius from Counsel's office. XYZ considers local and intrastate travel to be part of Counsel's ordinary overhead, and as such, XYZ will not reimburse Counsel for expenses related to intrastate travel.

X. Automobile travel (for other than local or intrastate travel):

1. Charges for automobile travel must be accompanied by the following information: date(s) of travel; purpose; number of miles; per-mile charge; and the amounts and nature of other expenses (tolls, parking, etc.). XYZ will reimburse Counsel according to the Internal Revenue Service's maximum mileage expense rate in effect at the time of travel or Counsel's internal rate, whichever is lower.
2. XYZ will not reimburse Counsel for the costs of fines and penalties related to driving and parking violations incurred by Counsel during business-related travel for SAE.
3. XYZ will not reimburse Counsel for the cost of towing and repair services incurred to service an automobile during business-related travel on behalf of XYZ.

Y. Photocopies:

1. Photocopies numbering fewer than 200 pages per billing period (usually monthly) are part of Counsel's overhead, and the cost of such photocopies will not be paid by XYZ.
2. If Counsel determines that it must copy single groups of documents numbering more than 100 pages, then Counsel must seek prior approval from XYZ, and endeavor to secure the most cost-effective means of making such photocopies. For approved photocopy projects completed internally by Counsel's firm, XYZ will reimburse Counsel at a rate of up to $.10 per page.

Z. Legal and Technical Research; Computerized Legal Research Services:

1. Performance of legal and technical research: XYZ hires Counsel based upon their experience, and expects that Counsel will be highly specialized and experienced in his/her field(s) of expertise. As such, XYZ expects that it will be rare for legal research by Counsel to be required. Before undertaking any legal research, therefore, Counsel should

obtain permission from XYZ, using the approval form attached hereto. In the few cases in which it is impractical for Counsel to procure prior approval, Counsel should inform XYZ as soon as possible after research has begun.

2. Computerized legal research: XYZ considers charges related to the use of computerized legal research services (e.g., Westlaw and LEXIS-NEXIS) to be part of Counsel's overhead, and such charges will not be reimbursed by XYZ.

AA. Charges for Messengers, Couriers, and Express or Overnight Delivery Services: XYZ discourages the use of such services, and will reimburse Counsel only for such charges that are reasonable under the circumstances and directly related to the defense or prosecution of the case.

BB. Other Non-Reimbursable Expenses: XYZ will not reimburse Counsel for the following expenses:

1. Photocopies (except as delineated above)
2. Computer, e-mail and word processing fees
3. Support staff pay
4. Overtime pay and shift differentials for staffers
5. Charges and rent for conference rooms
6. Office supplies
7. Postage
8. Library use and library staff charges
9. Clerks (billable time, expenses, etc.)
10. Proofreaders charges
11. Meals and food service (except during approved business-related travel)
12. Taxis/limousines to and from office (even at night; except for approved business-related travel)
13. Telephone charges
14. Facsimile charges
15. Cellular/wireless/Blackberry service charges
16. Document scanning charges (unless pre-approved by XYZ

NOTE : YOU CAN ADD MORE RESTRICTIONS

CC. Experts, consultants and other professionals: Counsel will consult with and seek approval from XYZ before retaining or otherwise incurring expenses for work performed by experts, consultants, investigators, translators or other professional service providers.

Agreement

_____________________ hereby agrees to abide by and follow "Requirements for Legal Counsel Retained by or on Behalf of XYZ Co, Ltd."

_________________________ (firm)

By: ______________________

Dated:

12. Litigation

The main issue facing companies involved in US litigation is that US litigation compared to litigation in many other countries is quite unique. US litigation is not only complex but can be quite costly, onerous, and burdensome. The key element of US litigation is that it is notice-based pleading in a common law setting, which means the facts of cases are to be developed through a complex discovery process in which lawyers for the parties play an adversarial role. The court is more of an umpire and will let the attorneys for both sides handle the case.

12.1 Discovery

Discovery, by its very nature, takes up time, adds a great deal of expense to the cost of litigation (for both parties) and can lead to the disruption of business.

The kinds of discovery vary but are primarily limited to the following formats:

- Depositions
  - Oral examination
  - May involve written questions
  - May involve key employees and/or officers of the company
- Interrogatories
  - Answers to written questions posed by the other side

- Production of documents and things and entry upon land for inspection and other purposes
- Production of ESI
- Physical examination of the evidence

It has been noted that discovery in the United States is like no other discovery process elsewhere. The United States, in fact, provides litigants a much greater ability to review all broadly relevant documents than any other jurisdiction in the world. The expense, delay, and business disruption associated with US discovery are unparalleled.[7]

12.2 Jury Trials

The USA, unlike most civil law jurisdictions, uses a jury system for civil proceedings. That means a jury composed of six to twelve people selected from the local area will decide the facts that are in dispute, effectively deciding the outcome of the case. The judge acts basically as an umpire by deciding legal questions. The problem this presents is that a group of ordinary laypeople from the area will decide the outcome of the case, no matter how technical or difficult it is.

The fact that a jury will decide the outcome of the case adds an element of unpredictability. Regardless of how strong the evidence is, a jury verdict is never guaranteed. Litigants, whether the plaintiff or defendant, often decide to settle, regardless of the strength of the merits of the claim or defense to the claim due to unpredictability, the cost and expense of trial, the potential disruption to business, and the negative publicity.

12.3 Absence of Fee-Shifting Statutes

Unlike many countries, the United States does not usually have fee-shifting statutes. Each party to a litigation bears his or her own legal expenses unless a statute or contractual agreement provides that the prevailing party should be awarded attorneys' fees. Courts are loath to award attorney fees to the prevailing party in absence of such contractual stipulation or statute.

---

7 Donald Donovan, *Introducing Foreign Clients to US Civil Litigation* (International Litigation Strategies and Practice, ABA Publishing, 2005), 34.

The absence of fee shifting, in most cases, is extremely important. The prevailing party in litigation may very well lose financially if the amount awarded at trial does not exceed the cost of litigation. This combined with the other costly factors of litigation, such as discovery, creates a litigation system that is more costly, time consuming, and burdensome than most litigation systems in other countries.

12.4 Strategy

In case where parties are unable to resolve the dispute prior to litigation or prior to trial, a litigant must develop a winning trial strategy. Such strategy will be based on complex rules of evidence allowing or disallowing the admission of certain evidence, including testimony or documents, etc. The parties will obviously try to position themselves to be in the strongest position possible up to and during trial, regardless of whether an out-of-court settlement is finally reached. What does this strategy mean to most litigants? It means:

- Time.
- Expense.
- Business interruption.
- The cost of business interruption.
- Potential bad or negative publicity.
- Negative impact on the company's brand.
- In the United States, trials are public. Does that matter to you?
- As trials are public, the media often plays a part in reporting the case. Do you want this?

12.5 Class Actions

Another unique aspect of US litigation is that of class actions. In the United States, groups of claimants are able to sue as a class. Such litigation is called "class action," and it exposes corporate defendants to potential life-threatening litigation where enough class members are involved. A class action could consist of thousands of claimants represented by one claimant. If a company is sued in a class action, it is potentially exposed to a jury award in the millions of dollars. Another issue is that there could be more than one class action or multiple class actions in a number of states. The potential legal exposure and high transactions costs of numerous trials are great.

12.6 LRM: US Litigation

To properly manage civil litigation in the United States, companies need to implement LRM strategies and processes by either creation of an in-house Law Department or a Risk Management Department that is capable of overseeing or managing outside litigation. Depending on the legal exposure of a company, it can be a full-time job. This management function will be key in properly coordinating litigation to avoid excessive costs, duplication of effort, and minimization of disruptions to a company's business, as well as setting an effective trial strategy.

What many foreign companies doing business in the United States fail to appreciate is that an outside litigation lawyer does not necessarily have the company's best interests in mind during litigation. A litigator wants to win, regardless of the cost. Many companies have paid millions of dollars to law firms during litigation when a resolution to the dispute was available had the parties tried to actively settle the case. Remember, a trial lawyer's business is trial work and not settlement.

An in-house legal manager or risk manager, representing the company's best interests, can help facilitate settlement once a legal risk assessment as to the validity, cost, and expense of litigation is made. In fact, during trial, a settlement is still possible and can be facilitated by in-house counsel or risk management. Therefore, the Law Department or the risk manager (if no Law Department exists) should maintain control and oversight of any litigation.

12.6.1 Reasons for an Internal Legal Risk Management Process

Companies facing US litigation are often exposed to excessive fees and costs, massive business disruption, lengthy litigation, and the unpredictability of the jury system. Though, obviously, outside litigation counsel is necessary in most cases, an in-house Law Department can save the company great sums of money by managing the litigation process. Such management involves the assessment, management, and potential transfer of risk through various LRM strategies, including:

- Effective coordination of legal defense efforts in order for the company to avoid duplication of costs and effort from case to case
- Coordination of witnesses, answers and interrogatory responses, documents, and depositions
- Acting as the central site for all facts, positions, decisions on legal issues, and motions
- Development, implementation, and coordination of a defense plan

12.7 Forms

12.7.1 Retainer Agreement

Re: XYZ v YYYY
Dear Mr. Smith:

We are pleased that the XXXX law firm has agreed to provide legal services to XYC, Inc. (the "Company") with respect to defending the above referenced lawsuit. The Law Department of the Company expects outside law firms to provide high quality services in a cost efficient manner. We wish to reach agreement with you in advance as to the conditions and guidelines that will govern our relationship, consistent, of course, with the rules of professional responsibility that apply to all attorneys.

First, to protect both of us and to comply with professional obligations, we have already discussed with you and have resolved any potential conflicts of interest with present or former clients of your firm. We expect that you will inform us of any additional potential conflicts which you may discover prior to commencing work for the Company, if possible, so that we can evaluate whether engaging you firm's services are appropriate. Moreover, we assume that if, during the course of your firm's services to the Company, your firm becomes aware of other potential conflicts of interest that may arise, we will be immediately provided all necessary information.

The services which your firm will provide shall be m accordance with the following terms and conditions:

A. *Professional Fees*—We understand that your fees will be based upon the reasonable value of your service as determined by the American Bar Association Model Code of Professional Responsibility and the New York State Code of Professional Responsibility. Your firm's fees will be based on the hourly billing rates charged by each attorney. I understand that a senior partner's billing rate is $250.00 per hour and that a partner's current billing rate is $200.00 per hour. Furthermore, I also understand an associate attorney's rate will be $175.00 per hour. Though all billing rates may be reasonably adjusted from time to time, they may not be adjusted more frequently than annually. Notice of any such adjustments must be given to us within reasonable time.

   No fees shall be paid separately for secretarial, clerical services or overhead. Any additional agreements regarding fees must be set forth in writing and signed by the responsible Company attorney.

B. *Costs and Expenses*—I understand that in the course of your representation, it may be necessary for your firm to incur certain costs or expenses. Our company will reimburse your firm for certain costs or expenses actually incurred and reasonably necessary for completing the assigned matter, as long as your charges for costs and expenses are competitive with other sources of the same products or services. Our billing procedure which outlines costs and expenses is attached.

   I expect that your firm will advance all such expenses and submit bills for reimbursement.

   1. *Court Costs*—We will reimburse for expenses incurred, but will not be responsible for sanctions or penalties imposed by a Court due to the conduct of your firm.

2. *Transcription*—We will reimburse for expenses of an original transcript at reasonable rates. Expedited transcripts may not be ordered without our prior approval.
3. *Photocopying*—We will reimburse at the rate of the firm's actual annualized per copy expense or 10 cents per page, whichever is lower, for normal photocopying.
4. *Telephone*—We will reimburse for long-distance telephone service at actual expense to your firm.
5. *Postage/Courier*—We will reimburse for postage at your firm's actual costs and for expenses of overnight courier or by-hand couriers only when such services are necessary or are requested by a Company attorney.
6. *Miscellaneous Expenses*—We will not reimburse for the cost of office equipment, books, periodicals or other office expenditures unless approval was obtained from us.

C. *Involvement of the Company*—We expect to be kept closely involved with the progress of your firm's services in this matter. Your firm will keep us apprised of all material developments in this matter, and, in the case of litigation or administrative proceedings, provide sufficient notice to us to enable a responsible Company attorney to attend meetings, discovery proceedings and conferences, hearings and other proceedings. A copy of all correspondence in the course of your firm's services should be forwarded to me.

D. *Budget*—If this matter will cost more than $5,000 I will need a budget. As you know the budget is designed to assist in our internal projections. It will also give me the opportunity to evaluate the defense strategy and approximate cost. Therefore, please provide me with a budget if you anticipate this costing more than the sum above.

E. *Termination*—We have the right to terminate your firm's engagement by written notice at any time. Your firm has the same right to terminate this engagement, subject to an obligation to give the Company reasonable notice to permit it to obtain alternative representation or services and subject to applicable ethical provisions. Your firm will be expected to provide reasonable assistance in effecting a transfer of responsibilities to the new firm.

For your reference, the Company's required billing format and expense procedure is attached to this letter.

Please review this agreement carefully, and if you have any questions concerning the foregoing conditions, do not hesitate to contact me. If this agreement is acceptable to you, please acknowledge that you have reviewed it, understand it, and desire to represent the Company on the basis of the terms of this letter by signing and delivering to me the enclosed copy. We recommend that you keep a copy of this letter in your file.

I look forward to working with your law firm on this matter.

Sincerely yours,

General Counsel
Encl.

13. Arbitration

13.1 What Is Arbitration?

Arbitration is a contractual mechanism that parties use to avoid litigation. As it is a contractual mechanism, the parties are free to determine the procedural requirements, number of arbitrators, governing law, and other key provisions, etc.

In other words, arbitration is a procedure that the parties select instead of availing themselves of a judicial system of a particular country, state, or province.

The primary characteristics of arbitration are:

- The parties select the arbitrator(s).
- It is a consensual process.
- It is a private process.
- It is a neutral process.
- It issues a final decision, with normally no appeal rights.
- It is very cost effective.

13.2 Justification for Arbitration

The main reasons that make arbitration a very attractive process over litigation, especially in the United States, are primarily: (1) it is a neutral process, (2) arbitral decisions are easily enforceable, (3) it offers flexibility (the ability to control and minimize electronic discovery and cost), and

(4) the arbitrations are sophisticated. Flexibility, sophistication of the arbitral process, and enforceability are set forth in more detail below.

- Flexibility: One of the most fascinating qualities of arbitration, both domestic and international, is its inherent flexibility. That quality principally arises from two sources: the fact that the contract of the parties creates the jurisdiction of the arbitrator, and the necessity to adapt to the procedural requirements of the claimants and respondents. Examples of flexibility include provisions for the type of arbitrator required, and rules regarding the admission of evidence and discovery of facts. That is particularly important for any company that engages in business in the United States due to the explosion of discovery requirements regarding electronic documents. US courts impose stringent requirements for the maintenance of electronic documents (such as e-mails) and enforce severe penalties for violating these rules. These rules are particularly onerous on companies that have documents stored in various countries and locations. The arbitration clause negotiated can protect a party from such requirements while still maintaining due process and the ability to prove one's case.
- Sophistication of arbitrators/process: Although arbitrators usually have legal training, they come from many different backgrounds—law professors, practicing lawyers, judges, government officials, etc. This fact creates an opportunity for the development of a sophistication that flows from the combing of many different experiences and points of view. Moreover, because all arbitral tribunals are ad hoc in the sense that they are created for a specific case and cease to exist when that matter is determined, an experienced arbitrator encounters numerous significant collegial experiences on a level and variety that is not available to the judge. This leads to a willingness to devise solutions to procedural and substantive matters that are sophisticated in the sense that they are worldly wise and are prepared to accept complexity. For example, if a dispute is of a technical nature, the parties can require that the arbitrator be experienced in specific fields (e.g., engineering, employment law, or commercial actions of a particular type). This leads to

sophisticated techniques of questioning expert witnesses, as well as other obvious benefits.

- Enforceability: It is a truism that an award issued by an arbitral tribunal and a judgment rendered by a court are worth very little unless it can be enforced. Happily, arbitral awards are easily enforced. Sometimes, in certain circumstances, they are more easily enforced than court-rendered judgments. In the United States, the enforcement of arbitral awards is guaranteed by the Federal Arbitration Act and numerous state laws. Indeed, if an international dispute exists between parties of different countries, the New York Convention (signed by the United States and most other nations) makes enforcement of arbitral awards easier than court-rendered judgments by virtue of limiting the defenses that may be interposed to enforcement of the arbitral award.
- Arbitration has long been viewed favorably as a dispute resolution mechanism for international disputes. This especially holds true for disputes in Asia.[8] In the past decade, arbitration in Asia has greatly increased which is an outcome or result of the rapid increase in trade.[9]

13.3 Arbitration Process: General Characteristics

General Characteristics: The arbitral process begins with the arbitration clause. When drafting an arbitration provision, several options are available. For example, an arbitration clause can include a provision first requiring mediation prior to proceeding with an arbitration. Thus, under this scenario a party can go to mediation, and if there is an agreement, the process ends there. If not, then the parties proceed to arbitration and a final award. The arbitration clause must also deal with the place of arbitration, the language of arbitration, and the type of arbitrators to be selected. The place of arbitration can be important, particularly in international disputes, because the law of the venue of the arbitration will be applicable on procedural matters where there is a dispute among the parties.

---

8 Bryan Hopkins, "A Comparison of Recent Changes in the Arbitral Laws and Regulations of Hong Kong, Singapore and Korea," *KLRI Journal of Law and Legislation* 3, no. 1 (2013).

9 Ibid

Arbitration clause: The first step in the arbitral procedure is the drafting of the arbitration clause. The following are the essentials of any arbitration clause:

- Include a mediation requirement if desired (strict time limits should be imposed and an administrative body selected to manage the mediation).
- A broad description of what is covered (e.g., "and dispute that arises from or is related to" a particular contract). This is important to make sure that the obligation to arbitrate is not avoided by a party arguing that a particular dispute is not covered by the arbitration provision.
- An institution to administer the arbitration (e.g., the International Chamber of Commerce (ICC), the American Arbitration Association (AAA), the London Court of International Arbitration (LCIA), etc. This is important to ensure that the process is not unduly delayed.
- Place of arbitration (make sure that the laws of the venue are arbitration friendly and provide for finality of the award).
- Arbitration award must be final.
- Number, process of selection, and qualifications of arbitrators.
- Law applicable to the dispute.
- Discovery concerns (how many depositions, limitations on E-discovery, etc.).
- Ability to obtain provisional remedies (e.g., injunctive relief) from courts without waiving rights to arbitration.
- Confidentiality.

13.3.1 Arbitral Procedure

Upon a dispute arising that is covered by an arbitration clause, the procedure regarding filing a demand or request for arbitration is simple. First and foremost, the rules of the administrative body selected to run the mediation must be consulted. However, the (very) general procedural steps are as follows:

- In the event mediation is called for in the arbitration clause, initiate mediation with a recognized mediation body. Several administrative bodies, such as the ICC (International Chamber of Commerce) and AAA (American Arbitration Association), provide for mediation rules as well. Typically a demand for mediation with a statement of the dispute and a filing fee are filed. The opposing party will then be entitled to file its own statement. The parties attempt to agree on a mediator; if not, the administrative body will select the mediator. The mediation is to be governed by strict time limits, at the conclusion of which the arbitration process can begin.

- A demand/request for arbitration is filed with the appropriate arbitral body, accompanied by a filing fee. What is included in the demand/request for arbitration is determined by the applicable rules and judgment of counsel at the time of filing. Typically the respondent will have to file its answer and will be responsible for half the costs of the arbitration. (Consumer arbitration differs significantly in this regard.)
- Arbitrators are selected, and the arbitration process begins. The production of documents and other evidence begins as circumscribed by the arbitral clause. In many circumstances, direct testimony will be provided in written form, and only cross-examination and limited redirect is allowed at the final hearings. Prehearing memorials are typically filed. A final hearing is held, after which the arbitral tribunal will issue a final award.
- Upon the issuance of a final award, if the losing party does not voluntarily comply with the award, then the award is presented to a court of competent jurisdiction, where it is confirmed and will be enforced as any other court judgment.

13.4 Arbitral Institutions

A number of arbitral institutions have become popular, especially in the international context. Many countries have their own arbitration laws as well as arbitral bodies that administer arbitration. The most popular are:

- The International Chamber of Commerce (ICC)
- The American Arbitration Association (AAA)
- The International Center of Dispute Resolution (ICDR)

Many companies that do business in Asia use the arbitration rules of Singapore (SIAC); Hong Kong (HKIAC) or Seoul (KCAB). To date, more arbitrations are beginning to take place in mainland China, as well. The increase of arbitrations in the Asia—Pacific countries are directly related to the increase in trade and rapid economic growth of the Asia region. This is expected to continue.

13.5 Arbitration Clause

The arbitration clause is the most important part of any contract when the parties are negotiating the use of arbitration.

A well-thought-out arbitration clause should contain:

- If possible, a mediation requirement—to possibly avoid arbitration
- A broad description of what is covered
- An institution to administer arbitration (ICC, AAA, ICDR, etc.)
- Place of arbitration (the laws of the venue should be arbitration friendly)
- An understanding that arbitration awards are final
- Number, process of selection, and qualification of arbitrators
- Applicable law
- Discovery concerns (limitations to E-discovery and use of ESI)

In light of the current climate, no one wants to incur costs associated with arbitration of litigation if avoidable. To help avoid arbitration or potential excessive costs, I recommend the following:

- The arbitration clause should also require a period of time (thirty days, etc.) where the dispute is first escalated to executive management to discuss. You will be surprised how easy it is to settle a dispute when the senior-level management, who understand the "big picture," gets involved.
- As stated before, try to make use of mediation as well. Having a neutral party look at a claim and provide an objective opinion on the claim could lead to a speedy resolution.
- Make certain the arbitration rules and administrative body fit the scope of the deal. How expensive is the deal?

- Limit the scope and length of arbitration as well as the discovery permitted. Limitations on discovery can help not only speed up arbitration but limit and control costs.
- Think about negotiating a prevailing party cost/recovery expense provision in the clause. This would certainly cause the parties to think more about settlement of a dispute instead of arbitration.
- In-house counsel must manage and control arbitration costs. Outside counsel needs to understand the need to control costs and should agree to an arbitration budget. A well-thought-out arbitration budget is very important. The costs of arbitration will depend on how well in-house and arbitration counsel manage the process.

13.6 Forms

13.6.1 Arbitration Clause

All disputes arising out of or in connection with this Agreement or related documents or agreements shall be submitted to the International Court of Arbitration of the International Chamber of Commerce and shall be finally settled under the Rules of Arbitration of the International Chamber of Commerce by an arbitrator appointed in accordance with said rules. Said arbitration shall take place in Hong Kong.

13.6.2 Model Arbitration Agreement for Employment Claims

A. Binding Arbitration

XXX is hopeful any claims related to employment will be satisfactorily resolved through XXX's internal problem resolution procedure. However, if the claim cannot be resolved through XXX's internal problem resolution process, (insert employee name) and XXX must submit the claim to binding arbitration before the American Arbitration Association ("AAA") as a final and binding means of resolving the claim.

XXX will pay all of the fees and expenses of the arbitrator, and the administration fees associated with the arbitration. Should ______________ choose to retain an attorney for the arbitration, _______ is solely responsible for ________'s own attorneys' fees and costs. The arbitration shall be arbitrated by a single arbitrator in accordance with the National Rules for the Resolution of Employment Disputes of the AAA. ________ understands that a copy of the AAA National Rules for the Resolution of Employment Disputes is available for review at the Human Resource Department. ________ further understands that may contact the AAA to request a copy of these rules at ____ or obtain them from AAA's website (www.adr.org).

B. XXX's Agreement to Alternative Dispute Resolution

Because this dispute-resolution procedure is intended to resolve all disputes between ________ and XXX (other than as explained below), XXX reciprocally and in consideration hereof, shall initiate or participate in arbitration as a final and binding means of resolving workplace issues, regarding any claim subject to this Agreement as set forth in section C

C. Claims Covered By This Agreement

This agreement to dispute resolution includes claims, controversies and disputes related to, arising out of, and in connection with your employment with XXX to include under Title VII of the Civil Rights Act; Civil Rights Act of 1991; Sections 1981 through 1988 of Title 42 of the United States Code; The Fair Credit Reporting Act; The Immigration Reform Control Act; The Americans with Disabilities Act; The Rehabilitation Act; The Age Discrimination in Employment Act; The Occupational Safety and Health Act; The Family and Medical Leave Act; The Equal Pay Act; The Fair Labor Standards Act; The Uniformed Services Employment and Reemployment Rights Act; Worker Adjustment and Retraining Notification Act; Employee Polygraph Protection Act; The New Jersey Equal Pay Act; The New Jersey Law Against Discrimination; The New Jersey Occupational Safety and Health Laws; The New Jersey Genetic Privacy Act; The New Jersey Conscientious Employee Protection Act; The New Jersey Smokers' Rights Law; The New Jersey Tobacco Use Discrimination Law; The New Jersey Family Leave Act and Rule; The New Jersey Wage and Hour Laws, New Jersey statutes regarding Workers' Compensation; Retaliation; Political Activities of Employees; Jury Duty: Employment Protection;

Lie-Detector Tests; Whistleblower Protection; Use of Tobacco Outside the Workplace; Plant Closings; Genetic Information Nondiscrimination Act of 2008; Consumer Reports; or any other law or cause of action; and, any other federal, state, or local law, ordinance or regulation, or based on any public policy, contract, tort, or common law or any claim for costs, fees, or other expenses or relief, including attorney's fees arising from _______ 's employment or cessation of employment with SEA, and which is otherwise not excluded by section D below. Further, notwithstanding any language to the contrary in this section, may retain the right to file a charge or complaint with appropriate governmental administrative agencies, and to assist or cooperate with such agencies in their investigation or prosecution of charges although understands that s/he will not be entitled to recover any monetary damages or relief as a result of such charges or complaints brought by such governmental agency. All claims and defenses which could be raised before a government administrative agency or court must be raised in arbitration and the arbitrator shall apply all applicable laws accordingly.

D. Claims Not Covered By This Agreement

Notwithstanding the language in section C identifying claims covered by this Agreement, claims not covered by this Agreement are claims: (i) for workers' compensation benefits; (ii) for unemployment compensation benefits; (iii) for injunctive, equitable or other relief relating to unfair competition, restrictive covenant (non-compete) and/or use of unauthorized disclosure of trade secrets or confidential information, as to which relief may be obtained from a court of competent jurisdiction; (iv) concerning the interpretation or application of XXX policies, practices, rules and procedures that result in disciplinary action consisting of a disciplinary notice, and/or suspension, and/or discharge, not alleged to be in violation of the statutes and laws, or other causes of action, identified in section C; (v) concerning changes to Company policies; performance evaluations; job descriptions; job classifications (grades); pay rates; changes to quality and quantity work standards; benefit plans under ERISA; disciplinary action that results from violation of the Company's substance abuse policy; (vi) based upon XXX's current employee benefits and/or welfare plans that contain an appeal procedure or other procedure for the resolution of disputes under the plan; (vii) concerning a violation of the National Labor Relations Act; (viii) brought by federal, state, or local governmental officials in criminal court against ________ or XXX; and, (ix) already filed with a court or government agency before implementation of this Agreement, which becomes effective upon execution.

E. Arbitrator's Decision is Final

The decision or award of the arbitrator shall be final and binding upon the parties. The arbitrator shall have the power to award any type of legal or equitable relief available in a court of competent jurisdiction including, but not limited to, attorney's fees, to the extent such damages are available under law. Because any arbitral award may be entered as a judgment or order in any court of competent jurisdiction, any relief or recovery to which the respective parties may be entitled upon any claim (including those arising out of employment, cessation of employment, or any claim of unlawful discrimination) shall be limited to that awarded by the arbitrator to the extent permissible under law.

F. Applicable Time limits

The parties understand that any claim for mediation and/or arbitration will be timely only if brought within the applicable statute of limitations for such claim, and/or other applicable administrative agency time limitations for the filing of such claim. If the claim for mediation and/or arbitration is made after the applicable statute of limitations or other applicable administrative agency time limitations have expired, such claim is barred.

G. Waiver of Jury Trial

The parties understand that, except as otherwise provided, by signing this Agreement, they waive their right to a court action, including a jury trial, in accordance with the terms of this Agreement. **The parties understand that they are waiving their right to a jury trial voluntarily and knowingly and free from duress or coercion.** If for any reason this Agreement is declared unenforceable in whole or in part as to any covered claims, the parties agree to waive any right they may have to a jury trial with respect to any such claims, and do so voluntarily and knowingly and free from duress and coercion.

H. At-Will Employment

Neither the terms nor conditions described in this Agreement are intended to create a contract of employment for a specific duration of time. Employment with XXX is voluntarily entered into, and _______ is free to resign at any time. Similarly, XXX may terminate the employment relationship at any time for any reason, with or without prior notice. Nothing contained herein or in any other statement, whether oral or written, can create a contract of employment or alter the at-will nature of ________'s employment.

I. Governing Law and Interpretation

This Agreement, as well as all terms and conditions of employment, shall be governed by and shall be interpreted in accordance with the laws of the State of New Jersey, without regard to its choice or conflict of laws provisions. If for any reason this Agreement is declared unenforceable, a court shall interpret or modify this Agreement, to the extent necessary, for it to be enforceable. If any term or provision of this Agreement is declared unenforceable by any court of competent jurisdiction and cannot be modified to be enforceable, such term or provision shall immediately become null and void, leaving the remainder of this Agreement in full force and effect.

Any dispute, controversy or claim arising out of, relating to employment (including but not limited to all issues regarding the jurisdiction, existence, scope, validity, performance, interpretation, and termination), shall be determined by arbitration administered by the American Arbitration Association (or International Centre for Dispute Resolution) in accordance with the National Rules for the Resolution of Employment Disputes of the AAA, and judgment on the award rendered by the arbitrator(s) may be entered in any court having jurisdiction thereof.

The parties agree that this Agreement may be interpreted or modified to the extent necessary for it to be enforceable and to give effect to the parties' expressed intent to create a valid and binding arbitration procedure to resolve all disputes not expressly excluded paragraph D of this Agreement. Other than as set forth in the above provisions, all other modifications of this Agreement shall be in writing and signed by the President/CEO of XXX and by ______.

The parties agree that the taking of evidence in the arbitration shall be governed by the ICDR's Guidelines for Arbitrators Concerning Exchanges of Information.

J. Consideration

______ understands that, as consideration for _______ signing this Agreement, XXX has agreed to pay all costs of mediation, and arbitration charged by the AAA, and to be bound by the arbitration procedure set forth in this Agreement. Other costs will be subject to Rule 54 of the Federal Rules of Civil Procedure. _______ further acknowledges that _______ has received additional consideration for signing this Agreement in the form of [bonus, salary increase, etc.].

K. Knowing and Voluntary Agreement

_________ has had the right to consult with counsel regarding this Agreement. _______________ and free from any duress or coercion signs this Dispute Resolution Agreement.

EMPLOYEE	**XXX, INC.**
_________________________	_________________________
Signature	Signature
_________________________	_________________________
Date	Date
_________________________	_________________________
Print Name	Print Name
	_________________________
	Title

14. Outsourcing

Outsourcing is another tool that can be used to mitigate, transfer, or reduce risk. Usually, outsourcing involves an arrangement under which a company transfers responsibility for the performance of an internal business function to an outside service provider.

A company may mitigate or transfer risk by turning over high-risk operations to a third party that is skilled in handling such operations. I was involved once in outsourcing a data center of a client to a third party that was skilled in maintaining such data centers as the client had problems in managing.

Outsourcing certain operations may not only save the company money and reduce financial risk, but may also reduce the risk of employee-related claims as well as risks associated with that function. Outsourcing, if used properly, can be quite effective in reducing and mitigating risk.

14.1 Structure

Outsourcing a departments function or even division normally involves:

- Providing a third party with hardware and equipment
- Developing and managing software or often deliverables
- Transfer of some key employees

Companies seek to minimize and transfer risk; outsourcing is a great tool if used properly. Normally companies will not outsource core functions of the company that generate cash but can outsource noncore functions involving such departments as:

- IT
- HR
- Facilities (mail, call center, food, maintenance)
- Training
- Legal

14.2 Outsourcing Arrangements

Outsourcing of a function involves the use and implementation of an outsourcing agreement that covers not only the transfer of the particular business function but the provision of services by the outsourcing company (i.e., service provider). Prior to developing the agreement, however, the company must really sit down and decide whether the outsourcing of a business function is worth it. What is the true basis of the decision to outsource and will it minimize or transfer risk? To answer that question, companies often conduct a study or approach potential outsourcing vendors to see what data they have to justify the decision to outsource.

There are numerous outsourcing arrangements companies can use to transfer risk, including:

- IT
    - Help desk
    - Software maintenance
    - Network management
    - Data center
- Corporate process
    - Claims processing
    - Payroll and employee benefits
    - Credit card processing
- Management
    - Labor based services such as:
        - HR

- Mail room
- Legal
- Compliance

14.3 Issues and Concerns

Before plunging ahead and outsourcing certain noncore functions, a business needs to be aware of the risks. Among the risks are:

- Labor and employment laws of the jurisdiction in which the outsourcing takes place
    - Is the vendor an established entity?
    - Is the vendor deemed an independent contractor under applicable laws?
    - Will it involve former employees who transfer over?
    - How much control will the company retain over workers?
- Restrictions in contracts
    - Are there contractual severance provisions in contracts of employees who are outsourced?
    - Bonus plan issues.
    - ERISA benefit plan issues.

The contract

An outsourcing arrangement by its very nature entails long-term relationship and the delivery of an ongoing service. Therefore, the contract is vital to the success of the outsourcing arrangement, especially the portion covering performance of services, which is normally set forth in a statement of work, or SOW. The SOW is arguably the most important part of the agreement.

Typically, the SOW sets forth and defines:

- The scope of services of each party
- Pricing
- The duties, functions, and responsibilities of the parties involved
- The applicable specifications, quantities, types, etc., as they relate to the services to be performed

It is of vital importance, therefore, that if you use an outsourcing arrangement you clearly define the specifications, scope, and responsibilities of both parties in the SOW. Some examples of SOW specification include:

- Transfer of equipment leases
- Types of hardware to be deployed
- Quantities of storage
- Deliverables to be provided
- Software licenses to be transferred
- Program modules to be migrated over
- Personnel to be transferred
- Project phases of arrangement

To help transfer or mitigate the risk involved in outsourcing itself, the following provisions or "tools" should be used in the contract and SOW:

- Performance levels
- Limitation of liability
- Insurance
- Changes in business
- Limited warranty
- Choice of law or dispute resolution mechanism
- Data security provisions

14.4 Dispute Resolution

Though dispute resolution itself is addressed in a different chapter of this book, as an outsourcing contract is a major contract, it is wise to mention it here as well.

Because outsourcing is a unique arrangement, it is best to consider what aspects of a company's organizational efforts should be used in facilitating and maintaining the outsourcing relationship. I think it best to consider management of the outsourcing relationship to be of primary importance when resolving disputes. When considering dispute management, a company should structure such process in the contract and SOW as follows:

- Corporate management services
    - Dedicated teams to manage outsourcing relationship
- Escalation of dispute to management and then executive management
- Nonbinding mediation
- Binding arbitration

14.5 Outsourcing Forms

14.5.1 Master Outsourcing Agreement

This Master Outsourcing Agreement together with the Attachments and supplemental agreement attached hereto ("Master Agreement") is made by and between ______(“____________”), a ____ corporation having an office at ____ and ____ (“__”), a _____, having an office at____________. The effective date of this Master Agreement is the date of the last party's signature ("Effective Date").

WITNESSTH

WHEREAS, ____________ has a testing facility providing testing services for itself and its customers;
WHEREAS, __________ has the business and technical know-how to run and desires to operate such testing facility;
WHEREAS, ____________ desires, and __________ agrees, to outsource the management and operation of the testing facility to __________ in accordance with the terms and conditions of this Master Agreement;

NOW, THEREFORE, in consideration of the mutual promises contained herein, the parties hereby agree as follows:

Article I. DEFINITIONS

Terms with initial capitalization, and as otherwise not defined in the provisions, shall have the meaning set forth below:

1.01 "Affiliate" means

1.02 "Services" means the testing services provided by __________ under the terms of this Master Agreement.

1.03 "Confidential Information" means information of a party to this Master Agreement which is provided or disclosed to the other and is marked as confidential or proprietary. If the information is initially disclosed orally then (1) it must be designated as confidential or proprietary at the time of the initial disclosure and (2) within twenty (20) days after disclosure, the information must be reduced to writing and marked as confidential or proprietary. No information of the disclosing party will be considered Confidential Information to the extent the information:

(a) is in the public domain through no fault of the recipient either before or after disclosure; or
(b) is in the possession of the recipient prior to the disclosure, or thereafter is independently developed by recipient's employees or consultants who have had no prior access to the information; or
(c) is rightfully received from a third party without breach of any obligation of confidence.

1.04 "Deliverable" means any written summary of results or any other written data, information or materials provided to ____________ including data, comments and conclusions pertaining to the Services performed under this Master Agreement. [Discussion Point: I am presuming that there will be Deliverables resulting from the Services.]

1.05 "Software" means the XXX Software and Third Party Software as set forth in the Software Licensing Agreement.

1.06 "Transition Period" means the time duration for which the Transition Plan set forth in Attachment C is in effect.

1.07 "Termination Transition Period" means the time duration for which the Termination Plans set forth in Attachment P or Attachment Q is in effect.

1.08 "Work for Hire" has the meaning prescribed to it under the Copyright Act of 1976, as amended.

Article II. SCOPE OF MASTER AGREEMENT

2.01 Background

Under the terms and conditions of this Master Agreement, ____ shall outsource to ________ the management and operations of the testing facility located at ______ ("XXX"). To effectuate this outsourcing arrangement, the parties shall undertake the execution of (i) this Master Agreement and (ii) the XXX Facilities and Equipment Agreement attached hereto as Attachment A and the Software License Agreement attached hereto as Attachment B ("Supplemental Agreements")

2.02 XXX Facilities

___ shall lease and/or sublease to __ the physical XXX facilities ("XXX Facilities") under the terms and conditions of the XXX Facilities and Equipment Agreement attached hereto as Attachment A and this Master Agreement. ___ shall remain the owner of the XXX Facilities and shall be solely responsible for the XXX Facilities, including, without limitation, all mortgage and/or lease payments, maintenance, insurance, security and landscaping of such XXX Facilities.

2.03 XXX Equipment

____ shall lease, sublease, and/or license to ___ the test equipment located in the XXX Facilities ("XXX Equipment") under the terms and conditions of the XXX Facilities and Equipment Agreement attached hereto as Attachment A and this Master Agreement. ___ shall remain the owner or lessee of such XXX Equipment and shall be solely responsible for any XXX Equipment purchase and/or lease payments, maintenance and insurance on such XXX Equipment.

2.04 Software

___ shall license to __ any of its software related to providing the Services under the terms and conditions of the Software License Agreement attached hereto as Attachment B. For any third-party software related to the provision of Services, ____ shall procure for ____ the right to use such third-party software, either by assignment, license or otherwise, under the terms and conditions of the Software License Agreement attached hereto as Attachment B.

2.05 Transfer of Third Party Agreements
_____ shall transfer all third party agreements under which is was responsible for the provision of Services.

2.06 XXX Employees
____ and ____ shall jointly work to transfer the employees and consultants working to provide the Services ("XXX Employees") from ______ to _______.

2.07 Provision of Services to ______ shall provide Services to ____ under the terms and conditions of this Master Agreement.

2.08 Marketing
__________ shall market the XXX capabilities to third parties, including to ____________ Affiliates, under the __________ name in accordance with the terms and conditions of this Master Agreement.

2.09 Splitting of Third Party Revenues
Subject to the terms and conditions of this Master Agreement, the parties shall split the revenue from the provision of Services to third parties.

Article III. GOVERNING BOARD

3.01 Membership of Governing Board
The parties hereby agree to the creation of an governing board to assist in the management of XXX and execution of the obligations set forth in this Master Agreement ("Governing Board"). Initially, the Governing Board members shall be comprised of three (3) ____________ (or S&T and client organizations) executives, three (3) __________ executives and one (1) XXX lead manager. Each party may replace any of its representative members upon notice to the other party.

3.02 Governing Board Responsibilities

The Governing Board's responsibilities shall include, but not be limited to:

(a) Establishing the strategy, objectives, policy and procedures of XXX.
(b) Setting XXX priorities.
(c) Evaluating the performance XXX with respect to the performance criteria set forth in this Master Agreement.
(d) Handle dispute resolution in accordance with the procedure set forth in Article XVIII.

Article IV. IMPLEMENTATION OF TRANSITION PLAN

The parties agree that to minimize disruption to the employees, consultants and third-parties, the parties shall implement the Transition Plan set forth in Attachment C commencing on the Effective Date. Part of the Transition Plan includes the transfer of employees as set forth in

Article V and transfer of third-party agreements for the Services as set forth in Article VI.

Article V. TRANSFER OF EMPLOYEES

5.01 Identification of Employees
No later than [xx] days from the Effective Date ____________ shall provide __________ with a list of all XXX Employees. The list shall include, at a minimum the information set forth in Attachment D.

5.02 Right to Interview Employees
__________ shall make an offer to all XXX Employees prior to or around the start of the Transition Period to apply to become __________ employees to manage and operate the XXX Facilities and Equipment and provide the Services. __________ shall have the right to interview any employee before deciding to extend or not extend an offer of employment to such employee or consultant.

5.03 Key Employees
__________ shall identify to ____________ a number of employees which __________ deems to be necessary for the viable and continued operation of XXX ("Key Employees"). __________ shall enter into employment negotiations with these Key Employees and ____________ shall exercise its best efforts to assist in the successful conclusion of these negotiations.

5.04 No Hire by ____________
____________ shall not continue the employment or the consultant relationship, hire, or make an offer to hire any XXX Employee during the initial term of this Master Agreement.

5.05 Transfer of Employees
The detailed process by which ____________'s XXX employees becomes __________ employees are set forth in Attachment E.

Article VI. THIRD-PARTY XXX AGREEMENTS

6.01 Assignment of Third Party Agreements
By the end of thirty (30) days of the Effective Date of this Master Agreement, ____________ shall have exercised its best efforts to assign all agreements with third-parties in providing them XXX testing services ("Third-Party XXX Agreements") to __________ and to obtain all third-party consents necessary so that __________ can provide the Services under the relevant Third-Party XXX Agreement.

6.02 No Assignment or Consent
In the event that ____________ has not been able to obtain the consent of third-parties for the Third-Party XXX Agreements, ____________ shall [_].

Article VII. PROVISION OF SERVICES BY __________

7.01 Description of Services
__________ shall provided to ____________ the Services in effect as of the Effective Date and consistent with past practices, in accordance

to the terms and conditions hereunder. These Services are set forth in Attachment F.

7.02 Provision of Services
__________ shall provide the Services described in individual Work Statements substantially in the form as set forth in Attachment G.

7.03 Service Level Commitments
In the provision of Services, __________ agrees to the service levels commitments set forth in Attachment H ("Service Levels").

7.04 Third-Party Testing Agreements
To the extent that ____________ has assigned existing Third-Party XXX Agreements to __________, __________ shall provide the Services in accordance with the terms and conditions of such Third-Party XXX Agreement, subject to prior review of the terms and conditions of such agreements.

7.05 Desktop and LAN Support
As part of the Services, __________ shall maintain the desktop computers listed the XXX Facilities and Equipment Agreement (see Attachment A), as well as the internal local area network ("Network Support Services") supporting provision of Services. The Network Support Services are described in Attachment I.

7.06 Day-to-Day Management
Except as otherwise set forth in this Master Agreement, __________ shall have sole authority and responsibilities for the operation and management of the XXX Facilities, XXX Equipment Software and testing programs in the provision of the Services.

7.07 Other Services
To the extent that ____________ desires __________ to provide other services related to the Services set forth in Attachment F, the parties shall negotiate a mutually acceptable agreement.

Article VIII. ______ PROVISION OF INFORMATION

_______ shall provide to ______ all documents, including, without limitation, all manuals, procedure manuals and forms related to the provision of Services.

Article IX. MARKETING OF SERVICES TO THIRD PARTIES

9.01 By ___ shall market the Services to third parties.

9.02 By ___

Article X. MAINTENANCE OF FACILITIES, EQUIPMENT AND SOFTWARE

10.01 XXX Facilities Maintenance
____________ shall be solely responsible for the upkeep and maintenance of the XXX Facilities in accordance with the XXX Facilities and Equipment Agreement (see Attachment A).

10.02 XXX Equipment Maintenance
____________ shall be solely responsible for the upkeep and maintenance of the XXX Equipment in accordance with the XXX Facilities and Equipment Agreement (see Attachment A).

10.03 Software Maintenance

(a) ____________ Software. ____________ shall provide __________ with maintenance and support for the ____________ software in accordance with the Software License Agreement (see Attachment B)
(b) Third Party Software. ____________ shall obtain maintenance for third party software used in the Equipment in accordance with the Software License Agreement (see Attachment B).

Article XI. UPGRADING OF XXX FACILITIES AND XXX EQUIPMENT AND SOFTWARE

11.01 Modifications to XXX Facilities to Meet Regulations

In the event that the XXX Facilities needs to be modified to meet federal, state or local laws or regulatory requirements, ____________ shall be solely responsible for such expenses and shall be solely liable for any claims and expenses arising out of such non-conformance.

11.02 Upgrading of XXX Facilities

(a) ____________ Network. ____________ shall be solely responsible for upgrading and expanding the XXX Facilities to ensure that the XXX Facilities are current with ____________'s network.

(b) Third Party Needs. ____________ shall be solely responsible for upgrading and expanding the XXX Facilities as requested by __________ to meet the additional market needs of third party customers. In the event that ____________ believes that such upgrade or expansion is not warranted, the matter shall be referred to the Governing Board.

11.03 Upgrade and Purchase of XXX Equipment

(a) ____________ Requirements. ____________ shall be solely responsible for upgrading and purchasing/leasing new XXX Equipment to keep the XXX Equipment current with the requirements of ____________'s network. Any new equipment purchases or leases shall be considered XXX Equipment.

(b) Third Party Requirements. __________ shall be responsible for upgrades and purchasing/leasing new XXX equipment over and above the upgrades made by ____________ in Section 11.03(a) or as needed for third party customers. These upgrades and purchases shall be owned by __________, but shall be considered XXX Equipment for purposes of this Master Agreement.

[Discussion Point: Who is responsible (and liable) for the maintenance of this __________ equipment? Maybe it would be better to ____________ to own such equipment and for approval to go to the Governing Board if there is a dispute.]

11.04 Upgrade and Licensing of Software

(a) ____________ Requirements. ____________ shall be solely responsible for upgrading and licensing new Software to keep the Software current with the requirements of ____________'s network. Any new Software license or upgrades shall be considered Software subject to the terms and conditions of the Software License Agreement.

(b) Third Party Requirements. ____________ shall be solely responsible for upgrading and licensing new Software to keep the Software current with the requirements of third party customers. Any new Software license or upgrades shall be considered Software subject to the terms and conditions of the Software License Agreement. In the event that ____________ believes that such upgrade or license is not necessary, the matter shall be referred to the Governing Board.

Article XII. CONSENTS

____________ shall obtain all consents or approvals necessary for __________, its employees, agents and subcontractors to use (i) the XXX Facilities, (ii) the XXX Equipment, (iii) ____________ and third party software.

Article XIII. CONFIDENTIAL INFORMATION

13.01 Use of Confidential Information.
Confidential Information disclosed by one party ("Disclosing Party") to the other ("Receiving Party") in connection with this Master Agreement will be used by the Receiving Party only in connection with the Receiving Party's obligations under this Master Agreement.

13.02 Disclosure of Confidential Information.
Confidential Information disclosed under this Master Agreement by the Disclosing Party will be protected by the Receiving Party from further disclosure, publication, and dissemination to the same degree and using the same care and discretion as the Receiving Party applies to protect its own confidential or proprietary information from undesired disclosure, publication and dissemination. Except as set forth in the following paragraph, neither party will disclose the other's Confidential Information to any Affiliate or other third party, without prior written consent from the other party. If Confidential Information is required by law, regulation, or court order to be disclosed, the recipient must first notify the disclosing party and permit the Disclosing Party to seek an appropriate protective order.

13.03 Disclosure to Employees and Consultants.
Confidential Information disclosed under this Master Agreement may be disclosed to a Receiving Party's employees (including contract employees) or consultants who participate in the provision of the Services if the employees and consultants have been made aware of their responsibilities under this Master Agreement and the consultants (including contract employees) have signed a statement agreeing to be bound by the terms of this Master Agreement with respect to confidentiality.

13.04 Misuse of Confidential Information.
Either party's failure to fulfill the obligations and conditions with respect to any use, disclosure, publication, release, or dissemination to any third person of the other party's Confidential Information or breach of any restrictions or obligations of any licenses granted by the other party, constitutes a material breach of this Master Agreement. In that event the aggrieved party may, at its option and in addition to any other remedies that it may have, terminate this Master Agreement, its obligations and any rights or licenses granted upon thirty (30) days written notice to the other party. In addition to any other remedies it may have, the aggrieved party has the right to demand the immediate return of all copies of Confidential Information provided to the other party under this Master Agreement. The parties recognize that disclosure of Confidential Information in violation of this Master Agreement will result in irreparable harm.

13.05 Right to Injunctive Relief
Each party shall have the right to injunctive relief in the event of a disclosure in violation of this Master Outsourcing Agreement.

Article XIV. INTELLECTUAL PROPERTY

14.01 Ownership of Deliverables
_______ owns all right, title and interest in and to any specific conclusions and recommendations which are contained in any Deliverable furnished to ______. _____ grants to _______ a personal, nontransferable, nonexclusive license to use and copy the Deliverable for ______ internal business purposes only. _____ shall include ______'s copyright notice on all copies of Deliverables. The Services and any Deliverables are not deemed to be Work For Hire.

14.02 Retention of Intellectual Property Rights
____________ retains all right, title or interest in any (a) patentable and unpatentable discoveries, and ideas, including methods, techniques, know-how, concepts, products ("Invention"), to all works fixed in any medium of expression, including copyright and mask work rights ("Works of Authorship"); and (b) other materials, created by or for __________ outside this Master Agreement, including those contained in any Deliverable. __________ retains all right, title or interest in any (a) Invention or Works of Authorship; and (b) other materials, created by or for __________ outside this Master Agreement, including those contained in any Deliverable.

14.03 Ownership of Newly-Created Intellectual Property
Except as expressly provided in Section 14.01 with respect to Deliverables, any Inventions or Works of Authorship or other intellectual property created by __________ relating to or arising from the provision of the Services are the sole and exclusive property of __________.

14.04 No Rights By Implication
No direct or indirect ownership interest or license rights in Inventions or Works of Authorship are created by implication. No direct or indirect ownership interest or license rights in any software or patents are granted by either party in this Master Agreement. Except as expressly set forth in

the Supplemental Agreements attached to this Master Agreement, any grant of an ownership interest or license rights in a patent or software must be negotiated in a separate agreement.

14.05 Similar Work for Other Customers
__________ may perform the same or similar services for others, including providing the same or similar conclusions and recommendations provided that ____________ Confidential Information is not disclosed.

Article XV. FEES

15.01 Fees for Services

(a) Fees and Discount Rate. _______ shall pay ______ fees for the provision of the Services at _________'s then current hourly rate, provided, however, that ________ shall be entitled to discounts in the hourly rate. These discounts are calculated for each fiscal year in advance of such fiscal year and is based on the revenue commitment by ______ to ______ for that fiscal year as a percentage of _________ revenue level forecasts for that fiscal year. The current revenue forecasts for the first four fiscal years are set forth in Attachment J. ______ must provide such percentage revenue commitment levels and fiscal year forecasts to ______ at least thirty (30) days in advance of the start of the fiscal year. The discount rate schedule is forth in Attachment K.

(b) Initial Revenue Commitments by ____________. Notwithstanding any provision to the contrary, ____________ agrees to provide the minimum revenue levels for each fiscal year set forth in Attachment J.

(c) Failure to Meet Revenue Commitment Levels. __________ shall calculate any shortfalls in revenues committed by ____________ at the end of the fiscal year. To the extent that discounts were applied, the discounts will be recalculated based on the actual revenue level achieved and the fees for the Services provided in that fiscal year shall be adjusted to account for the new discount. __________ will issue a bill to ____________ for such shortfall and fee adjustments.

15.02 Lease of XXX Facilities and XXX Equipment
As consideration for the XXX Facilities and XXX Equipment, __________ shall provide a credit to the ____________ with respect to the fees due __________ of the provision of Services ("Capital Credit"). These credits shall be as follows:

(a) Depreciation Relief. __________ shall assist ____________ with depreciation relief for the capital improvements made by ____________ to the XXX Facilities and XXX Equipment ("Depreciation Recovery"). This Depreciation Recovery is calculated as follows:

   (i) Calculate depreciation costs for the consulting revenue stream as __% of the revenue stream generated;
   (ii) Calculate the Depreciation Recovery as the sum of the results of 15.02(a)(i) and 15.02(a)(ii), less depreciation costs associated with __________'s incremental capital investments.

(b) Capital Cost Relief. __________ shall provide ____________ with credit according to Attachment L, depending on the level of __________ profits ("Capital Cost Relief"). ____________ shall only be entitled to Capital Cost Relief for the lesser of the life of the Master Agreement or the average remaining life of the current investment as of the Effective Date.
(c) Revenue Sharing. The parties agree that __________ and ____________ shall share equally the net revenues generated from the provision of Services to non-____________ customers ("Net External Revenues"). The Net External Revenues are calculated as follows:

15.03 Termination Fee
In the event of termination of this Master Agreement the terminating party shall pay the other party a termination fee in accordance with Attachment M.

Article XVI. PAYMENTS

16.01 Payments by ____________

(a) _____ shall submit bills to ______ on a quarterly basis and _______ shall pay the billed amounts within thirty (30) days of the date of the bill. [Discussion Point: Is a quarterly basis acceptable?]

(b) All payments to __________ must be in United States dollars and may be either wire transferred to:

(i) Bank of America_________
ABA No. ________________
Account No. ______________

or

(ii) mailed to ________________

16.02 Overdue Payments

Overdue payments are subject to a late payment charge, calculated and compounded monthly, and calculated at an annual rate of one percent (1%) over the lowest prime rate available in New York City, as published in The Wall Street Journal on the first Monday (or the next bank business day) following the payment due date. If the amount of the late payment charge exceeds the maximum permitted by law, the charge will be reduced to that maximum amount.

16.03 Taxes

_________ shall pay or reimburse _____ for all sales or use taxes, duties, or levies imposed by any authority, government or government agency (other than those levied on ________'s net income) in connection with this Master Agreement. If _______ is required to collect a tax to be paid by _____, _____ shall pay this tax on demand. If ____ fails to pay these taxes, duties or levies, ___ shall pay all reasonable expenses incurred by ___, including reasonable attorney's fees, to collect such taxes, duties or levies.

Article XVII. PERFORMANCE CRITERIA

17.01 Performance Matrix

The parties agree to periodically assess the performance of the parties. Performance shall be assessed by the use of mutually agreed performance matrices and criteria as set forth in Attachment N. Performance shall be assessed by the Governing Board.

17.02 Failure to Achieve Performance Goals

Failure to meet the performance criteria by a mutually agreed upon margin by one party shall permit the other party the option to terminate this Master Agreement. The parties agree that a party may request the use of a mutually agreeable independent third party to assess any failure to meet the performance criteria and the party requesting such third party shall bear the cost of such third party assessment, provided, however, that if the party requesting evaluation by a third party was correct, the other party shall bear the cost of such third party assessment.

Article XVIII. DISPUTE RESOLUTION PROCEDURE

Any dispute, disagreement, claim or controversy arising hereunder or referring or relating to this Master Agreement and the performance or nonperformance by a party of its obligations hereunder (singularly or collectively a "Dispute") shall be submitted to the Dispute Resolution Process pursuant to the provisions in Attachment O. Notwithstanding the foregoing and anything to the contrary herein, each party shall have the right to seek preliminary, temporary and/or permanent injunctive relief to prevent misuse or unauthorized use of its Intellectual Property Rights or Confidential Information.

Article XIX. CHANGE CONTROL PROCEDURE

The parties hereby agree that any change in the scope of the services or rates shall accomplished in accordance with the following procedure:

(a) Any change to the scope of services, schedules or rates ("Change") desired by a party shall be in writing signed by that party's Project Manager ("Change Order") and shall be submitted to the other party's Project Manager. Each Change Order shall set forth in detail, at a minimum, (i) the requested Change, (ii) the impact in the services, schedules and/or rates, if any, and (iii) the cost for such Change, if any.

(b) The party receiving the Change Order shall submit a written response to the requesting party within thirty (30) calendar days of receipt of such Change Order. Subsequently, the Parties shall discuss the proposed Change and such discussion shall result in either (i) a written agreement not to proceed further with the requested Change, (ii) a written and executed amendment to the applicable provision(s) of the Master Agreement to effectuate the Change.

(c) Notwithstanding any provision to the contrary, the Change Order shall have no effect unless agreed to by both parties' Project Managers in a written and executed amendment. The obligations of the parties shall not be changed, nor shall the applicable party have the obligation to proceed with, or accept, such Change until such amendment has been executed by both parties.

Article XX. REPRESENTATIONS AND WARRANTIES

20.01 General

Each party represents and warrants to the other party that the execution and delivery by such party of this Master Agreement and the consummation of the transactions contemplated hereby have been fully authorized by all necessary company or corporate action, and this Master Agreement constitutes a legal, valid and binding obligation of such party enforceable in accordance with its terms, except to the extent that such enforceability is subject to or limited by bankruptcy, insolvency or similar laws relating to enforcement of creditors' rights generally.

20.02 By ________ represents and warrants that:

(a) it has the rights to grant, transfer and/or assign to __________ the rights granted in (i) the XXX Facilities and Equipment Agreement attached hereto as Attachment A and (ii) the Software License Agreement attached hereto as Attachment B;
(b) until the completion of the Transition Plan pursuant to Attachment C it shall operate and maintain the XXX business in the ordinary course consistent with past practices and consistent with achieving its revenue forecasts;
(c) there are no pending or imminent lawsuits or proceeding against the XXX business;
(d) there are no claims of infringement of third party rights against the XXX business;

Article XXI. DISCLAIMER OF WARRANTIES

THE WARRANTIES SET FORTH HEREIN ARE IN LIEU OF ALL WARRANTIES OF MERCHANTABILITY AND FITNESS FOR A PARTICULAR PURPOSE.
Article XXII. INDEMNIFICATION

22.01 General
Each party agrees to indemnify and hold harmless the other party and its successors and assigns and their respective affiliates, agents, employees, officers and directors ("Indemnified Parties") from any and all damages, liability, fines or penalties resulting from or arising out of any claims or demands whatsoever, including the costs, collection costs, expenses, and reasonable attorneys' fees incurred on account thereof, that may be made:

(a) as a result of any breach or alleged breach of a representation or warranty of such party under this Master Agreement;

(b) by the party or any other person for bodily injury or damage to property occasioned by the acts or omissions of such party or its subcontractors, or the employees or agents of any of them;
(c) by the other party or its subcontractors or the employees or agents of any of them under workers' compensation or similar acts;

22.02 Intellectual Property Indemnification
Each party agrees to indemnify and hold harmless the other party and its Indemnified Parties from a claim of infringement of any patent, copyright, trademark, misappropriation of trade secrets or other property right only pursuant to those express terms and conditions set forth in the relevant agreements attached as Attachments to this Master Agreement.

Article XXIII. LIMITATION OF LIABILITIES

Except as otherwise set forth in the applicable agreements attached as Attachments to this Master Agreement, no party shall be liable to the other for any consequential, indirect, special, exemplary, or punitive damages, or any lost revenues or lost profits, even if advised of the possibility of such damages. Each party's aggregate liability, if any, shall be limited to [__] and liquidated damages as set forth in Section 15.03.

Article XXIV. TERM AND TERMINATION

24.01 Term
This Master Agreement shall commence as of the Effective Date and continue for a period of five (5) year thereafter. After such initial five (5) year term, the term of this Master Agreement shall automatically renew for successive five (5) year terms unless a party provides notice to the other party at least sixty (60) days prior to the end of the then current term that such party does not want to renew this Master Agreement.

24.02 Termination Events

(a) For Cause. Except as expressly set forth in an applicable provision, if either party materially breaches any provision in this Master Agreement and such breach is not cured within sixty (60) days after receiving written notice of such breach from the other party, the party giving notice may then deliver a second written notice to the breaching party, terminating the Master Agreement, and the licenses granted hereunder shall terminate on the date specified in such second notice.

(b) Insolvency. In the event that a party is (a) adjudged insolvent or bankrupt, or (b) upon the institution of any proceedings by it seeking relief, reorganization or arrangement under any laws relating to insolvency, or (c) if an involuntary petition in bankruptcy is filed against such party and said petition is not discharged within sixty (60) days after such filing, or (d) upon any assignment of the benefit of creditors, or (e) upon the appointment of a receiver, liquidator or trustee or any of its assets, or (f) upon the liquidation, dissolution or winding up of its business, or (g) upon the filing of any liens against such party (including, without limitation, against the Equipment or XXX Facilities) (collectively an "Event of Bankruptcy"), then such party shall immediately give notice thereof to the other Party, and the other Party may, at is option and without liability or any further obligation, terminate this Master Agreement.

(c) Change in Control. If there is a direct or indirect change in the effective voting control of a party, or if such party merges into or is acquired by a third party, or if such party sells or transfers all or substantially all of the assets of the business or the XXX Facility or Equipment to the third party (collectively a "Change in Control"), then such party shall provide written notice to the other party within thirty (30) days, and the other party, at its option, may, within thirty (30) days after receipt of such notice, terminate this Master Agreement, without liability, by delivering written notice to such party. To the extent a party is aware of a proposed Change in Control, such party may notify the other party in writing ninety (90) days in advance of any such proposed Change in Control prior to its effectiveness, and the other party shall, within thirty (30) days after receipt of such notice, notify such party whether the other party would exercise or reserve its right to terminate this Master Agreement if such proposed Change of Control were consummated.

(d) Employees. In the event that less than 75% of employees or contractors offered to join __________ do not agree to be employed or be hired by __________, __________ shall have the right to terminate this Master Agreement without and liability or obligation, including to any employees extended offers.

(e) Key Employee. In the event that any Key Employees decides not become an employee of __________, __________ shall have to right to immediately terminate this Master Agreement without any liability or obligation.

(f) Failure to Meet Performance Criteria. Failure to meet the performance criteria as set forth in Article XVII by a mutually agreed upon margin by one party shall permit the other party the option to terminate this Master Agreement and the Termination Plan set forth in Attachment Q shall take effect.

(g) Checkpoint Termination: Either party has the option to terminate this Master Agreement three (3) years after the Effective Date and thereafter at two (2) year intervals and the Termination Plan set forth in Attachment Q shall take effect.

(h) Telecommunications Act of 1996.

    (i) Statutory Constraints. __________ is subject to the terms of the Telecommunications Act of 1996 (the "Act") and will only provide Services or products to ____________ consistent with the limitations and obligations imposed by the Act. __________ will not provide any Services directed to the manufacture, including design, of any telecommunications products or customer premises equipment.

    (ii) Inconsistent with the Act. This Master Agreement may be terminated or modified by __________, without liability, upon written notice if __________ receives notification from any United States agency or court that __________'s performance under this Master Agreement or of similar Services is or may be inconsistent with the terms of the Act.

    (iii) No Cause for Claim. Termination or modification of this Master Agreement as provided under this Section 24.02(h) will not be cause for a claim by ____________ against __________ for any damages whatsoever, whether direct, indirect, special or consequential.

24.03 Effect of Termination

(a) Return of Deliverables, Confidential Information. Upon termination of this Master Agreement, each party shall destroy or return all Confidential Information of the other party to the other party, including all copies in whole or in part, and, if requested by the other party, certify by an authorized representative of the party, in writing to the other party, the destruction or return thereof.
(b) Accelerated Payment of Revenues. Upon the termination of this Master Agreement, ____________ shall pay any minimum revenue commitments to __________ for the years in the term prior to such termination.
(c) Termination Transition Period. In the event of the termination of this Master Agreement by either party for cause as set forth under Section 24.02(a), the parties shall be subject to the Termination for Cause Plan set forth in Attachment P. All other termination shall use the Termination Plan set forth in Attachment Q.
(d) License Termination. Notwithstanding any provision to the contrary, any licenses granted by ____________ to __________ shall continue until such Termination Transition Period is complete.

Article XXV. GENERAL

25.01 Duty to Cooperate
Each party agrees to execute all documents and take all other actions that may be reasonably required to accomplish the purposes of this Master Agreement, so that the parties, and their permitted successors and assigns, will hold all rights as contemplated herein.

25.02 Notice

(a) Manner of Delivery. All notices, requests, consents and other communications ("Notice" or "Notices") hereunder shall be in writing, shall be addressed to the receiving party's address set forth below (or to such other address as that party may designate by Notice hereunder), and shall be delivered, postage prepaid, (a) international postal mail, return receipt requested, (b) by overnight courier; or (c) by facsimile or electronic mail and confirmed by overnight courier.

If to ________:	If to ________:
Attn:	Attn:
With a copy to:	
With a copy to:	
Attn:	Attn:

(b) When Deemed Received. All Notices shall be deemed to have been given to, and received by, the receiving party (a) if by international postal mail, five (5) business days after such mailing; or (b) if by overnight courier, facsimile or electronic mail, on the next business day after delivery to the courier (unless such courier fails to complete delivery overnight).

25.03 Assignment

Neither party may assign this Master Agreement, or sublicense, assign or delegate any right or duty hereunder, by operation of law or otherwise, without the prior written consent of the other party. Any such purported assignment, sublicense or delegation without such prior written consent shall be null and void and of no effect.

25.04 Amendment

This Master Agreement may not be amended except in a writing executed by authorized representatives of each party.

25.05 Force Majeure Event

Neither party shall be deemed in default of this Agreement to the extent that the performance of its obligations or attempts to cure any breach of this Agreement are delayed or prevented by reason of an act of God, fire, electrical outage, computer network failure, software malfunction, natural disaster, accident, act of government, or any other cause beyond the control of such party (a "Force Majeure Event"). In the event of a Force Majeure Event, the time for performance or cure shall be extended for a period equal to the duration of the Force Majeure Event.

25.06 Relationship of the Parties

Nothing in this Master Agreement shall be construed as creating a partnership, joint venture, principal/agent or any other relationship between the parties for any purpose whatsoever. Except as may be expressly provided herein, neither party may be held liable for the acts either of omission or commission of the other party, and neither party is authorized to, or has the power to, obligate or bind the other party by contract, agreement, warranty, representation, covenant or otherwise in any manner whatsoever.

25.07 Employee Taxes, Insurance And Other Charges

Each party shall be responsible for any withholding, payroll and unemployment taxes, disability insurance and other employee insurance payments and other taxes or charges incurred in the performance of this Master Agreement with respect to its employees, servants, agents and subcontractors.

25.08 Governing Law

This Master Agreement shall be governed by, and construed in accordance with, the laws of the State of New Jersey, United States, applicable to contracts wholly made and wholly performed in the State of New Jersey, United States. This Master Agreement will not be governed by the United Nations Convention on Contracts for the International Sale of Goods.

25.09 Joint Negotiations

The parties have participated jointly in the negotiation and drafting of this Master Agreement. In the event an ambiguity or question of intent or interpretation arises, this Master Agreement (and any applicable or relevant provision) shall be construed as if drafted jointly by the parties, and no presumption or burden of proof shall arise favoring or disfavoring any one party by virtue of the authorship of any of the provisions of this Master Agreement.

25.10 No Waiver
The failure of either Party at any time to require performance by the other Party of any provision hereof shall not affect the full right to require such performance at any time thereafter, nor shall the waiver by either Party of a breach of any provision hereof be taken or held to be a waiver of any succeeding breach of such provision or as a waiver of the provision itself.

25.11 Survival
The rights and obligations in ____ shall survive the termination or expiration of this Master Agreement.

25.12 Headings
Headings in this Master Agreement are for convenience only and shall not be construed to affect the interpretation of the Master Agreement.

25.13 Precedence
In the event of a conflict between the provisions of this Master Agreement, and any Work Statements, Exhibits or fees, the order of precedence shall be as follow: (i) the Work Statement, (ii) the Supplemental Agreements, and (iii) this Master Agreement.

25.14 Severability
If any provision of this Master Agreement or its application in a particular circumstance is held to be invalid or unenforceable to any extent, the remainder of the Master Agreement, or the application of such provision in other circumstances, shall not be affected thereby, and each provision shall be valid and enforced to the fullest extent permitted by law.

25.15 Counterparts
This Master Agreement may be executed in one or more counterparts, each of which shall be deemed an original, but all of which together shall constitute one and the same agreement.

25.16 Entire Agreement

This Master Agreement, including all exhibits, contains the final and entire agreement of the parties on the subject matter herein and supersedes all previous and contemporaneous verbal or written negotiations or agreements on the subject matter herein.

IN WITNESS WHEREOF, each of the parties has caused this Master Agreement to be executed on its behalf by its duly authorized representatives as of the Effective Date.

AGREED TO BY:

____

____

By:	By:
Name:	Name:
Title:	Title:
Date:	Date:

__________ Legal Approval

ATTACHMENT A
XXX FACILITIES AND EQUIPMENT AGREEMENT

ATTACHMENT B
SOFTWARE LICENSE AGREEMENT

ATTACHMENT C
TRANSITION PLAN

ATTACHMENT D
EMPLOYEE INFORMATION
Employee Name:
Position:
Salary:
Brief Job Description:
Commendations by ___________:
Employment Problems:
Disciplinary Actions Taken by ___________:

ATTACHMENT E
EMPLOYEE TRANSFER PROCEDURE

ATTACHMENT F
SERVICES

ATTACHMENT G
SAMPLE WORK STATEMENT

XXX SERVICES WORK STATEMENT
Contract No. < ######>
This Work Statement is under the XXX Master Agreement dated _________ and is between ______________ ("Customer") and __________ ("__________"). __________ shall provide the following Services under the terms and conditions of the Master Agreement and any additional terms contained in this Work Statement.

1. SCOPE OF SERVICES

2. DESCRIPTION OF SERVICES
   __________ shall provide the following services:
3. NO YEAR 2000 SERVICES
4. CUSTOMER RESPONSIBILITIES
5. FEES AND PAYMENTS
6. DELIVERABLES
7. SCHEDULE OF SERVICES
8. __________'S CONTACT(S)
9. CUSTOMER'S CONTACT(S)
   The parties to this Work Statement agree to the terms of the Master Agreement and this Work Statement and further represent that this Work Statement is executed by duly authorized representatives as of the dates below.

AGREED BY:
< CUSTOMER'S FULL LEGAL NAME>

____

By:	By:
Name:	Name:
Title:	Title: Contract Manager
Date:	Date:

ATTACHMENT H
SERVICE LEVEL COMMITMENTS

ATTACHMENT I
NETWORK SUPPORT SERVICES

[Insert description of network support services here]

ATTACHMENT J
MINIMUM REVENUE COMMITMENTS

Year Fiscal Year Revenue Forecasts Percentage Revenue Commitment

Year 1	90% of fiscal year forecast
Year 2	75% of fiscal year forecast
Year 3	65% of fiscal year forecast
Year 4	50% of fiscal year forecast

ATTACHMENT K

HOURLY DISCOUNT RATE SCHEDULE

Percentage Revenue Commitment Level	Discount Rate
>110% of the fiscal year forecast	12%
90% to 110% of the fiscal year forecast	10%
70% to 90% of the fiscal year forecast	8%
60% to 70% of the fiscal year forecast	7%
50% to 60% of the fiscal year forecast	6%
50% of the fiscal year forecast	0%

ATTACHMENT L

CAPITAL COST RELIEF

__________ Profit Capital Cost Relief

ATTACHMENT M

TERMINATION FEE

Termination Event ____________Termination by ____________

Termination by __________

For Cause (Section 24.02(a))

Insolvency (Section 24.02(b))

Change in Control (Section 24.02(c))

Employees (Section 24.02(d))

Key Employees (Section 24.02(e))

Failure to Meet Performance Criteria (Section 24.02(f))

Checkpoint Termination (Section 24.02(g))

$0 $0

Telecommunications Act (Section 24.02(h))

Not Applicable $0

ATTACHMENT N
PERFORMANCE MATRICES

Performance Metrics
Metrics Measurement Approach Acceptance Criteria Non-financial

1 Meeting committed time schedules for delivery of project results. For each project, identify end-date, dates for key milestones, critical contingencies. 95% of the time delivering within one week of the deadlines

In case of delays caused by ____________ customer's action (e.g., critical info/funding not provided), dates must be adjusted. Initial dates may also be adjusted with customer concurrence.

2 Satisfactory acceptance rate for work not committed in the annual baseline plan Work outside the annual plan will be considered "Out-of-plan" Acceptance rate of 95% for Qualified Requests

Reviews will be held quarterly with key customer groups to identify potential out-of-plan requests as early as possible. 90% of the time delivering within one week of the deadlines

Work accepted contingent upon agreements on: timely investment funding (when needed), schedule of the new work, and adjustments to annual plan work (if necessary in case of critical resource constraints)—"Qualified Requests"

3 Satisfactory handling of emergency requests—either by reprioritizing work or by a 20%-40% rate premium (to cover any losses and overtime) Work accepted contingent upon agreement on: timely investment funding (when needed), schedule and pricing of the new work, and adjustments to annual plan work (if necessary in case of critical resource constraints)—"Qualified Requests" Acceptance rate of 95% for Qualified Requests

(e.g., request for completion of testing two weeks sooner, testing with very short notice) 80% of the time delivering within one week of the deadlines

4 Satisfactory customer feedback, using a customer satisfaction survey (sample provided below) Executive surveys of key customer groups twice a year Aggregate satisfaction score of 4.0 or better for at least 90% of surveys.

Surveys for all "strategic" projects and a sample of other projects at project completion. Strategic projects could be defined as those involving important new technology or supporting deployment of critical new services/applications.
Each project would be categorized at the time of acceptance.

5 Field support: Timely and effective isolation and resolution of field-reported problems Time to call-back Less than one-hour for 75%+ calls Financial

6 Reduction in capital investment as a percentage of forecast __________ business and technical evaluation of proposed capital investments __________ proposals to ____________ for reductions of at least 10%. Acceptance at the discretion of ____________.

7 Revenue and profitability attainment, from services to non-XXX customers, as a percentage of the forecast Segment the market for non-XXX services as follows: Suppliers, carriers (ILECs and new entrants), ____________ affiliates/partners
Agreement on Segment Definitions (e.g., Sample companies comprising the segment) and growth parameter (e.g., Revenue, profits)
When healthy conditions (growth in Supplier segment of >20%, Carrier segment of >15%, Affiliates segment of >15%) 75% of Forecasts
When "Deteriorating" conditions (growth in Supplier segment of 10-20%, Carrier segment of 5-15%, Affiliates segment of <5-15%) 50% of Forecasts
When poor conditions (Growth in Supplier segment of <10%, Carrier segment of <5%, Affiliates segment of <5% can be considered indicator of poor conditions) 25% of Forecasts
_Negative growth rate in Supplier market 0% of forecasts

ATTACHMENT O

DISPUTE RESOLUTION PROCEDURE

1. Internal Mediation. The Dispute (as such term is defined in Article XVIII), subject to provisions of Article XVIII of the Master Agreement, shall be referred to the Governing Board

or such other senior executives as may be mutually agreed upon by the parties from time to time for resolution ("Internal Mediation"). If such persons do not agree upon a resolution within twenty (20) days after referral of the matter to them (or such other period of time as the parties may agree for a particular Dispute), then the parties shall proceed to Outside Mediation or as set forth below.

2. Outside Mediation. Either party, upon written notice and within ten (10) days after the conclusion of Internal Mediation, may elect to utilize a non-binding resolution procedure whereby each party presents its case at a hearing (the "Hearing") before a panel consisting of a senior executive of each party and a mutually acceptable neutral mediator (the "Outside Mediator"). If a party elects to utilize Outside Mediation, the other party hereby agrees to participate. The Hearing will occur no more than ten (10) days after a party serves written notice to use Outside Mediation. Each party may be represented at the Hearing by its attorneys. If the matter cannot be resolved at such Hearing by the senior executives, the Outside Mediator may be asked to assist the senior executives in evaluating the strengths and weaknesses of each Party's position on the merits of the Dispute. Thereafter, the senior executives shall meet and confer to try to resolve the Dispute.
3. Litigation. If the Dispute has not been resolved by in accordance with Paragraphs 1 and/or 2 above, each party, subject to the provisions of Paragraph 2, may commence an action and/or proceeding in equity regarding the Dispute. Subject to the provisions of Article XVIII, no party shall commence an action and/or a proceeding in equity regarding a Dispute until after the expiration of a fifteen (15) period after the last day of the Hearings, if any.

[or]

4. Arbitration Provisions.

    (a) The Disputed Matter shall be settled by final and binding arbitration in accordance with the Commercial

Arbitration Rules of the American Arbitration Association (the "AAA"); provided, however, that if such Rules are inconsistent with any provision of this Master Agreement, this Master Agreement shall control;

(b) Any such arbitration shall be conducted in the New Jersey metropolitan area at a place and time mutually agreed upon by the parties or, failing mutual agreement, selected by the arbitrators;

(c) Any arbitration shall be conducted before a panel of three (3) arbitrators who shall be compensated for their services at a rate to be determined by the AAA in the event the parties are not able to agree upon their rate of compensation, but based upon hourly or daily consulting rates for the neutral arbitrator reasonably consistent with such arbitrator's normal charges or fees. Within fifteen (15) days of notice by a party seeking arbitration under this provision, the party requesting arbitration shall appoint one arbitrator and within fifteen (15) days thereafter the other party shall appoint the second arbitrator. The persons so appointed shall meet the qualification requirement set forth in Paragraph (d) below. Within fifteen (15) days after the appointment of the second arbitrator, the two arbitrators so chosen shall mutually agree upon the selection of the third, impartial and neutral arbitrator who must be employed in the computer industry with a minimum of five years experience in a testing environment. In the event the chosen arbitrators cannot agree upon the selection of the third arbitrator, the AAA Rules for the selection of such an arbitrator shall be followed, provided that the selection is from among such persons who meet the above-stated requirements;

(d) Each person so appointed shall have substantial experience with respect to testing of sophisticated computer hardware and software products.

(e) In any dispute in which the amount of controversy, exclusive of interest and costs, is less than $25,000, there shall be only one arbitrator agreed to by the parties who shall meet the requirements set forth above for the neutral arbitrator; in all other cases, there shall be three (3) arbitrators.

(f) Each party shall bear its own costs and expenses of arbitration including, but not limited to, filing fees and attorneys' fees, and each party hereby agrees to pay one-half of the administrative fees of the AAA and of the compensation to be paid to the arbitrators in any such arbitration and one-half of the costs of transcripts and other expenses of the arbitration proceedings, subject, however, to allocation of costs and expenses (excluding attorneys' fees) by the arbitrators consistent with the award.

(g) The parties agree to make available to the arbitrator(s) all non-privileged books, records, schedules and other information reasonably requested by them. Such materials are to be made available to the arbitrator(s) at such times as are deemed necessary by them to make their decision as herein provided. Each party will be entitled to take discovery in accordance with the Federal Rules of Civil Procedure;

(h) The arbitrator(s) may conduct any pre-trial proceedings by telephonic conference call rather than by a face-to-face meeting;

(i) The arbitrator(s) shall, prior to rendering their decision on the arbitration matter, afford each of the parties an opportunity, both orally and in writing, to present any relevant evidence (the formal rules of evidence applicable to judicial proceedings shall not apply) and to express, orally and/or in writing that party's point of view and arguments as to the proper determination of the arbitration matter; provided, however, that either party submitting written material shall be required to deliver a copy of such written material to the other party concurrently with the delivery thereof to the arbitrator(s) and such other party shall have the opportunity to submit a written reply, a copy of which shall also be delivered to the other party concurrently with the delivery thereof to the arbitrator(s). Oral argument shall take place only at a hearing before the arbitrator(s) at which all parties are afforded a reasonable opportunity to be present and be heard;

(j) In the event of a willful default by any of the parties hereto in appearing before the arbitrator(s) after due written notice shall have been given, the arbitrator(s) are hereby authorized to render a decision upon the testimony of the party(ies) appearing before the arbitrator(s);

(k) The arbitrator(s) shall (by decision of a majority of the arbitrators) make a decision and award resolving the dispute within forty-five (45) days after the selection of the last arbitrator, or the first arbitrator if only one arbitrator is to decide the dispute; and within fifteen (15) days of the last hearing held concerning such dispute(s);

(l) Any judgment upon the award rendered by the arbitrator(s) may be entered in any court having jurisdiction thereof;

(m) Within thirty (30) days after the arbitrators make their decision and award, the arbitrators shall render findings of fact and conclusions of law and a written opinion setting forth the basis and reasons for any decision and award rendered by them and deliver such documents to each party to this Master Agreement along with a signed copy of the award;

(n) The arbitrator(s) chosen in accordance with these provisions shall not have the power to alter, amend or otherwise affect the terms of these arbitration provisions or the Master Agreement, and without limiting the foregoing, any award is subject to the limitation of liability provisions contained in the Master Agreement.]

ATTACHMENT P
TERMINATION FOR CAUSE PLAN

- Exit Arrangement:
- Assessment of increase in valuation of the facility, and each party's share thereof, by an independent third-party. Value enhancement could be from both tangible sources (e.g., incremental capital investment from __________) and

intangibles (e.g., improved brand equity of the XXX facility, improved customer relationships, technology primarily developed from the resources in XXX)

- ____________ would compensate __________ for __________'s share of the value enhancement
- Facilities and infrastructure would revert to ____________
- People would have freedom to transfer to either of two parties

ATTACHMENT Q
TERMINATION PLAN

- Exit Arrangement:
- Assessment of increase in valuation of the facility, and each party's share thereof, by an independent third-party. Value enhancement could be from both tangible sources (e.g., incremental capital investment from __________) and intangibles (e.g., improved brand equity of the XXX facility, improved customer relationships, technology primarily developed from the resources in XXX)
- ____________ would compensate __________ for __________'s share of the value enhancement
- Facilities and infrastructure would revert to ____________
- People would have freedom to transfer to either of two parties

14.5.2 Mail Center Services Outsourcing Agreement

This Agreement ("Agreement") is made as of this ____ day of April, 2002 by and between <Client> ("__") and Leasing Company, a Division of ___, a _____ Corporation with its principal office at _, __, _ ("__").

WHEREAS, Client wishes to retain Leasing Company to manage and perform <outgoing mail fulfillment functions, on-site mail center functions and related services> ("Services") in the capacity of an independent contractor, at Client's facilities located at _________, _________, ________ (the "Facility") and such other off-site locations as the parties may agree upon; and

WHEREAS, Leasing Company desires to provide such Services to Client on the terms and conditions set forth in this Agreement.

NOW, THEREFORE, in consideration of the mutual covenants contained herein, and for good and valuable consideration, receipt of which is acknowledged, Client and Leasing Company agree as follows:

1. Integration of "Whereas" Clauses

   The above "Whereas" clauses are incorporated in and form a part of this Agreement as if set forth in their entirety in this Agreement.

2. Services

   In return for the fees and compensation described in Paragraph 5, Leasing Company shall coordinate, manage and perform the outgoing mail fulfillment functions, incoming mail processing and distribution at the Facility and provide mail center operation and supervisory personnel for an on-site mail center at the Facility and such other related functions as Client may designate. In providing the Services, Leasing Company shall be responsible for the following:

   (a) The coordination, management and control of all outgoing mail fulfillment functions for the Facility. Initially, for a period to be agreed to in writing between Client and Leasing Company, Leasing Company will oversee, control and manage the outgoing mail handling process that has been performed to date by ___________ ("Vendor"), a vendor who has performed such functions for Client. Leasing Company will coordinate with Client management the transfer of such functions from Vendor to an automated process staffed and maintained by Leasing Company either on-site at the Facility, off-site at Leasing Company's facilities or on the premises of an approved contractor of Leasing Company Provided, in the event Leasing Company seeks to contract with any third party to perform any Services within the scope of this Paragraph 2(a) or any other provision of this Agreement, Leasing Company shall be obligated to provide Client with advance written notice of such proposed contracting arrangement, including the identity of any contractor, a statement as to where the contractor will perform any such services and such other information as Client may request, to confirm that such contractor has the capacity to perform the Services in accordance with the agreed upon service standards. Leasing Company further acknowledges and agrees that any such contractor shall be required to comply with all of the obligations and responsibilities applicable to Leasing Company under this Agreement and that Leasing Company shall provide Client with such proposed subcontractor's written agreement to be bound by and comply with all applicable provisions of this Agreement;

(b) Leasing Company shall provide an appropriate number of cross-trained (i.e., sufficiently skilled) mail center/distribution personnel to perform all required daily and other functions in accordance with established levels of services and compliance parameters, including all personnel necessary to meet peak demands in accordance with such levels and parameters. All personnel supplied by Leasing Company shall be employees of Leasing Company, independent contractors retained by Leasing Company or employees or independent contractors of Leasing Company's approved contractors;

(c) Leasing Company shall provide training for all personnel required to appropriately staff the on-site mail center and otherwise required to provide Services. Leasing Company and Client agree that certain personnel of Leasing Company assigned to perform work in connection with the provision of Services under this Agreement shall be designated "Key Employees of Leasing Company." Leasing Company agrees that no Key Employee of Leasing Company shall be removed (unless the employee voluntarily severs his/her employment with Leasing

Company) from Leasing Company's work for Client or have his/her position functionally changed without Client's express prior written consent. Leasing Company shall provide full time staffing and supervision for continuity of Service during all absences of its personnel;

(d) The Services shall include all those itemized in Leasing Company's ________________ proposal to Client and any other services Client may reasonably request from time to time;

3. Facilities

Client will be responsible, at the sole cost and expense of Client and not as a part of the operating costs of the on-site mail center, for the following:

(a) Providing, on an initial and ongoing basis, Information Technology and/or other support for the automation of Client's outgoing mail function as Client may deem appropriate;

(b) Providing and maintaining a fully furnished and equipped on-site mail center, in good and safe condition and good working order, which mail center shall be equipped with such furniture, fixtures, furnishings and other equipment and accessories as the parties agree are necessary for the operation of the on-site mail center, and for providing replacements thereof required due to ordinary wear and tear of same. Leasing Company shall give Client prompt notice of any required maintenance, repairs or replacements, and Client shall reasonably maintain, repair or replace the same. Leasing Company shall exercise reasonable care over all Leasing Company provided equipment, so as not to cause damage or waste and shall assist Client in connection with maintenance repair and replacement of same;

(c) Providing appropriate space, including storage areas, necessary for the operation of the on-site mail center, including hot and cold water, heat, air-conditioning, ventilation, lighting, telephone and utility service necessary for the operation and maintenance of the fixtures and equipment on Client's premises for use on providing Services. Leasing Company shall exercise reasonable care over same, so as not to cause damage or waste and shall cooperate with Client with respect thereto;

(d) Furnishing access to toilet and washroom facilities for Leasing Company's personnel at the Facility;

(e) Providing management review and consultation with respect to Client developed performance standards and operating procedures;

(f) Appointing and identifying to Leasing Company a representative or representative of Client as Leasing Company's primary point of contact for various matters concerning the services and this Agreement;

(g) Providing reasonable security for all equipment owned or leased by Client maintained at the Facility at such times as Leasing Company personnel are not on-site, in a manner the same as or similar to that provided for Client equipment. Provided, Leasing Company shall be required to maintain all necessary and appropriate insurance against damage to, loss or destruction of Leasing Company's property and equipment.

4. Term of Agreement

This Agreement shall be effective for a term of one (1) year, beginning on the effective date set forth on page 1 of this Agreement (the "Term"), unless terminated earlier pursuant to Paragraph 21. Following the Term, unless either party provides the other with written notice not less than ninety (90) days prior to the expiration of the Term or any subsequent one (1) year renewal period that it wishes to terminate or modify this Agreement and/or any terms of the Agreement then in effect, the Agreement shall continue and remain in effect for an additional one (1) year period on the terms and conditions then in effect.

5. Fees for Services

(a) Client shall compensate Leasing Company for its <on-site mail center services> at a monthly rate of $_________. The monthly rate is based on a forty (40)-hour week for a manager and clerk and includes all salaries, benefits, backup, overheads and profit, and the risk of loss or profit shall be Leasing Company's. Leasing Company is authorized to bill an overtime rate for all personnel of $____.00 per hour, but only for actual overtime hours worked by an employee in excess of forty (40) hours in any week. Client's authorized representative must approve all overtime in advance. Leasing Company guaranties the rates provided for in this Paragraph 5(a) for the initial one year Term. Thereafter, rates may be modified only upon the express written agreement of the parties, but shall not be raised in any one year by more than six percent (6%).

(b) Client shall temporarily compensate Leasing Company for the off-site outgoing mail fulfillment function at a rate equal to that being paid to Vendor. Payment is due within forty-five (45) days of invoice date. A permanent and fixed fee shall be negotiated by Client and Leasing Company when the outgoing mail fulfillment function is automated.

(c) Leasing Company shall issue invoices to Client for Services on a monthly basis. Each invoice shall identify with specificity the Services and charges for which payment is requested, including whether the invoiced amounts are for on-site mail center services, outgoing mail fulfillment or other functions. Client shall pay undisputed invoiced amounts within forty-five (45) days of Client's receipt of an invoice from Leasing Company. Leasing Company may add a monthly service charge equal to the lesser of (i) one and one-half percent (1.5%), or (ii) the highest lawful rate allowed by law, on the unpaid balance of an undisputed invoice after sixty (60) days. In the event of any dispute on the part of Client concerning any invoice issued by Leasing Company, Client shall notify Leasing Company in writing of the dispute within thirty (30) business days after Client's receipt of the disputed invoice, including the reason(s) for dispute. The parties shall meet promptly in person, through designated managers, to attempt to resolve any such dispute. Any dispute that cannot be resolved in that manner shall be subject to resolution through binding arbitration pursuant to Paragraph _ of this Agreement.

(d) Upon reasonable notice to Leasing Company, Client shall have the right, during normal business hours, to inspect and audit all records of Leasing Company which pertain to any Services performed pursuant to this Agreement, including but not limited to for the purpose of determining the accuracy of any invoice issued by Leasing Company to Client

6. Non-Employee Status

(a) Leasing Company will at all times in the course of furnishing Services to Client be an independent contractor as regards Client. This Agreement does not create a relationship of agency, partnership or employment between the parties hereto, and no act or obligation of either Client or Leasing Company shall in any way bind the other except as expressly set forth herein. All persons retained by Leasing Company to perform Services, including but not limited to <on-site mail center personnel,> shall be employees of Leasing Company for all purposes and at all times during the term of this Agreement. Leasing Company and Client agree that this Agreement establishes Leasing Company solely as an independent contractor.

(b) It is agreed that all persons employed or retained by Leasing Company to perform Services pursuant to this Agreement, are and shall at all times be employees and/or contractors of Leasing Company only and in no respect shall be considered employees, contractors, or agents of Client. Leasing Company's employees, contractors and agents are not eligible for, and shall not be eligible to participate in and shall not participate in, any profit-sharing, pension, health, dental, education reimbursement coverage, compensation incentives or other benefit plan or program provided to or maintained for the benefit of contractors to or employees of Client. Leasing Company shall promptly notify all Leasing Company employees, contractors and agents, who perform any work in conjunction with Leasing Company's provision of Services under this Agreement of these facts and obtain written acknowledgement thereof in a manner acceptable to Client.

(c) Leasing Company agrees that it shall, where legally required, pay for all persons performing work of any type in connection with this Agreement, all federal state and local payroll, withholding and other required taxes, including but not limited to all Federal Insurance Contribution Act (FICA), Federal Unemployment Tax Act (FUTA), state and local unemployment insurance taxes and all other payroll withholding taxes. leasing Company will supply W-2 Forms to its employees and 1099 Forms to its contractors and, upon request, will provide copies thereof or other evidence satisfactory to Client, as proof that required withholdings have been and continue to be made and that such tax forms have been and continue to be issued. Neither federal, state, nor local income taxes nor payroll taxes of any kind shall be withheld or paid by Client on behalf of leasing Company or any employee or contractor of leasing Company.

(d) Leasing Company agrees it shall comply with all applicable workers' compensation laws concerning its employees, contractors and agents, and shall provide to Client a certificate of workers' compensation insurance or other proof of coverage acceptable to Client upon Client's request. As Client shall not be the employer, co-employer, joint employer or principal of any such employee, contractor or agent of leasing Company, Client shall not maintain workers' compensation insurance coverage with respect to such persons, regardless of whether they perform work on Client's premises or in connection with this Agreement.

(e) leasing Company agrees that it shall indemnify Client and hold Client harmless from and against any liability or expense (including reasonable attorneys' fees, as incurred by Client) arising from or based upon (i) any claim by any person, including by way of example any employee, contractor or agent of Client or any taxing or other governmental entity, that Client stands in any relationship, including but not limited to employment, co-employment, joint employment, principal/agent and/or master/servant, with respect to leasing Company or any of leasing Company's employees, contractors or agents, or (ii) any breach by leasing Company or any of its employees, contractors or agents of any provision of this Agreement.

(f) Client reserves the right to review the qualifications of any person assigned or to be assigned by leasing Company to perform work for Client in connection with this Agreement prior to such assignment. When requested by Client, leasing Company agrees to provide resumes of such persons for review by Client. Before assignment of any leasing Company employee, contractor or agent to perform work at Client premises or in concert with any Client personnel, leasing Company will advise such persons of leasing Company's obligations under Paragraphs 12, 13 and 14 and as otherwise affect the rights and responsibilities of and standards of conduct applicable to any personnel of leasing Company assigned to perform any work in connection with the Services.

(g) In the event that the performance of any leasing Company employee or contractor is found by Client to be unacceptable to Client for any reason, Client shall notify leasing Company and leasing Company shall immediately take appropriate corrective action up to and including removal of the employee or contractor from performing Services under this Agreement and providing a qualified replacement. In the event that leasing Company provides a replacement for an employee, contractor or agent for any reason, leasing Company shall not charge Client for any time required to train such replacement or for such replacement to become familiar with any work performed prior thereto, so that such replacement is capable of performing the same assignments as the replaced employee, contractor or agent at the time of departure.

7. Service Standards

The parties shall measure and evaluate leasing Company's performance, consistent with service levels to be established in writing and reviewed and adjusted at regular periodic monthly and quarterly meetings. In addition, leasing Company shall provide Client with monthly reports concerning Services provided and work performed during each month. At the parties' quarterly meetings, they shall discuss what steps, if any, shall be taken to adjust staffing, performance, procedures and any other aspect of leasing Company's provision of the Services, including but not limited to staffing levels and leasing Company employees, contractors or agents.

8. Compliance with Laws and Regulations and Insurance

(a) leasing Company represents and agrees that leasing Company as well as employees, contractors and agents of leasing Company shall comply with all applicable federal, state, county and local laws, ordinances, regulations and codes, and any applicable foreign laws, ordinances, regulations and codes, applicable to Client and/or its employees, contractors and agents and to the performance of their obligations under this Agreement, including, without limitation, laws, executive orders and regulations relating to employment (including equal opportunity, harassment and nondiscrimination), and for the procurement of licenses, qualifications, visas, permits or certificates where required. leasing Company further agrees to hold harmless and indemnify Client and its parents, subsidiaries and affiliates against any liability or expenses (including reasonable attorneys' fees) arising from or based on the failure of leasing Company or any employee, contractor or agent of leasing Company, to comply with any such law, rule, ordinance, regulation or code. leasing Company represents and warrants that it carries sufficient insurance to cover any and all costs and possible judgments related to any claims that might be brought against Client by any employee, contractor or agent of leasing Company, or any third party, for wrongs caused by Client and/or its employees, agents and representatives, with such insurance including but limited to comprehensive general liability coverage for not less than One Million Dollars and not less than Five Hundred Thousand Dollars per claim, and such other insurance against other risks as Client may from time to time reasonably identify. All such insurance will be evidenced by policies that are satisfactory to Client and that will not be cancelable or subject to reduction of coverage or other modification on less than thirty (30) days prior written notice to Client. Leasing Company will deliver to Client certificates or other evidence satisfactory to Client of any insurance required to be maintained by leasing Company.

(b) leasing Company understands that Client is firmly committed to a policy against discrimination in employment and that discrimination against or harassment of any person on the basis of his or her race, color, religion, creed, sex, national origin, citizenship, age, disability, genetic predisposition or carrier status, marital status, sexual orientation, uniformed service or any other characteristic protected by law, that such discrimination is strictly prohibited and that Client also prohibits sexual and other forms of unlawful harassment of its employees and agents in any form or manner. Leasing Company further acknowledges that Client intends to comply fully with applicable laws that prohibit retaliation against employees who may complain in good faith of discrimination, harassment or other improper or unlawful conduct directed against them. If, during the Term of this Agreement or any renewal or extension, leasing Company or any of its employees, agents or representatives, violates Client's "Anti-Discrimination and Sexual Harassment Policies" (attached hereto and as may be modified by

Client during the term of this Agreement), as determined by Client in its sole discretion, or otherwise acts in a manner inconsistent with the policies and practices referenced in this paragraph, Client shall notify leasing Company and leasing Company shall be responsible to immediately take appropriate corrective action, up to and including removal of such person or persons from performing Services under this Agreement.

(c) Leasing Company agrees to obtain any and all necessary certificates, registrations, licenses and permits including but not limited to those required by law, for leasing Company to operate in accordance with the provisions of this Agreement. Leasing Company agrees to comply with all applicable federal, state, local laws and regulations relating to its performance. In addition to the foregoing, leasing Company acknowledges that the following clauses of the Federal Acquisition Regulations will apply to the employment practices of Client for all persons who shall perform services for the benefit of the leasing Company hereunder:

Federal Acquisition Regulation (48 FAR CFR Chapter 1)

Clauses:
Clause No.
Clause Title

16 Equal Opportunity
15 Affirmative Action for Handicapped Workers
16 Affirmative Action for Special Disabled and Vietnam Era Veterans

Leasing Company agrees at all times, comply with the foregoing provisions, which are incorporated herein by reference.

9. Placement Fee

(a) In the event Client employs any employee of leasing Company who has performed work in connection with leasing Company's provision of Services under this Agreement, Client will compensate leasing Company in an amount equal to one (1) month's billing based on four (4) thirty-five (35.0) hour weeks for such employee at their leasing Company rate of payment or its hourly equivalent. No compensation will be due in the case of Client's hiring or retention a current or former employee of leasing Company more than three (3) months after the date such person's assignment to Client's work in connection with leasing Company's provision of Services has concluded. The foregoing represents the complete understanding between leasing Company and Client with respect to fees that may be payable by Client in such event. These fees will not be increased in any instance, but may, subject to written agreement between leasing Company and Client be reduced.

(b) Leasing Company shall perform or have performed appropriate background checks on all employees or other persons otherwise present on prior to their assignment at Client including, but not limited to, education and employment history checks. leasing Company agrees to maintain detailed records regarding such checks. Upon reasonable request, leasing Company will forward results of any background check for personnel assigned to perform work at the Facility or for the benefit of Client. Client agrees that all such information be used for legitimate business purposes Client agrees to take reasonable steps to limit access to such information to those persons wish a legitimate business reason for access.

(c) Ensuring that leasing Company employees assigned to work at Client's facilities shall not keep elsewhere than at the Facility, nor remove from the Facility, any of Client's property. In the event an ____________ employee or contractor ceases to work at the Facility, Leasing Company shall cause such person to immediately return to Client any of Leasing Company's property.

No Restriction of Client's Direct Performance

Nothing contained in this Agreement shall restrict or limit the right of Client or any of its affiliates to hire or employ employees or retain independent contractors during the term of this Agreement to perform any work and/or function related to any aspect of Client's business and/or operations.

10. Indemnification

(a) Leasing Company agrees to promptly and fully indemnify Client, its directors, employees and agents and hold them harmless from all loss, damage, liability and expense, including damages and injury to persons (including Client's employees) and property (including Client property), arising out of it's employees and agents.
(b) Client agrees to promptly and fully indemnify Leasing Company, its directors, employees and agents and hold them harmless from all loss, damage, liability and expense, including damages and injury to persons and property, arising out of it's employees and agents.
(c) Notwithstanding Paragraphs 10(a) and 11(b) hereof, Leasing Company and Client each hereby releases the other, its directors, employees and agents, from liability for any loss or damage to property of the other covered by fire insurance with special form causes of loss endorsement, even if such fire or other casualty shall have been caused by the negligence of the other party or anyone for whom such party may be responsible. However, this release shall be applicable only with respect to loss or damage (i) for which there has been an actual recovery from an insurance carrier by the releasor, recognizing that any releasor deductibles shall be considered the same as a recovery from an insurance carrier, and (ii) occurring during such time as the releasor's insurance shall not have been adversely affected by this release. Client and Leasing Company each agrees that any physical damage insurance policies will include a waiver of subrogation clause or endorsement, but if the same shall have a charge associated with it, only so long as the other party pays for such extra cost. If

there is an extra cost to the waiver, the party carrying the insurance shall advise the other of the amount of the extra cost, and the other party, at its election, may, but shall not be obligated to, pay the same.

(d) Client shall be permitted to inspect the on-site mail center facilities and equipment utilized by Leasing Company on Leasing Company's premises or those of its contractors at any time, as long as such inspection does not unreasonably interfere with Leasing Company's on-site mail center operations.

(e) If either party shall be in default with respect to its obligations hereunder, then the non-defaulting party may give to the defaulting party written notice specifying the default and the intent of the party giving such notice to terminate this contract. If the default specified in such notice shall continue and not be cured at the expiration of forty-five (45) days from the date of giving such notice, or, if the default results from the failure of either party to pay the other in a timely manner, at the expiration of five (5) business days from the date of giving such notice, this contract shall, upon the expiration of said period of forty-five (45) days or five (5) business days, as applicable, terminate and expire at the election in writing of the party giving such notice with the same force and effect as if said date were specified as the termination date of the contract. The defaulting party agrees to indemnify and hold harmless the non-defaulting party from and against all loss, costs and expenses, including reasonable attorneys' fees, but excluding consequential or punitive damages, arising out of the default.

(f) In addition to any and all other obligations Leasing Company may have to indemnify Client under this Agreement, Leasing Company shall indemnify, defend and hold Client harmless against all claims, demands, liabilities, losses, damages, costs or expenses, including attorneys' fees, resulting from any suit or proceeding brought for any claim of breach of contract, infringement of copyrights, patents, trademarks or other proprietary rights, or for unfair competition arising from compliance with or utilization of Client's designs, specifications or instructions, or for any claims to which Client is subjected by reason of any act or omission by Leasing Company, or any employee or agent of Leasing Company, including but not limited to acts or omissions by employees and/or contractors of Leasing Company, in connection with the provision of Services under this Agreement.

11. Confidential Information and Client's Property

(a) Leasing Company acknowledges that, during the Term of this Agreement and any extension or renewal period, Leasing Company, and its employees, contractors and agents will use, have access to and possession of trade secrets, confidential business information and proprietary information belonging to and/or about Client, its parent, subsidiaries and affiliates and their respective customers, distributors, end users and suppliers. Leasing Company agrees that during the term of this Agreement and at all times thereafter, Leasing Company and its employees, contractors, agents and representatives will keep secret and not use or disclose to any person or entity other than Client, in any fashion or for any purpose whatsoever, any Confidential Information (as defined below) relating to Client, except at the request of Client or as required by an order of a court or governmental agency with jurisdiction. Leasing Company agrees to give prompt written notice to Client of any such request or requirement or any threatened requirement, by a court or governmental agency in order to allow Client the opportunity to resist such request or requirement. Leasing Company agrees that it shall cooperate with Client in connection with any action by or on Client's behalf to oppose or reject such request or requirement or any effort by Client to oppose, restrict or otherwise narrow the scope of any such request or requirement. For purposes of this Agreement, "Confidential Information" includes but is not limited to, information in written, graphic, recorded, photographic or any machine readable form or that is orally conveyed to Leasing Company, concerning: Client's business, operations, plans, strategies, prospects or objectives; Client's structure, products, product development, technology, distribution, sales, services, support and marketing plans, practices, and operations; the prices, costs and details of Client's products and services; Client's financial condition and results of Client's operations; Client's research and developments, Client's customers and customer lists (including, without limitation, the identity of distributors, clients, and end users names, addresses, contact persons and distributors' and end users' business status and/or needs); information received from third parties under confidential conditions; management organization and related information (including, without limitation, data and other information concerning the compensation and benefits paid to officers, directors, employees, and representatives of Client); Client's personnel, commission and other compensation policies; Client's operating policies and manuals; Client's financial records and related information; means of gaining access to Client's computer data systems and related information; or any other financial, commercial, business or technical information related to, or any of the products or services made, developed, or sold by, Client, its distributors, end users or Client's parent, subsidiary and related companies.

(b) Leasing Company further agrees to store and maintain all Confidential Information in a secure place and manner. On the termination of this Agreement or upon Client's request during the Agreement, Leasing Company agrees to promptly deliver all records, data, information and any other documents produced or acquired during its performance under this Agreement, as well as any and all copies thereof, to Client. Such material shall at all times remain the exclusive property of Client, unless otherwise expressly agreed to in writing by Client. Upon any termination of this Agreement or any extension or renewal or any other direction by Client, Leasing Company agrees to refrain from making any further use of any Confidential Information on its own behalf or on behalf of any person or entity other than Client.

(c) Upon termination of this Agreement or upon any prior request by Client, Leasing Company shall return to Client all other Client property, including but not limited to, beepers, keys, computers and laptops, which employees, contractors and agents of Leasing Company were given by Client or otherwise obtained from Client. Leasing Company acknowledges that all such items shall at all times remain the exclusive property of Client, unless otherwise agreed to in writing by Client.

12. Inside Information

Leasing Company acknowledges that during the term of this Agreement, Leasing Company and its personnel including but not limited to employees and contractors, may have access to "inside" information. Use of "inside" or Confidential Information in making any investment is absolutely prohibited, and Leasing Company, and its employee, contractors and agents must not make any investment in a security under circumstances that would indicate reliance on information they obtained while performing services for Client and that is not generally known or available to non-client employees. Also, in the course of performing services for Client, Leasing Company and its employees, contractors and agents may learn of business opportunities offered to Client and/or its distributors, end users, customers and suppliers. Neither Leasing Company nor any of its employees, contractors or agents may take advantage of any such knowledge for their own benefit or for the benefit of any other person or party. Leasing Company personnel, including their family members, may invest in securities, but such investments may not be in conflict with the following principles:

- All decisions to buy or sell securities must be based on public information.

- No purchase or sale of securities may be effected while in possession of material, non-public information that in any way concerns such securities or their issuer(s).

If, during the engagement, any employee, contractor or agent of Leasing Company violates this paragraph, as determined by Client in its sole discretion, Client shall notify Leasing Company and Leasing Company shall immediately take appropriate corrective action, up to and including removal of such person from performing Services under this Agreement.

13. Ownership Rights

(a) Leasing Company agrees that except as otherwise expressly provided herein, all copyrights, patents, trade secrets and other intellectual property rights associated with any work performed by Leasing Company for Client under this Agreement, including but not limited to any and all ideas, concepts, techniques, inventions, processes or works of authorship developed or created by Leasing Company, and its employees, contractors and agent who participate in providing Services, during the course of Leasing Company's engagement by Client (collectively referred to as "Work Product") shall belong exclusively to Client and will, to the extent possible, be considered "work made for hire" for Client within the meaning of Title 17 of the United States Code. Leasing Company, further agrees on behalf of itself and any employees or contractors of Leasing Company who have or may have any rights with respect to such Work Product that if any Work Product is deemed not to be a "work made for hire" under Title 17 of the United States Code, Leasing Company shall automatically assign to Client at the time of the creation of such Work Product, without any requirement of any further consideration, any and all rights, titles and other interests Leasing Company and its employees and contractors may have in the Work Product, including any copyrights and other intellectual property rights pertaining thereto, throughout the universe and in perpetuity. Leasing Company further agrees that upon Client's request, Leasing Company and its employees and contractors will take such further actions, including execution and delivery of instruments of conveyance by Leasing Company and/or its employees and contractors, as Company may deem appropriate to give full and proper effect to any such assignment without any further consideration.

(b) Leasing Company warrants that its performance of the Services provided for under this Agreement does not and will not violate any applicable law, rule, regulation, or contract between Leasing Company and any third-party and that Leasing Company's performance hereunder will not infringe upon the rights of any third parties, including property, contractual, employment, trade secret, proprietary information and non-disclosure rights, or any third-party rights in any trademark, copyright or patent rights, nor shall its performance breach any other agreement to which Leasing Company is a party or under which Leasing Company may otherwise be bound. Leasing Company further warrants that it is the lawful owner or licensee of any and all software, programs and other materials used or to be issued by Leasing Company in the performance of the Services hereunder (except for any software, programs or other material made available to Leasing Company by Client for use under this Agreement), and that Leasing Company has all rights necessary to convey to Client the unencumbered ownership of any Work Product.

(c) Leasing Company on its own behalf and on behalf of all employees and contractors, hereby waives any so-called "moral rights of authors" in connection with any Work Product. Leasing Company acknowledges and agrees that Client may use, exploit, distribute, reproduce, advertise, promote, publicize, alter, modify or edit any Work Product or combine any Work Product with other works, in Client's sole discretion, in any format or medium hereafter devised. Leasing Company, on behalf of itself and employees and contractors, further waives any and all rights to seek or obtain any injunctive or equitable relief in connection with any Work Product. Leasing Company agrees to indemnify and hold Client harmless from and against any and all claims, liabilities and/or expenses including court costs and reasonable attorneys' fees incurred by Client in connection with such matters resulting from, arising out of, or relating to the Services to be performed under this Agreement or any breach of the warranties made hereunder.

14. Non-Solicitation

During the Term and for a period of one (1) year following any termination of this Agreement or any extension or renewal period, whether for Cause or without Cause, Leasing Company will not without Client's prior written authorization (a) directly or indirectly, recruit, solicit or hire any employee or contractor of Client or any of its affiliates to work for Leasing Company or any other person or entity, (b) directly or indirectly solicit the business of any Client distributor, end user, customer or prospective customer of Client or any of its affiliates for any purpose other than to obtain, maintain and/or service the party's business for Leasing Company or its affiliate, without Client's express prior written authorization or (c) directly or indirectly recruit any employee, independent contractor or agent or representative of any other contractor or supplier of Client to work for Leasing Company or any other person or entity.

15. Background Checks and Drug Testing

Leasing Company agrees, upon the request of Client, to perform or have performed investigative background checks on persons to be assigned to perform Services under this Agreement. Leasing Company agrees to have drug tests acceptable to Client conducted prior to assigning any person to perform services at Client's premises or upon the request of Client during the assignment of any person to perform Services under this Agreement.

16. Supporting Documentation

Upon execution of this Agreement, Leasing Company shall provide to Client with copies of the following documents: (a) a certificate of good standing as a corporation under the laws of its state of incorporation; (b) any governmental licenses or permits that may be required for the proper and lawful conduct of Leasing Company's business; (c) evidence of compliance with all insurance requirements described herein, including, but not limited to, workers' compensation and liability insurance coverage; (d) evidence of Leasing Company's federal employer identification number, and (e) copies of any software or other licenses confirming Leasing Company's authority to use such programs in connection with its provisions of the Services to Client. Failure by Leasing Company to provide Client any documents required under this paragraph shall be grounds for withholding payment of Leasing Company's invoices and/or termination of this Agreement without further obligation.

17. Injunctive and Other Equitable Relief

Leasing Company acknowledges that the actual or threatened breach by of any of its employees, contractors or agents, including Employees and Consultants, of any obligation under of Paragraphs 12, 13 or 14 will cause Client great and irreparable harm, for which Client will have no adequate remedy at law, and that, in addition to all other rights and remedies that Client may have including the right to recover reasonable attorneys' fees: (a) Client shall be entitled to obtain injunctive and other equitable relief to prevent a breach or continued breach of this Agreement; (b) this Agreement shall be specifically enforceable in accordance with its terms; and (c) in the event of any unauthorized publication of Confidential Information, Client shall automatically own the copyright in such publication.

18. Notices

All notices, consents and demands hereunder shall be in writing and shall be personally delivered or sent by certified or registered mail, return receipt requested, addressed to the other party at its address set forth in this Agreement, and shall be deemed given upon receipt. Notices to Client shall be addressed to the attention of ____________. Notices to Leasing Company shall be addressed to the attention of _______.

19. Termination of Agreement

(a) Client may terminate this Agreement for Cause upon notice to Leasing Company without any obligation other than to provide Leasing Company with payment for Services provided through the date of such termination. For purposes of this Agreement a termination for Cause shall mean a termination because of (i) the material failure by Leasing Company to perform its duties under this Agreement after reasonable notice to Leasing Company of such failure; (ii) misconduct by Leasing Company that is materially injurious to Client or any of its affiliates; (iii) Leasing Company or any principal shareholder's, officer's or director's conviction of, or entry of a plea of guilty or nolo contendere to a crime that constitutes a felony; (iv) the material breach by Leasing Company of any written covenant or agreement with Client or any of its affiliates, including but not limited to its obligations under Paragraphs 12, 13 and 14 of this Agreement not to utilize or disclose any of Client's Confidential Information or (v) Leasing Company's voluntary filing or becoming the subject of an involuntary bankruptcy petition.

(b) Client may terminate this Agreement without Cause by providing Leasing Company with sixty (60) days' written notice or a payment equal to two month's base fee under Paragraph 5 and compensation for all Services provided through the date of the Termination of this Agreement and Leasing Company's appointment.

(c) If Client terminates this Agreement, whether for Cause or without Cause, Leasing Company shall immediately deliver to Client: (i) a written invoice for the pro rata value of Services performed by Leasing Company and unpaid by Client as of the termination date; (ii) any then-existing Work Product, resulting from the Services of Leasing Company hereunder; and (iii) any property of Client then in the custody, possession or control of Leasing Company. In the event of any termination of this Agreement, Client shall have no further obligation to Leasing Company or to any employee, contractor or agent of Leasing Company, other than the payment to Leasing Company of all amounts theretofore payable hereunder for Services previously performed.

20. No Assignment

Except as otherwise expressly provided in Paragraph 1, Leasing Company may not assign, transfer, or subcontract this Agreement or any of Leasing Company's obligations hereunder without the prior written consent of Client. However, Leasing Company may assign its right to receive payments to such third parties as Leasing Company may designate by written notice to Client.

21. Disputes

Any dispute arising between Client and Leasing Company, including those concerning compensation, benefits or other terms of this Agreement, will be determined by arbitration, as authorized and governed by the Arbitration Law of the State of New Jersey, without regard to choice of law rules, under the auspices and rules of the American Arbitration Association ("AAA") in New York City or such other location as the parties may designate, in accordance with the Commercial Rules of the AAA, and the decision of the Arbitrator(s) will be final and binding on both parties. Nothing in this paragraph shall detract from Client's right to seek and obtain injunctive relief in an appropriate judicial forum as provided under this Agreement.

22. No Third Party Beneficiaries

Client and Leasing Company agree that it is their understanding and intent that no third party, including but not limited to any contractor, employee, agent, representative or supplier of Leasing Company, are intended to be third party beneficiaries to this Agreement. Accordingly, it is the understanding and agreement of the parties that no third party shall have any rights to enforce or claim damages under this Agreement.

23. No Waiver

The failure by any party to insist upon strict performance of any of the provisions contained in this Agreement on any occasion shall not be deemed a waiver of its rights under that or any other provision hereof.

24. Severability

If any provisions of this contract or portion of a provision or the applications thereof to any person or circumstance is for any reason held invalid or unenforceable, the remainder of this contract (or the remainder of such provision), and the application thereof to other persons or circumstances, shall not be affected thereby.

25. Entire Agreement

This Agreement contains the entire understanding of the parties with respect to the subject matter contained herein and supersedes all previous written or oral communications between the parties concerning the subject matter of this contract. This contract shall not be amended in any manner except by a written instrument referring to this contract and duly executed by both parties.

IN WITNESS WHEREOF, the parties hereto have caused this Agreement to be executed by their duly authorized officers to be effective as of the day and year first above written.

By: Leasing Company

Name: ______________________________
please print

Title: ___________, a Division of_____, Inc.

By: Client

Name: ______________________________
please print

Title:____________

Date:____________

Index